Five Overtimes

ALSO OF INTEREST
AND FROM MCFARLAND

World Series '48: The Cleveland Indians and Boston Braves in Six Games (John G. Robertson and Carl T. Madden, 2023)

The Bruins in 25 Games: Boston's Most Unforgettable Wins and Heartbreaking Losses (John G. Robertson and Carl T. Madden, 2023)

Cold War on Ice: The NHL versus the Soviet Union in Hockey's Super Series '76 (John G. Robertson and Carl T. Madden, 2023)

The Mustache Gang Battles the Big Red Machine: The 1972 World Series (John G. Robertson and Carl T. Madden, 2022)

Hockey's Wildest Season: The Changing of the Guard in the NHL, 1969–1970 (John G. Robertson, 2021)

Amazin' Upset: The Mets, the Orioles and the 1969 World Series (John G. Robertson and Carl T. Madden, 2021)

When the Heavyweight Title Mattered: Five Championship Fights That Captivated the World, 1910–1971 (John G. Robertson, 2019)

Too Many Men on the Ice: The 1978–1979 Boston Bruins and the Most Famous Penalty in Hockey History (John G. Robertson, 2018)

The Games That Changed Baseball: Milestones in Major League History (John G. Robertson and Andy Saunders, 2016)

A's Bad as It Gets: Connie Mack's Pathetic Athletics of 1916 (John G. Robertson and Andy Saunders, 2014)

The Babe Chases 60: That Fabulous 1927 Season, Home Run by Home Run (John G. Robertson, 1999; paperback 2014)

Baseball's Greatest Controversies: Rhubarbs, Hoaxes, Blown Calls, Ruthian Myths, Managers' Miscues and Front-Office Flops (John G. Robertson, 1995; paperback 2014)

Five Overtimes

*The Habs and the Leafs
in the 1951 Stanley Cup Finals*

John G. Robertson *and*
Carl T. Madden

McFarland & Company, Inc., Publishers
Jefferson, North Carolina

ISBN (print) 978-1-4766-9520-4
ISBN (ebook) 978-1-4766-5254-2

LIBRARY OF CONGRESS AND BRITISH LIBRARY
CATALOGUING DATA ARE AVAILABLE

Library of Congress Control Number 2024019128

© 2024 John G. Robertson and Carl T. Madden. All rights reserved

*No part of this book may be reproduced or transmitted in any form
or by any means, electronic or mechanical, including photocopying
or recording, or by any information storage and retrieval system,
without permission in writing from the publisher.*

Front cover: Defenseman Bill Barilko is lifted up by his teammates
Cal Gardner (left) and Bill Juzda after his goal in overtime on April 21, 1951,
won the Stanley Cup for the Toronto Maple Leafs
(Michael Burns, Sr./Hockey Hall of Fame)

Printed in the United States of America

McFarland & Company, Inc., Publishers
Box 611, Jefferson, North Carolina 28640
www.mcfarlandpub.com

This book is dedicated to you,
the stalwart fans of NHL playoff hockey.

You are the loyal fanatics who long for lengthy games and are prepared to sit in the arena for the duration of any overtime contest.

You are the frugal fans who purchase overpriced tickets in anticipation of getting more than your money's worth.

You are the armchair warriors who are prepared to forego bathroom visits until the game's outcome is settled.

This book is also dedicated to those overtime-scoring hockey heroes who gain notoriety, albeit briefly at times, for their fleeting moments of fame.

Those goals make for stories that can be immortalized in print.

Acknowledgments

The authors are grateful for the special assistance of...

- Toronto Maple Leaf superfan Mark Fera for his alacrity in inviting the authors of this book to see his huge and remarkable collection of team memorabilia and game-used treasures, especially those from the 1950–51 NHL season, and for answering our many questions;
- Bill Doucet, a writer from the *Cambridge* [Ontario] *Times*, who innocently asked, "What became of the Bill Barilko puck?"—thus unwittingly beginning our journey of inquiry that led us to a remarkable story and the opportunity to meet Mark Fera;
- the Cambridge (Ontario) public library system, specifically its inter-library loan department, for their help in acquiring Kevin Shea's out-of-print biography of Bill Barilko and for being the keepers of the microfilm of the defunct *Galt Evening Reporter*;
- the staff at the Dana Porter Arts Library at the University of Waterloo for their gracious assistance in accessing their archives of the *Toronto Star*, *Montreal Star*, and *Winnipeg Free Press* on microfilm;
- the Boston Public Library, specifically Bob Cullum, for the generous use of nine images from the Leslie Jones Collection of photographs;
- the good folks at HockeyReference.com for compiling and maintaining their wealth of statistics for the benefit of hockey fans and researchers—and for being open and welcoming enough to correct obvious errors when they are pointed out to them (yes, we did catch some boo-boos in their stats and records for the 1951 Stanley Cup finals);
- and Joseph Bowman for providing information about Ted (Teeder) Kennedy and his connection to what is now Port Colborne, Ontario.

Table of Contents

Acknowledgments — vi
Notes on Spellings — ix
Introduction — 1

1. The 1950–51 NHL Regular Season: A Two-Team Race — 5
2. Semifinal Series "A": Montreal vs. Detroit — 30
3. Semifinal Series "B": Boston vs. Toronto — 45
4. Montreal vs. Toronto: Their Histories and Rivalry — 61
5. The 1951 Stanley Cup Finals: The Anticipation — 70
6. Game One: Sid Smith Settles Matters — 76
7. Game Two: Rocket Richard Responds — 82
8. Game Three: Ted Kennedy Gives the Leafs the Edge — 93
9. Game Four: Harry Watson's Goal Puts Toronto in Control — 104
10. Game Five: Bill Barilko Becomes Famous — 114
11. Post-Series Miscellany — 131
12. Studs and Duds of the 1950–51 Stanley Cup Finals — 137
13. The Short Life, Disappearance and Recovery of Bill Barilko — 142
14. The Curious Case of the Two Barilko Pucks — 163

Table of Contents

15.	Oops! The Stanley Cup Engraver Had a Bad Day	171
16.	Postscripts	173
17.	1951 Stanley Cup Finals: Series Statistics	198

Chapter Notes   201
Bibliography   209
Index   211

Notes on Spellings

- Throughout the book the authors have used the Anglicized spelling of Montreal (without the acute accent on the e) rather than the French version (Montréal). This is in keeping with the preferred format used in English-language sports periodicals of the early 1950s. However, we have strived to place the correct accents on the first and last names of French-Canadian players based on the spellings of their names that appear on today's hockey websites—even though that was seldom done outside of Quebec in the early 1950s. If we have overlooked any player whose name properly requires an accent, it is purely an oversight and we apologize for the omission.
- Although the Chicago franchise entered the National Hockey League in the 1926–27 season as the "Blackhawks" (one word), it was routinely written as "Black Hawks" (two words) for more than six decades—even appearing on the team's jerseys for a time in that manner. In keeping with the practice of sportswriters during the 1950–51 hockey season, the authors have opted to follow the common (albeit technically inaccurate) two-word spelling of the Chicago NHL team's nickname at the time.
- Bill Barilko's mother's first name was officially Feodosia, but after she immigrated to Canada, she was typically addressed by a nickname. It was spelled as either "Fay" or "Faye" in 1951 newspaper reports when her hockey-hero son became a missing person, with the three-letter version being far more common than the latter. However, her gravestone at Timmins Memorial Cemetery is inscribed with the four-letter spelling, so we have opted to use that version of her nickname.
- The Vezina Trophy was donated to the NHL by the Montreal Canadiens to honor the memory of their outstanding goaltender Georges Vézina, who died from tuberculosis in March 1926 at

Notes on Spellings

age 39. Vézina's surname was spelled with an acute accent on the e. However, the accent almost never appears in print in English-language references to the goaltender or the trophy named for him. Rightly or wrongly, we are sticking to the established practice of not spelling the trophy's name with an accent.
- The NHL officially began referring to its championship series as a singular "final" circa 2006. However, much of the North American media—and a great many hockey fans—continue to refer to it in the plural form as the Stanley Cup "finals" to this day. Those two terms are interchangeable. You will see both in this book.

Introduction

In all of sports, there is nothing quite like hockey's sudden-death overtime for its inherent excitement. Once the puck is dropped at center ice, a game can literally end at any moment with either team emerging victorious. No ticketholder worth his salt dares to venture to a concession stand, a souvenir shop, or anywhere else in the arena once the fourth period of a hockey game starts. Similarly, few fans watching the action at home on television choose to take a bathroom break with overtime action underway—unless nature absolutely forces them to do so. NHL playoff overtime is intrinsically riveting.

Baseball has had extra innings to break ties since the 19th century, but because each team is required to get its at-bats, the format is more designed for sustained drama rather than an opportunity for instant thrills and an unexpected climax. Basketball's overtime is merely a five-minute extension of its regulation time. Regardless of how much scoring occurs, the game will continue until the buzzer ending the extra time sounds. It has no frenzied action or high drama remotely comparable to an overtime period of hockey. Despite its overwhelming popularity, American football—in both the college and pro ranks—has yet to come up with a format for breaking ties that is simple, efficient, and, at the same time, fair. Because of these flaws, there is a strong belief among some football followers that regular-season ties should not be broken at all. Soccer fans generally despise penalty shootouts to break deadlocks in elimination matches that 30 minutes of extra time has failed to settle. They decry the gimmick that they believe unsatisfactorily ended both the 1994 and 2022 FIFA World Cup tournaments.

Hockey is unique in its sudden-death format: fans observing the game have no clue if they are in for a few additional seconds of on-ice entertainment or several hours of exciting end-to-end action. NHL history has shown that either outcome is just as likely.

According to an article written for hockeyresponse.com, the average overtime in an NHL playoff game lasts about 13 minutes. Of course,

Stanley Cup playoff overtimes can be wildly brief. It took just nine seconds of bonus time for the Montreal Canadiens to defeat the Calgary Flames on May 18, 1986, courtesy of rookie Brian Skrudland's quick strike. There have been three other postseason games in the NHL's century-long history that took exactly 11 seconds of overtime to decide. On the reverse side of the coin, a deadlocked playoff game can drag on until the wee hours of the morning, testing the stamina and nerves of the fittest of players and the hardiest of fans. It is doubtful there is anyone still alive who witnessed or who can honestly recall either of the NHL's two six-overtime games that were played three years apart in the 1930s. However, scholarly hockey fans born decades afterward are usually able to name the men who scored the overtime tallies in both of those famous games: Modere (Mud) Bruneteau of the Detroit Red Wings on March 24–25, 1936, and Ken Doraty of the Toronto Maple Leafs on April 3–4, 1933. Although neither man is enshrined in the Hockey Hall of Fame, both Bruneteau and Doraty have achieved an enduring type of celebrity status that many Hall of Famers have subsequently lost as the years progressed after their retirements from the sport. All glory is certainly *not* fleeting for those two Stanley Cup overtime heroes.

As the cases of Bruneteau and Doraty dramatically prove, NHL playoff overtime heroics can lift an obscure player to instant fame if he is the man who happens to notch the winning goal. Cam Connor, a rugged member of the dynastic Montreal Canadiens who never got much ice time in his one season with the powerful Habs, was not nearly as well-known as Roger Doucet, the team's operatic national anthem singer. (Connor once joked on his own *View from the Penalty Box* podcast that if he ever wrote his autobiography, it ought to be titled *Cam Who?*) Nevertheless, Connor was the toast of Canadiens fans for his double-overtime tally versus the Toronto Maple Leafs during the 1979 Stanley Cup playoffs. It occurred on his only shift in that marathon game! More than 40 years later, Connor is still frequently asked to revisit and comment on his memorable goal as it was easily the most noteworthy occurrence in his 109-game NHL career.

There is absolutely no accounting for whom the hockey gods may favor during the Stanley Cup playoffs. Joe Sakic scored a remarkable eight overtime winners in playoff competition in his stellar career. That is a record, two better than Maurice Richard's total of six—which was once thought to be unbreakable. Evander Kane and Corey Perry are close to Richard's runner-up mark with five apiece. At the other end of the spectrum, some of the NHL's greatest superstars—Gordie Howe and Frank Mahovlich, for example—never once scored a playoff overtime goal. Notables such as Sidney Crosby, Jean Béliveau and Bobby Orr got just one each. Yet Boston's Mel Hill fired home *three* within a 12-day stretch in a single 1939 playoff series versus the New York Rangers—he had never scored one before and he never scored another after—after netting just 10 goals during the 1938–39 regular season. It is no wonder he acquired the catchy, flattering and enduring nickname "Sudden Death Hill" for his feat. It remained with him for the rest of his life. (By comparison, Hill's three overtime tallies place him just one behind the four notched by Wayne Gretzky over his long and storied career.)

Given the tremendous drama connected to overtime games, it is somewhat surprising that few NHL fans today know much about the 1951 Stanley Cup finals. That spring, the Toronto Maple Leafs defeated the Montreal Canadiens in the best-of-seven matchup in five thrilling games. Remarkably all five contests required an overtime period to determine a winner! (They were all settled quickly, however. None of the five extra sessions lasted more than six minutes. Such facts did not stop a United Press reporter from hyperbolically calling the series "one of the most grueling Stanley Cup finals in history."[1]) Be that as it may, such a quirky occurrence had never happened before 1951—and, not too surprisingly, it has not happened again. It was quite a month of playoff hockey. Even during the two Stanley Cup semifinal series that season, additional periods were almost the norm. "All those fans around the National Hockey League who were yelling for a return of overtime play have found it on the menu virtually every night,"[2] gushed Dink Carroll, the sports editor of the *Montreal Gazette*, well before the Maple Leafs and Canadiens clashed in the Cup finals.

Apart from the widespread but tragic fame attained by Bill Barilko, one of the series' overtime heroes, it is likely that only the most devoted fans of hockey history know very much about the '51 finals. Perhaps it is because that particular Stanley Cup series occurred just before the beginning of the NHL's partnership with television. *Hockey Night in Canada* did not begin its weekly TV broadcasts until October 1952. Thus, any hockey fan who wanted to follow the goings-on of the NHL's 1951 championship series as it happened had to listen to *HNIC*'s descriptions on the radio and let the power of words paint the images for him or her. Interestingly, in a June 2023 poll, not even one of those five games from April 1951 made the cut when journalist Jeff Mazydlo compiled his list of the 25 best games ever played in the Stanley Cup finals for the website Yardbarker.com.

"It was a great, great hockey series. [It was] certainly the best I was ever in," said Toronto's Howie Meeker in an interview half a century later.[3] *The Hockey News* wholeheartedly concurred, stating that fans could not have asked for a more exciting finale to the season than five overtimes in the five games. Upon the series' conclusion, that same publication called the 1951 Stanley Cup finals "tight as bark." It was.

Introduction

Such a wonderful championship series deserves to be revisited—and that is what this book will do. To give a thorough picture of how that riveting Stanley Cup championship series came to be, both semifinals and the 1950–51 finals will be examined in detail. As well, the regular season will be recapped for its trends, highlights and curiosities. In the end, there was a great fight for both first place in the league standings and for fourth place as well—the NHL's final playoff spot in its famous and nostalgic six-team era.

At a time when the Korean War was escalating and expanding,

Bill Barilko's Stanley Cup ring. Presented posthumously to his family, it represented the fourth championship Barilko had won in five seasons with the Maple Leafs (photo by Carl T. Madden).

President Harry Truman was quarreling with General Douglas MacArthur, a vast college basketball game-fixing scandal was unfolding, and various geopolitical goings-on were dominating the front pages of daily newspapers, it was NHL playoff hockey—overtime hockey—that provided a pleasant diversion for the sport's passionate followers on both sides of the Canada-U.S. border. In April 1951, 60 minutes of action often decided absolutely nothing.

1

The 1950–51 NHL Regular Season

A Two-Team Race

From the moment the six member clubs of the National Hockey League began playing meaningful games on Wednesday, October 11, 1950—the earliest opening date in the circuit's 34-year history—until the regular season reached its climax in late March, only two teams seemed to have the makings of a Stanley Cup champion: the Detroit Red Wings and the Toronto Maple Leafs. The other four outfits played as if they were also-rans. In fact, no other team posted a .500 record. Furthermore, for the first half of the 1950–51 season, it looked like Toronto would have no serious opposition at all until Detroit improved steadily and got themselves back into the race for first-place. Nevertheless, as in all NHL campaigns, there were enough peripheral stories to keep fans interested and talking about the league throughout its six months and 210 games of regular-season play.

Before the season began, the NHL instituted a new rule which required the home club have an emergency backup goaltender present at every game for use by either team. It might be a retired pro netminder or a capable amateur. He basically got a free ticket to the game and had to be ready at a moment's notice to rush down to either team's dressing room to replace a starting goalie. This mandate, of course, was to be used only in case a team's regular goaltender was so seriously incapacitated by an injury that he was unable to return to the ice to finish a game. As they had always done in the past, the NHL's gallant, bare-faced goaltenders were expected to "tough it out" as best they could. As it turned out, none of these use-if-necessary replacements was needed in any game during the 1950–51 NHL regular season. Only nine different goalies saw action in the NHL over its entire 210-game schedule.

On July 1, the Boston Bruins announced that coach George (Buck)

Boucher would not be returning for a second year after a disappointing 1949–50 season. Boucher had been a longtime NHL player, his 17-year career spanned from 1915 to 1932, most of it with the original Ottawa Senators. Previously, Boucher had three brief NHL coaching stints, none of which lasted more than one season. Oddly, each of the three NHL teams Boucher had coached in the past were now defunct: the Montreal Maroons, Ottawa Senators, and St. Louis Eagles. In 1948–49, Boucher had coached an amateur version of the Ottawa Senators—a team that played in the Quebec Hockey League—to the Allan Cup, the symbol of amateur hockey supremacy in Canada. Bruins general manager Art Ross hoped Boucher would bring some of that winning magic to Boston in 1949–50. It did not work out that way. The Bruins finished the league's lengthy new 70-game schedule in fifth place with a disappointing 22-32-16 record. Boucher did not take his sudden dismissal especially well, calling it "the dirtiest deal I ever had in my 15 years [sic] in hockey."[1] He never again coached in the NHL.

Ross lured a former foe, Lynn Patrick, to replace the dismissed Boucher and fill the vacancy. Patrick, a longtime player with New York Rangers, had coached that club to within one goal of the 1950 Stanley Cup, but the Rangers refused to match the $12,000 offer the Bruins had made to him. (Rookie coach Neil Colville would be hired as the Rangers' new bench boss for 1950–51.) Ross publicly stated it was his intention to slowly groom Patrick to eventually take over the GM position with the Bruins—the role the former now occupied—by 1952. Patrick, alas, did not enjoy much immediate success in Boston.

"The Bruins are termed the 'mystery team' because nobody knows much about them," wrote journalist Austin (Dink) Carroll in an October 14 *Montreal Gazette* article that ran just prior to Boston's first appearance at the Montreal Forum in 1950–51. He continued,

> They had the shortest training period of any of the NHL clubs. Lynn Patrick, their new coach, has been doing considerable experimenting with the players. Boston writers, who have had a good look at the club, say that Jack Gelineau, the Bruins goaltender who won the Rookie of the Year award last season, is vastly improved and appears to be headed for a great season.

The Bruins held their training camp in Kitchener, Ontario. Just before it closed, coach Patrick optimistically declared his team was 25 percent better than the previous year and almost a certainty to qualify for the Stanley Cup playoffs come springtime.

The preseason confidence in Boston initially seemed to be ill-founded as Patrick's club got off to a disappointingly sour start. The 1950–51 campaign was a difficult one for the Bruins as they suffered both on the ice and

Lynn Patrick, the New York Ranger player pictured in this photograph from his playing days, became the coach of the Boston Bruins in 1950. His uncle, Frank Patrick, is at the left. His father Lester is at the right. The other man is not identified (courtesy Boston Public Library, Leslie Jones Collection).

at the Boston Garden turnstiles. After playing their first eight games, the club had three ties and five losses. The team's first win did not come until November 4 at the Montreal Forum where they prevailed, 3–2, over the Habs. "After eight futile attempts, the Boston Bruins finally won their first game of the National Hockey League season," reported the next day's Sunday *Boston Globe*. Despite picking up two points, the Bruins were still at the bottom of the NHL standings. Four more games went by before the Bruins recorded their second victory of 1950–51, this time beating the Chicago Black Hawks at home on November 11. Qualifying for the playoffs at the end of March seemed to be out of the question for this lackluster Boston outfit.

There were also changes afoot in Toronto where the Maple Leafs were a dominant force. Team owner Conn Smythe had been in less-than-perfect health in recent years. With his overall well-being a big question mark,

Smythe relinquished some of his duties to his underlings, but that did not necessarily mean that Smythe would take a hands-off approach in the club's management. Taking a backseat was simply not Smythe's way to operate. Hap Day, who had won five Stanley Cups as the team's coach, was promoted to the position of general manager. Joe Primeau, who had starred for the Leafs during the 1930s, was hired as the team's new coach to replace Day behind the bench. Primeau had been offered the vacant coaching position in Boston by Art Ross, but he politely declined the job. It proved to be a very wise choice for the affable man whom the press sometimes referred to as "Gentleman Joe."

Months before the first puck was dropped for the 1950–51 season, the largest trade in NHL history occurred on Thursday, July 13. It involved a whopping nine players. The participants were the defending Stanley Cup champion Detroit Red Wings and the always-struggling Chicago Black Hawks. It was certainly an eye-catcher. Detroit sent their very capable 23-year-old goaltender, Harry Lumley, and four other players to the Hawks. The departing Wings were defensemen Jack Stewart and Al Dewsbury, center Don Morrison, and forward Pete Babando. (Just a few months earlier, Babando had dramatically scored the winning goal in overtime to defeat the New York Rangers in the seventh game of the 1950 Stanley Cup finals. Apparently, even that rare and memorable feat was not good enough to keep Babando on the roster of the defending Cup champions.)

In return, the Red Wings acquired four players from the struggling Chicago organization. Those players were journeyman goaltender Jim Henry, defenseman Bob

Toronto owner Conn Smythe was still an omnipresent figure within the Maple Leafs organization in 1950–51 despite being told by his physician to reduce his involvement in the day-by-day operations of the club (courtesy Boston Public Library, Leslie Jones Collection).

Goldham, and forwards Gaye Stewart and Metro Prystai. According to general manager Jack Adams, Prystai was acquired to eventually replace the aging Sid Abel as Detroit's first-line center. That part of the deal made sense. To many outsiders, however, trading the promising Lumley seemed an odd thing for Adams to do, as the young Lumley had been quite good for the Red Wings during the successful 1950 Cup playoffs. However, Adams had an even more highly regarded goaltending newcomer named Terry Sawchuk under contract. He simply oozed quality. Sawchuk had played a handful of games for the Wings in 1949–50 and was seeking an opportunity to play regularly in the NHL. By abruptly shipping Lumley to the downtrodden Black Hawks, Adams saw to it that Sawchuk got the job opening in Detroit he desired. Over the next decade, Lumley would become something of an itinerant netminder, playing for every NHL team except Montreal in a fine career that lasted until 1960; he would be elected to the Hall of Fame in 1980.

Sawchuk was on another level, however. The Winnipeg-born netminder would quickly establish himself as one of the top NHL goalies of all-time—the best ever, in the eyes of a great many hockey historians. Over his career he amassed 445 career wins—a lifetime statistical category Sawchuk led when he played his last game in 1970. (As of the start of the 2023–24 NHL season, he holds down the eighth spot.) In 1950–51, Sawchuk's skills were first displayed before a large gathering of hockey writers at the annual All-Star Game in Detroit on October 8. At the time, it was a preseason game contested between the defending Stanley Cup champions and a team comprised of top players from the other five NHL teams. It was an impressive outing for the 20-year-old Sawchuk. Before a less-than-capacity crowd of 9,600 patrons, the Red Wings won the All-Star Game easily, 7–1. Despite the seven tallies, it was the newcomer guarding the pipes for the champions in the wide-open contest who got the most praise. It was well deserved. Dink Carroll wrote in his October 10 column for the *Montreal Gazette,*

> This brings us to Terry Sawchuk, the Red Wings' rookie netminder. How good is he? Consensus was that he is very, very good. He is big, fast, and rarely loses sight of the puck, which is quite a feat in the type of hockey they are playing today. Indeed, Baz O'Meara [the veteran *Montreal Star* sports editor], who has seen a lot of puck-stoppers come and go, pronounced him as the best young goaltender he had ever seen.

At the time of the massive Red Wings-Black Hawks trade, Chicago president Bill Tobin gleefully crowed that his club had gotten the better of the deal, but time would prove otherwise. Two months into the season, on December 2, the Red Wings and Black Hawks arranged another trade, with Detroit picking up Bert Olmstead and Vic Stasiuk from Chicago in exchange for Steve Black and Lee Fogolin (Sr.). As it turned out, Olmstead never played a game for Detroit. He was traded by the Red Wings to Montreal 17 days later for Leo Gravelle and an unspecified amount of cash. The Habs absolutely fared better than Detroit in that deal.

The Chicago Black Hawks would have a new coach in 1950–51, too. It was 43-year-old Ebenezer (Ebbie) Goodfellow, a former defenseman who had played his entire 14-year NHL career in Detroit. His tenure dated back to the time when the club was nicknamed the Cougars and the Falcons. Goodfellow replaced Charlie Conacher, the former Maple Leaf star player of the 1930s, who had finished out of the playoffs in each of the three seasons he had been the man guiding the Hawks. Thus, three of the NHL's six clubs would have a new face behind the bench as the 1950–51 season opened. Goodfellow had achieved success coaching in the American Hockey League, leading the St. Louis Flyers to a divisional championship. However, Goodfellow had an uphill climb waiting for him in Chicago. The Black Hawks had finished in the league's cellar in 1949–50. Not much improvement was expected from them.

The NHL scheduled a rematch of the 1950 Cup finals on opening night of the league's 34th season, with the New York Rangers visiting the Red Wings in Detroit. Ranger coach Neil Colville cautiously predicted his club would have only a moderately successful season because of the strength of the defending Stanley Cup holders his team was about to face. "I don't think we'll finish first or second," he told the Associated Press the day before the first puck was dropped. "We'll have a good chance for third. It will be between us and Boston." He then added, "Detroit is the team to beat."[2]

It was the earliest opening night in NHL history—October 11. The hometown Red Wings prevailed in a tight affair, 3–2, with Ted Lindsay scoring the first goal of the new season against Chuck Rayner who was guarding the New York net. Surprisingly, the game did not draw a full house to the Detroit Olympia. The announced turnstile count was just 11,321. It was the first indication that the league's attendance—or lack thereof—in American cities would be a hot and sometimes sensitive topic throughout the long grind. Similarly, the first Sunday of NHL play saw fewer than 11,000 fans turn out for the Boston Bruins' home opener against the Montreal Canadiens. That attraction would have been a guaranteed sellout at Boston Garden just a few short years before. The game, a 2–1 victory by the visitors, featured a wild third-period brawl that cleared both benches. Among the witnesses was a more technically gifted scrapper: Sugar Ray Robinson, the supremely talented world welterweight boxing champion. His views of the impromptu hockey punch-up were not

1. The 1950–51 NHL Regular Season

The supremely talented world welterweight boxing champion Sugar Ray Robinson was at Boston Garden for the Boston Bruins' 1950–51 home opener versus Montreal. He witnessed a few fights of a different nature (courtesy Boston Public Library, Leslie Jones Collection).

sought. (Robinson was in town, preparing for a non-title bout at Boston Garden on October 16 versus Joe Rindone who was efficiently dispatched in six rounds. The win raised Robinson's professional ring record to a mind-boggling 114–1–2.)

Those Montreal Canadiens were a team with unusually low expectations for 1950–51. Coach Dick Irvin promised the media, in a speech at a luncheon, that his team would make the playoffs when springtime arrived, but nothing more than that. Nevertheless, a record turnout of 14,224 fans filled the Forum for the campaign-starter on Thursday, October 12, to see the visiting Chicago Black Hawks put a scare into the home team. The game ended in a 3–3 tie with the Habs having to stage a comeback to overcome a two-goal deficit in the third period to salvage a draw. "It looked grim for the Habitants," Dink Carroll wrote in the next day's *Montreal Gazette*, "but they caught fire in the last seven minutes to tie the count on markers by Kenny Mosdell and Floyd Curry."[3] Maurice (the Rocket) Richard did not figure in on any of Montreal's three goals, but the fiery 29-year-old would be the main headline-grabber for the Canadiens throughout the team's 70-game grind and beyond, for both good and bad reasons.

Prior to the game, there was a somber moment of silence observed at the Forum for George Hainsworth, Montreal's small but superb goaltender from the late 1920s and early 1930s. On October 9, the 57-year-old Hainsworth had been killed in a head-on accident with a truck near Gravenhurst, Ontario. When the fatal mishap occurred, Hainsworth and his wife, Alma, were returning to their home in Kitchener where he was a city councilor and an accomplished hockey coach. They had been to Val D'Or, Quebec, to visit their son. Alma and three other people suffered relatively minor injuries, but her ex-goalie husband was pronounced dead at the scene. Hainsworth had compiled 94 career shutouts in regular-season play—22 of them in one 44-game season!—a career NHL mark that would eventually be topped by Terry Sawchuk who finished his stellar career with 103 whitewashes.

The Toronto Maple Leafs, who had won three of the last four Stanley Cups, got off to a roaring start to their 1950–51 campaign, as was expected. They disappointingly lost their season-opener at home to Chicago by a 2–1 score to start on a sour note, but they rallied from a 4–1 third-period hole in the space of about three minutes to tie the Red Wings, 4–4, in Detroit the next night. It was certainly an inauspicious start for Toronto, but the Leafs did not taste defeat again for nearly a month—a stretch of 11 games without enduring their second loss. Detroit ended the Maple Leafs' impressive point streak on November 11 with a 3–1 triumph at Maple Leaf Gardens. It was somewhat fitting as the Red Wings would soon emerge as the only serious challenger Toronto truly had in the chase for the Prince of Wales Trophy. At the time, that bauble was awarded each season to the NHL team that finished atop the standings. When December 23 dawned, Toronto led the NHL with 44 points to Detroit's 41, although the Leafs had played three more games than the Red Wings. The other four clubs were far in arrears. Not one of them even had accrued 30 points.

The Maple Leafs tried something that was heretofore unknown in NHL hockey. They had two goaltenders who regularly shared the team's netminding duties throughout the 1950–51 season: Rookie Elwin (Al) Rollins and hugely popular veteran Walter (Turk) Broda. On February 28, a Canadian Press story lauded Toronto's goaltending heir apparent. It stated,

> There isn't a hotter goaltender in the league than Al Rollins, the lanky rookie from Vanguard, Saskatchewan. He's threatening to walk off with the Vezina goaltending prize as well as the NHL's rookie prize as well. Rollins hasn't pushed Broda to the sidelines yet. Leaf plans are to leave the rookie in until

Turk Broda was hugely popular and successful in his long tenure as the Toronto Maple Leafs goaltender. When the 1951 playoffs began, however, Broda's career was rapidly winding down, and he had been replaced by the much younger Al Rollins (courtesy Boston Public Library, Leslie Jones Collection).

he's beaten or looks bad. Then the Turk—in what is probably his last season—will get the call again.[4]

By the end of the 70-game season, the much younger Rollins—who turned 24 shortly before the Maple Leafs' opening game—had appeared in 40 contests to the 36-year-old Broda's 31. (There was one Toronto game in which both Rollins and Broda appeared—a true rarity in the early 1950s.) In contrast, three of the six NHL teams used just one goalie for every minute of every game. The Leafs unusual ploy worked out well for them as the team led the circuit in fewest goals allowed, with 138. Detroit was second-best with 139. (Rollins, keenly mindful of the goals-against stats for both the Maple Leafs and Red Wings, allowed just three goals in Toronto's final five games. Over his final five games, Sawchuk allowed nine goals to Detroit's opponents even though the Wings' last game—versus Montreal—was a shutout.)

However, the rotating goalie system created an unforeseen problem for the NHL. Under the league's rules at the time, the Vezina Trophy was awarded to the team that allowed the fewest goals over the course of the season and specifically to the goaltender on that team who played in the most games. Based on those criteria, the Vezina Trophy—and its $2,000 prize—was given to Rollins instead of Detroit's sensational rookie, Terry Sawchuk, who played all 4,200 minutes of the Red Wings' 70 games in 1950–51 and compiled a 1.97 goals-against average (GAA). (Despite Sawchuk's rapid ascension to NHL star status, his surname was often misspelled with an extra C before the K by many sports reporters during his breakout season.) Rollins had the superior GAA (1.77), but had played just 2,367 minutes during the season—slightly more than 56 percent of Sawchuk's workload. Tellingly, Sawchuk was voted the winner of the Frank Calder Memorial Trophy as the NHL's Rookie of the Year, however. Rollins finished second in the Calder voting.

Conversely, at the other end of the NHL standings sat the disappointing New York Rangers. They were faring poorly in the season's first two months. Based on how close New York was to winning the Stanley Cup in 1950, their slow start surprised many NHL fans. "We had the makings of a winner the second time around," former Rangers general manager Frank Boucher—a younger brother of ex–Boston coach George Boucher—sadly recalled, "but then everything went wrong."[5]

The previous year's Stanley Cup finalists got out of the gate slowly under the guidance of their young, new coach Neil Colville. New York lost their opening game on Wednesday, October 11, by a 3–2 score in Detroit, but won their next contest four nights later in Chicago by the same close score. Then followed a dreadful winless skein for New York that did not end until Wednesday, November 22, in Montreal. After 17 games, the Rangers had just one victory, but they had played seven tie games over that stretch, so their record was not quite as dismal as it seemed.

Nevertheless, in a combination publicity stunt and desperation move, the Rangers boldly hired a psychologist—something completely new to hockey—to try to shift their players into a positive-thinking mode. Dr. David F. Tracy was brought aboard for the task. A passionate sports fan, the portly Tracy used hypnotism in his methods. Tracy did have some experience on his résumé dealing with underperforming top-tier sports teams. His talents had allegedly turned the St. Francis College basketball team into winners. But when a Major League Baseball club, the bottom-feeding St. Louis Browns, secured the services of Tracy in 1950, it did not pay dividends for them. The dismal Browns failed to turn their fortunes around. (In fairness, some of the St. Louis ballplayers defiantly refused to cooperate with Tracy. They believed him to be a quack.) Tracy was on the payroll for 33 games. St. Louis won just eight of them. The Browns finished in seventh spot in the eight-team American League in 1950 with a 58–96 record, 40 games out of first place. Tracy put the blame for his dismissal squarely on the shoulders of St. Louis manager Zack Taylor, claiming the old-school pilot of the Browns did not fully embrace his unique and modern ideas. He later told a reporter,

> From the start, [Taylor] displayed no interest in my work. He neither helped nor hindered me. Had he stepped in and gone along with me, I think I could have helped him win some games. When I joined the Browns, I had an idea I'd have the status of a coach, with authority to call the players together, possibly once a week for meetings. Also, I thought I'd be given the privilege of talking to certain players just before they took the field for a game, so I could cement in their minds the theories transmitted to them earlier, but the Browns didn't approve of my plan.

In a parting shot at the club, Tracy bitterly added, "The Browns got a million dollars' worth of publicity, but they failed to get the benefits of my work."[6]

The disappointing outcome did not seem to dissuade Tracy at all. Shortly thereafter, he wrote a detailed book about his experiences with the Browns titled *The Psychologist at Bat*. The *New York Daily News* was certainly skeptical about New York's NHL team giving the doctor a second chance to influence a professional sports outfit. It ran the following negative headline: "Rangers Need Victory—Get Dr. Tracy Instead."[7]

Be that as it may, Dr. Tracy reported to Madison Square Garden at 1 p.m. on the afternoon of Thursday, November 15, 1950, to try his luck with the minds of the struggling New York Rangers. That night, at 8:30, they would host their traditional rivals, the Boston Bruins. Years later, Boucher recalled the scene.

> Tracy came into our dressing room an hour or so before our game against Boston. He was a burly, jovial man with sleek black hair, beautifully tailored clothes ... [but] he had a peculiar eye. There was a white dot in it that made him look very odd indeed.[8]

Tracy immediately went to work. He selected forward Tony Leswick at the beginning of his hypnotic phase. Tracy stared into Leswick's eyes and talked quietly while teammates, Pentti Lund, Alex Kaleta and Buddy O'Connor all listened closely to him. "Then, he spoke to all the players [individually]," Boucher remembered. "When it was Nick Mickoski's turn, Nick fled the room. He was afraid that Tracy was going to hypnotize him."[9]

With Mickoski purposefully absent, Tracy ignored the unexpected snub and spoke to the rest of the team collectively. In a quiet, deliberate tone, he stressed the importance of a positive attitude for success. His work done for the night, Tracy exited the dressing room and the Rangers prepared to play the visiting Boston Bruins.

Perhaps Dr. Tracy had helped the Rangers—but not at the box office. As a publicity stunt, Dr. Tracy was a bust. *The Boston Globe* reported that fewer than 7,000 fans paid to watch the game—one of the lowest single-game attendance totals in Rangers' club history, one which dated back to the 1926–27 season. Be that as it may, it was a tightly played contest. New York and Boston were even, 2–2, after the second period. Sadly for the home team, they surrendered a pair of third-period goals and lost the game, 4–3. It was their 13th straight outing without posting a win (0–7 with six ties). Tracy publicly blamed the team's defeat on the unlucky number 13—and on New York goaltender Chuck Rayner's subpar netminding. Dr. Tracy's services were never sought by the Rangers again.

On January 1, 1951, Dink Carroll of the *Montreal Gazette* sent out New Year's greetings to everyone in the sports world whom he thought deserved special praise. One such person was Frank Boucher, who, according to the scribe, "never dodged a rap for the Rangers' lowly position in the NHL standings, whether it was coming to him or not."[10]

Remarkably, by the end of the season, the Rangers were a Stanley Cup playoff contender and a threat to finish as high as third place. However, that was truly more a reflection of how weak the bottom four teams in the NHL were in 1950–51 than any great improvement made by the New Yorkers in the campaign's final three months.

The NHL's feel-good story of the 1950–51 season came out of Detroit where 23-year-old Gordie Howe won the league's scoring championship with a record total of 86 points by accruing 43 goals and 43 assists. That sum bested the old NHL mark of 82 points set by Herbie Cain of the Boston Bruins in the substandard wartime season of 1943–44 when most of the league's stars were in some branch of the Canadian or American military. (The NHL's regular season was just 50 games long then, and Cain had played in 49 of Boston's games.) Howe had nearly died from a serious on-ice head injury during the opening round of the 1950 Stanley Cup playoffs, so his scoring title the following season was an unexpected, delightful bonus for the Red Wings.

The date was March 28, 1950. It was the first game of the 1950 Stanley

Cup playoffs. Detroit was hosting Toronto in a match the home team would lose badly, 5–0. (It was the twelfth straight playoff game Toronto had won versus Detroit.) The main story coming from the Olympia was a scary one, involving one of the NHL's greatest young stars. A United Press report said, "Gordie Howe, brilliant wingman of the Detroit Red Wings, underwent an emergency operation earlier today, less than three hours after he suffered severe head injuries in a Stanley Cup hockey game here on Tuesday."[11]

What exactly happened to the 22-year-old Howe in the third period is subject to debate, even to this day. There is no known film of the incident, and newspaper reports from that time vary greatly. It is the NHL's *Rashomon* moment in which numerous eyewitnesses cannot come close to agreeing on what they saw. Everyone, however, agrees that with Toronto holding a 4–0 lead in the third period, the Maple Leafs esteemed captain, 24-year-old Ted (Teeder) Kennedy, was rushing the puck along the left boards. He was being pursued from behind by Detroit defenseman Jack Stewart and from the side by Gordie Howe. This is where the various accounts of what occurred between Kennedy and Howe differ wildly.

One version has Howe attempting to bodycheck Kennedy, missing him, and awkwardly crashing head-first into the side boards at the Olympia with Stewart then adding to Howe's woes by accidentally falling on top of him. A more sinister version has Kennedy subtly butt-ending Howe in the face as he deftly eluded Howe's check after which the already injured Detroit star slammed heavily against the boards and then was flattened by teammate Stewart. There was no penalty called against Kennedy, who had accrued a moderate total of 34 penalty minutes during the 1949–50 NHL season.

Although Detroit coach Tommy Ivan and the team's general manager, Jack Adams, insisted the latter butt-ending tale was indeed accurate, in an Associated Press story that ran following day, Kennedy maintained that he had made no contact whatsoever with Howe. "I don't know how he got [injured]," Kennedy insisted. "I avoided his check along the boards and didn't feel anything hit me, although he may have hit my stick."[12] Kennedy further stated that he was so oblivious to what had happened to Howe that he had to be alerted by his Maple Leaf teammates that Howe was lying injured near the boards.

Upon hearing those remarks, Detroit goalie Harry Lumley angrily declared, "Kennedy is a damned liar."[13] NHL president Clarence Campbell sided with Kennedy's account. Campbell was among the spectators at the Olympia that night and he saw nothing untoward happen on the fateful play. The game officials' postgame report supported this version of the events, too. Furthermore, Campbell publicly rebuked Ivan and warned him that his remarks about Kennedy were potentially libelous.

Among the hockey writers who staunchly defended Kennedy from any wrongdoing was Ted Reeve of the *Toronto Telegram*. Reeve thought the butt-ending accusation was nonsense. He asked, "How would a right-handed stickhandler [Kennedy] going down the left boards give anyone a butt-end?"[14] During his recuperation, Howe bluntly and graciously said to a reporter, "Ted is too good a player to deliberately injure another player."[15] Years later, Howe, who always believed he had been struck somehow by Kennedy's stick, described his injuries as accidental and self-inflicted. Until he died at age 83, Kennedy lived with the enduring suspicions of having maliciously injured Howe—suspicions held by numerous people who were not even born when the incident occurred. In Kennedy's lengthy obituary that appeared on the NHL's website on August 14, 2009, the controversial 1950 playoff incident with Howe was not even mentioned.

Besides the life-threatening head injury, Howe also suffered a lacerated right eyeball, along with a fractured nose, cheekbone, and skull. Bleeding profusely, Howe was sprawled unconscious on the ice; he did not move in the slightest.

Rushed to the nearby Harper Hospital, Howe, vomiting blood, was diagnosed with a brain hemorrhage from a ruptured blood vessel. He endured a three-hour emergency procedure where a hole was drilled into his skull to drain the excess blood that had collected around his brain. Over the next few days, frequent radio bulletins from the hospital kept concerned Michiganders and Canadians from coast to coast updated about Howe's serious condition. It was widely assumed that if Howe survived the ordeal—and that was a huge "if"—his promising professional NHL career was certainly over. The Montreal Canadiens, to a man, all became very silent when they heard the grim news while waiting to check in at a New York City hotel for their Stanley Cup semifinal playoff series with the Rangers. Goaltender Bill Durnan spoke for them all when he told a newspaperman, "That's an awful thing to happen to a kid like that. Why, he's only 22 ... or is it 21? This may mean the end of his hockey career."[16]

That was a gross miscalculation. Howe did not play in the rest of the 1950 playoffs, but he was present, in street clothes, when the Red Wings won the Stanley Cup 26 days later. As a souvenir of the awful incident, Howe would have a steel plate embedded in his skull for the rest of his life. He would also become a beloved icon within the sport, playing on and off until 1980 at the age of 52, and earning the endearing sobriquet "Mr. Hockey."

In 1950–51 the New York Rangers did not top the league in points, but they certainly led the NHL in oddball publicity stunts. Case in point: After the underachieving New York Rangers had failed with Dr. David Tracy's psychology experiment early in the season, in late December a diehard fan took it upon himself to try something completely new to get his favorite NHL team out of their doldrums. It was restaurateur Gene Leone, the owner/operator of Leone's, an Italian restaurant located a short distance from Madison Square Garden. For the sake of his beloved Rangers, Leone concocted an elixir of mysterious portions to give them a boost in their New Year's Eve game versus the Boston Bruins.

With the blessings of Ranger general manager Frank Boucher—who was a good friend of the restaurant owner—Leone brought a black bottle into the home team's dressing room. It was accompanied by a note that got straight to the point: "Drink it and win." Most of the Rangers were brave enough to sample the stuff. Its taste got mixed reviews. One imbiber said it tasted like the Atlantic Ocean, while another praised it for its kick. "One gulp and we feel like a bunch of war horses,"[17] claimed center Edgar Laprade. But there was no denying its effect on the team. The result was wholly positive for New York. The visiting Bruins were dispatched, 3–0, by the New Yorkers to end 1950 on a high note, even though the team's record was now 7–14–13 after 34 games. Laprade had scored 32 seconds into the first period for New York. It was really the only tally the home team required. A pair of third-period goals by Nick Mickoski put the game out of reach. Many fans among the sellout crowd came equipped with noisemakers in preparation for the New Year's Eve festivities. They used them well before the midnight hour struck.

Over the next little while, Leone's Magic Elixir, as the Gotham press gleefully dubbed it, was downed with regularity by the Broadway Blueshirts. The Rangers lost, 3–2, on January 1 in Boston, in a game where goaltender Charlie Rayner was struck in the face by a deflected puck, delaying the game by about 35 minutes while he got patched up in Boston Garden's infirmary. After that setback, New York promptly rolled off three straight wins. The middle of those three games was a road victory. The bottle almost never made it to the game. Leone's liquid so rattled Toronto owner Conn Smythe that he tried to have the bottle impounded by customs when the Rangers crossed the border into Canada for a game at Maple Leaf Gardens on Saturday, January 6. The Rangers had to use some subterfuge to get the bottle to the arena in time for the game. New York won that contest, 4–2.

Overall, quaffing the brew got only mixed results for the Broadway Blueshirts. Whatever positive effects the elixir had on the Rangers; they were short-lived ones. New York missed qualifying for the Stanley Cup playoffs. Gene Leone later admitted that there was nothing sinister or mysterious whatsoever about the bottle's contents. It contained only a benign combination of orange juice, ginger ale, and honey.

In early March, Maurice Richard's volatile temper got him into trouble with NHL president Clarence Campbell. The trouble began at a Detroit-Montreal game at the Forum on Saturday, March 3. Detroit won the game 3–1, but that was only a secondary talking point for all those who witnessed the contest.

"Virtually everybody in the rink thought it was a poorly officiated game," bluntly wrote Dink Carroll in the March 5 edition of the *Montreal Gazette*. "Tension reached a peak near the halfway mark in the final period with the Canadiens trailing 2–1. Referee Hugh McLean gave the Rocket a misconduct penalty, which he later raised to a game misconduct."[18]

Richard was livid because he had been tripped and cut by a wayward Detroit stick, held by Sid Abel, that had opened a gash on his face. Abel also allegedly applied some wrestling holds to impede the Rocket's progress. Those violations went unnoticed—and unpenalized—by referee McLean. "A man can only take so much," Richard later told Montreal hockey writer Elmer Ferguson. He also told McLean, "This is the damnedest thing yet"[19]—which got him a misconduct penalty.

Richard, still steamed, trudged to the penalty box. There Detroit's Leo Reise laughed at the angry Hab and said something derisive that set off Montreal's #9. (It seems unbelievable by modern standards, but players from both teams typically shared the same penalty box in 1951.) Richard promptly punched Reise. Linesman Eddie Mephan tried to intervene, but all he got for his efforts was a poke from the Montreal superstar. That was when Richard was banished from the game. In a more philosophical frame of mind, Richard would later say, "There is no use in making protests about a thing like that because the referees are always right. They always punish the guy who finishes the argument, never the one who starts it."[20]

In his description of the goings-on, Dink Carroll wrote, "When it was announced over the loud speaker that [Richard] had been given a game misconduct, the crowd showered the ice with overshoes, programs, and newspapers. There was a long delay while the ice was being cleared. One overshoe struck referee McLean on the back."[21]

The Habs were playing the Rangers in New York City the very next night. When the team arrived at the Picadilly Hotel, whom did the Rocket glimpse in the lobby? It was none other than referee McLean! Always one to carry a grudge, Richard grabbed McLean by his necktie and wound up to throw a haymaker at him. Luckily for McLean, he was accompanied by linesman Jim Primeau who had also worked the Saturday game at the Montreal Forum. Amid plenty of colorful language, Primeau quickly intervened before a brawl erupted. Nevertheless, when Clarence Campbell heard about the unseemly scuffle at the hotel, he promptly fined Richard $500 for conduct detrimental to the welfare of hockey. Sports editor

1. The 1950–51 NHL Regular Season

Tommy Shields of the *Ottawa Citizen* commented on March 6, "Maurice Richard is not doing his cause any good. Untoward actions in the heat of a game can be understood and overlooked, but his run-in with referee McLean took place hours after the game was over." Shields also noted that a recent Pacific Coast League game featuring Babe Pratt as a coach saw the ex-NHLer punch out referee Eddie Powers and earn an indefinite suspension. Oddly, Pratt's New Westminster team was *ahead* of Portland 6–1 at the time of the assault.

The Rangers and Habs played to a 2–2 draw that night at Madison Square Garden. It had been an important game for both clubs who were battling for a playoff spot. The next morning the NHL standings showed Montreal sitting in fifth place, slightly behind both Boston and New York. However, the Habs were about to embark on a much-needed hot streak— one that vaulted them over both the Boston Bruins and New York Rangers by the end of the season.

There were a few memorable donnybrooks and other incidents during 1950–51 that required the NHL to enforce discipline. On January 25 at the Detroit Olympia during a Boston-Detroit Game, Ted Lindsay battled Bill Ezinicki in a heated, prolonged scuffle that lasted three full minutes—the length of a boxing round, noted the Canadian Press. There was no doubt about which scrapper won that one contest. It ended with Ezinicki of the Bruins lying flat on the Detroit ice bleeding profusely from a head wound behind his ear. Lindsay himself finished the fracas with a head wound and a cut on his hand. Both players received match penalties. Later, NHL president Clarence Campbell slapped them both with $300 fines and three-game suspensions. The brawl spawned several negative editorials about violence in hockey—especially at the professional level.

The last-place Chicago Black Hawks had their share of run-ins with Campbell, too. On February 3, in a 4–3 loss at Toronto, Chicago coach Ebbie Goodfellow was ejected by referee Hugh McLean, but he stubbornly refused to leave the visitors' bench area. He was tagged with a $250 fine by the league president for defying the requirement that an ejected coach had to go to his team's dressing room for the rest of the game. In another incident involving a misbehaving Hawk, Chicago's 34-year-old Roy Conacher was fined for shoving a referee. Sometimes the Black Hawks themselves were the victims of dangerous play. In March, Toronto's Gus Mortson was fined $250 for high-sticking Chicago forward Adam Brown. According to reports, the stick violence in that incident was hardly one-way: Mortson left the ice bloodied—and needing six stitches to close the wound in his gashed face.

But the top stories in hockey in 1950–51—as they often were in the top league's fabled six-team era—was the tight, two-team battle for first place

NHL president Clarence Campbell is flanked by Ted Lindsay (left) and Bill Ezinicki not long after the two players engaged in a nasty stick-swinging battle (courtesy Boston Public Library, Leslie Jones Collection).

and the even tighter struggle for the fourth and final berth in the Stanley Cup playoffs. The closeness of these twin races made just about every game in the last half of the season very meaningful one way or the other.

On January 3, with about half the schedule completed, Detroit held a slim one-point lead over Toronto for first place in the NHL, 48 points to 47. Three teams—Boston, New York, and Montreal—all sat deadlocked at 30 points. (Dink Carroll, writing a roundup column in the *Montreal Gazette* on New Year's Day, declared that the Canadiens' publicity department "did not have much to crow about" as 1950 ended.) Even last-place Chicago was within easy striking distance of the threesome directly above them with 27 points. By that time, however, the Black Hawks, were mired in a horrendous 21-game streak in which they failed to win a single contest throughout January. Dink Carroll's report in the January 12 edition of the *Montreal Gazette* of the Habs' 4–1 victory at the Forum against the Black Hawks the previous night was typical of how things went all year for the woebegone Chicagoans. It said,

> The Canadiens, to the fore, outskated and outhustled the Black Hawks all the way. Harry Lumley, the Hawks' good goaltender, kept his team in the game for

two periods behind a wobbly defense, but Harry himself tired of the peppering and did not look good on the last two shots that beat him.

By the time Chicago defeated Boston 5–2 on February 1 to end their embarrassing dry spell, they were well off the pace of the playoff contenders. On February 28, it was announced by the Black Hawks that their top scorer, Doug Bentley, was lost to the team with a season-ending groin injury. That bit of bad news basically terminated all hope for a miraculous Black Hawk ascension into a playoff spot. Chicago would end the season in the NHL cellar with just 36 points, a whopping 25 points behind the fifth-place team and 26 points out of the playoff chase. In their worst defeat of the season, on March 4, the Hawks were thrashed, 10–2, by the Boston Bruins, a game in which Woody Dumart scored four times for the victors. Dumart modestly told Herb Ralby of the *Boston Globe* his feat had merely been an example of "dumb luck." (It was the first time any Bruin had scored even a hattrick since 1947.) The reeling and injury-prone Black Hawks won just two of 35 games during the second half of the 1950–51 season.

At about the same time that the Black Hawks were badly collapsing, the Detroit Red Wings began to soar and establish themselves as the Stanley Cup favorites for 1951. On January 7, the Wings shut out the Boston Bruins at Olympia Stadium, 3–0, to begin a nine-game undefeated streak. Detroit dropped two consecutive games to end January, but then romped through February with only a single loss in 11 games. Their torrid streak continued into the next month. The Red Wings began March by winning nine straight games. That impressive streak ended on March 24—the penultimate game of the regular season—with a hard-fought 3–2 loss in Montreal in which the visitors nearly erased a two-goal Montreal lead. Detroit responded to the setback by soundly beating the Habs, 5–0, in a rematch at home the following night to end the season on a high note. That shutout victory also clinched first place for Detroit and ensured they would face the third-place Canadiens in the best-of-seven Stanley Cup semifinals two evenings hence. Remarkably, the Red Wings desperately needed that last win to capture the regular-season championship. The strong Toronto Maple Leafs only trailed Detroit by a single point in the NHL standings after the schedule's full 70 games had been played by each team.

Far from the struggle for first place, it seemed like the Montreal Canadiens were not going to be part of the NHL's postseason festivities in 1950–51. Entering the last week of February, the Boston Bruins and New York Rangers were battling each other for third place in the NHL's standings. The Habs were back in fifth place, clearly struggling, with a month left in the league's 70-game schedule. When Boston and New York skated to a

2–2 tie at Madison Square Garden on February 21, it was the worst possible outcome for the Habs as both teams gained a crucial point on them.

Yet, as March approached, Montreal suddenly began surging up the standings, losing just one of 10 games from February 24 to March 18. Meanwhile, the slumping Rangers and Bruins now fought to keep pace with the onrushing Habs. New York's offense noticeably sputtered. After the Rangers had dropped two weekend games to Toronto, by scores of 2–0 and 5–2, a headline in the *New York Telegram-Sun* comically alluded to a Theodore Roosevelt maxim. It read, "Rangers talk big but carry little stick." A seven-game Ranger winless streak (that included six losses) ultimately settled who would and would not make the NHL playoffs in 1950–51. Boston had not fared very well at the end of the season either, accruing just three victories in their final dozen games, but it was enough—just barely—to get them a fourth-place finish a single point ahead of fifth-place New York.

Those two teams' respective fates were decided on Wednesday, March 21. A Boston home win over Chicago and a Ranger home loss to Detroit ensured the Rangers could finish no higher than fifth, as Boston held a three-point edge over New York with just one game left on the Rangers' schedule. It seemed like the Gotham hockey fans had already given up hope. Fewer than 6,000 fans turned out for the game at Madison Square Garden to see their Rangers lose to the Red Wings, 4–1. In fairness, only about 8,100 fans attended the Chicago-Boston game at Boston Garden, but they cheered wildly when Johnny Peirson got the game-winning tally for the home side with about three and a half minutes left in the third period. Boston eked out a 6–5 win. "Well, the Bruins are in, folks," wrote Tom Fitzgerald in the opening line of his coverage in the *Boston Globe* of the home team's important victory. It was difficult to tell whether he was excited, disgusted or nonplussed by that development. After all, the Bruins had finished eight games below .500 with a thoroughly mediocre 22–30–18 record for 62 points, nearly 40 behind the front-running Detroit Red Wings.

Mel Sufrin, a Canadian Press hockey writer, was outwardly less cynical than Fitzgerald about the fourth-place Bruins. He basically said the B's had earned their playoff berth. "The Boston Bruins have qualified for the Stanley Cup playoffs—something they missed last season when they wound up in fifth place," he noted. "The Bruins entered the charmed circle when they defeated the last-place Chicago Black Hawks, 6–5, while the New York Rangers were being eliminated by the Detroit Red Wings, 4–1."[22]

The New York Rangers, Stanley Cup finalists from 1949–50, had remarkably tied more games than they had won in 1950–51 with their peculiar 20–29–21 record. They would be on the outside looking in when the playoffs began in a few days. Had even half of those tied games been wins for the Rangers, New York, would have comfortably qualified for the postseason.

The day after the regular season concluded, the Bruins began advertising that playoff tickets were on sale at Boston Garden, with a top price of $3.50 for a choice seat. The club's home attendance had been lackluster all season long—they were dead last in the six-team league in that department, averaging only 8,819 fans per home game. But this turnstile disappointment was also the case in New York and Chicago. It was a worrisome trend. Many longtime hockey people, including Toronto owner Conn Smythe, blamed fan apathy on the expanded schedule the NHL introduced in 1950–51 that added 10 more regular-season games for each club. A decade earlier, when there were seven clubs in the NHL, each team played a balanced, 48-game schedule. Smythe believed the extra games—a 46 percent increase since the 1941–42 campaign—were unnecessary and created a watered-down regular season that was driving away casual fans. This, Smythe surmised, was especially true in American cities where hockey was clearly secondary to other team sports in overall spectator interest.

Smythe was not alone in that belief. Indeed, declining attendance in the four American NHL teams' home buildings in 1950–51 was noticeable—so much so that the subject merited an article in March 1951 issue of *Sport* magazine. It was penned by veteran journalist Al Hirshberg who covered sports for the *Boston Post*, one of the Hub's daily newspapers. He led off with these ominous words of warning to the men in charge of the NHL:

> A red line and a few greedy magnates are strangling big-time hockey. What used to be the fastest, most exciting, and utterly thrilling spectacle on the North American sports scene is becoming a routine go-as-you-please game which is going nowhere and pleasing few. Unless somebody does something about the situation soon, the National Hockey League might as well strip the boys of their skates and send them home to grow potatoes.

Hirshberg's reference to the center red line goes back to its introduction into NHL play in 1943. Prior to that year, the defensive team could not pass the puck to a teammate from the defensive zone to the neutral zone; it had to be carried over the defensive blue line. The adoption of the center red line meant that a player could now pass the puck from his own zone as long as it was touched by a teammate before he went beyond center ice. The newfangled rule took some getting used to—especially by defensemen who now had to contend with opponents' passes entering the neutral zone—but it certainly opened up the game. Very high-scoring games became the norm in the NHL during the last two war years. Many people saw it as a gimmick, however, and longed for the days when a team had to skillfully extract themselves from a defensive bind with fancy stickhandling. Apparently, writer Hirshberg was one of them. He wrote that if the NHL moguls are not worried about the state of their sport, they ought to be.

The Boston scribe continued with his worrisome diatribe, "What has happened to their game? Why is hockey hanging on the ropes after nearly a quarter of a century of prosperity? What have these people at the top done to kill the goose that laid the golden egg? What can they do to bring it back to life again?"

Hirshberg blamed the increased length of the NHL's regular season, and argued it should be cut back to 60 games—perhaps even fewer—to make each contest more meaningful in the league's playoff chase. (He was no fan of fourth-place teams getting hot in the playoffs at the expense of teams that excelled over the long haul.) The expanded season meant there were too many tired teams today, Hirshberg opined, and the game's former dizzying pace was no longer very dizzy. Hirshberg also noted that the mid–October start to the 1950–51 NHL season—which used to occur in November or December—was causing conflicts with both the football and baseball schedules—and that American fans would favor either of those sports over hockey in most cases.

Another Hirshberg gripe was the discontinuation of regular-season overtime and the proliferation of tie games. "There isn't another sport in the world," he claimed, "that would draw flies if there was a [substantial] chance of the game resulting in a tie, for nothing irks the customers more." (Hirshberg obviously was not a soccer fan.) Be that as it may, the writer suggested, "if the schedule of games was not so tight, overtime periods could be restored, and it wouldn't make any difference if a team had to spend a night in a visiting town in case a train should be missed."

Dink Carroll of the *Montreal Gazette* disagreed with most of Hirshberg's list of reasons for declining attendance in the four American NHL cities—although he did concede the obvious fact: hockey was lagging in popularity with American fans. It was well behind both baseball and football. In his March 1 column, Carroll instead blamed the economy's rising prices, the growing television coverage of hockey in the United States, and substandard clubs that were all located south of the border. He wrote this thoughtful reply to Hirshberg's gripes.

> It wasn't so long ago that games in all NHL cities were automatic sellouts, no matter where the clubs were in the standings. That was in the era of wartime prosperity. That was in the era when everyone had money and a yen to be entertained. If they wanted to see a hockey game, they went, and it didn't seem to bother them if the home club was in fifth or sixth place.

1. The 1950–51 NHL Regular Season 27

Hockey has never played the major role in American sport that it has in Canadian sport. That role is reserved for baseball and football in the United States. Attendance at major league ballgames stood up remarkably well last season, just as it is standing up in Canada now at hockey games. An American might give up something to see a ball game, but we doubt if he would [do so] to see a hockey game.

The playoff system, the lack of overtime and the red line have been there so long now that any fans who resented them enough to quit have quit long ago. Those fans who lamented the decline of stickhandling and body checking so much that they no longer wished to attend games departed about the same time. A whole new generation of fans grew up to pack the rinks. If some of them are staying away now, it isn't because they regret the passing of a style of play which they never saw or never knew.

As the 1950–51 regular season headed toward its finish, Boston had a mathematical chance to overtake Montreal and move into third place, but they lost their final two games on their schedule to Toronto on March 24 and 25. Meanwhile, the Canadiens split a home-and-home series with Detroit on those same dates to end their 70-game campaign three points ahead of the Bruins. Coincidentally, those pairs of games from the final weekend of the regular season were, by chance, both previews of the two upcoming Stanley Cup semifinals.

Montreal's successful charge toward the final playoff spot—and the team's eventual third-place finish—impressed quite a few people around the NHL. One was Lynn Patrick. "You know," the Bruins coach frankly told the *Montreal Star*, "I didn't think Montreal would make the playoffs. Our team wasn't so strong, but I thought we had the better club [compared to the roster of the Habs]."[23]

Of course, finishing third overall presented a problem for Montreal: It meant their first-round opponents in the Stanley Cup playoffs would be the feared Detroit Red Wings as the NHL used a playoff format that seems odd today: 1st vs. 3rd and 2nd vs. 4th. However, Basil (Baz) O'Meara of the *Montreal Star* thought the Habs were up to the challenge presented by the formidable Red Wings based on the outcome of the Canadiens' final two games of the regular season. He wrote in his March 26 column,

> With the fight they are showing, the [Canadiens] proved that the Wings could be had. That statement may cause raucous laughter, but don't sell the Habs too short. It may sound like heresy, wishful thinking, or sheer optimism, but they may pull off the most stunning upset of several seasons.[24]

The books were now closed on the NHL's thirty-fourth regular season with all 210 scheduled games for 1950–51 having been played. Of those completed contests, 165 games had produced a winner. There had been a record number of tie games—45—a sizeable chunk (21 percent)

A youthful Milt Schmidt (15) with teammate Cooney Weiland in a photograph from the late 1930s. By the 1951 playoffs, the 33-year-old Schmidt was the wily, veteran captain of the Boston Bruins. He was the Hart Memorial Trophy winner in 1950–51, voted as the most valuable player to his team (courtesy Boston Public Library, Leslie Jones Collection).

that probably irked a certain sports writer employed by the *Boston Post*. Exactly 1,139 goals had been scored, an average of about 5.4 per game and almost 190 per team. There had been a total of 36 shutouts recorded by seven different goaltenders. Most importantly, two of the six teams had been eliminated from postseason play following the final games on Sunday, March 25. The Rangers and Black Hawks were both now on the outside looking in on the impending playoff action. The four remaining clubs could now focus on the real goal of every NHL season—to win Lord Stanley's famous silverware.

1950–51 National Hockey League Final Standings

		GP	W	L	T	GF	GA	DIFF	Pts
1	Detroit Red Wings	70	44	13	13	236	139	+97	101
2	Toronto Maple Leafs	70	41	16	13	212	138	+74	95
3	Montreal Canadiens	70	25	30	15	173	184	−11	65
4	Boston Bruins	70	22	30	18	178	197	−19	62
5	New York Rangers	70	20	29	21	169	201	−32	61
6	Chicago Black Hawks	70	13	47	10	171	280	−109	36

NHL Individual Statistical Leaders and Trophy Winners for 1950–51

Scoring champion: Gordie Howe (DET)—86 points
Goals: Gordie Howe (DET)—43
Assists: Gordie Howe (DET) and Ted Kennedy (TOR)—tied at 43
Penalty Minutes: Gus Mortson (TOR)—142
Wins by Goaltender: Terry Sawchuk (DET)—44
Goals-Against Average: Al Rollins (TOR)—1.77
Shutouts: Terry Sawchuk (DET)—11
Most Valuable Player to His Team (Hart Trophy): Milt Schmidt (BOS)
Vezina Trophy Winner: Al Rollins (TOR)
Rookie of the Year (Calder Trophy): Terry Sawchuk (DET)

2

Semifinal Series "A"

Montreal vs. Detroit

"By the form sheet, the Wings rate as heavy favorites over the Canadiens."—*Montreal Gazette*, March 27, 1951

"We'll win it in six games. The spirit on this team is the best I've seen in 21 years of coaching in the National Hockey League. Spirit like that will carry you a long way."—Montreal coach Dick Irvin, *Montreal Gazette*, April 9, 1951

When the 1950–51 regular season ended, the Detroit Red Wings were a whopping 36 points ahead of the third-place Montreal Canadiens. The Canadiens had finished their schedule five games *under* .500—and only managed four wins and two ties versus the Red Wings in the 14 times they had faced each other during the 70-game schedule. (In fairness, Montreal's four victories against the defending Stanley Cup champions were the most that any team managed in 1950–51. Detroit lost just 13 times all season.) Even Stanley Cup playoff history was against Montreal. The Habs had faced Detroit four times in previous playoff series (in 1937, 1939, 1942 and 1949) and came out the losers in every instance. However, the Habs could take a degree of solace that each of those four series required the maximum number of games to determine a winner.

All indications were that the teams' upcoming best-of-seven semifinal—officially called Series "A" by the NHL's office and statisticians—ought to be a cakewalk for the Michigan squad that accrued 101 points from 44 wins and 13 ties and lost just three home games out of 35 in 1950–51. Indeed, an Associated Press preview article reported, "Many of Detroit's old-time hockey fans have been saying for weeks that the present Red Wing club is the best in [NHL] history."[1] Few fans outside of Montreal gave the outgunned Habs much of a chance against the heavily favored Wings.

With such a daunting opponent facing his underdog team, 58-year-

2. Semifinal Series "A"

old Montreal coach Dick Irvin was happy to attempt to shift all the pressure onto the shoulders of the favorites with some carefully chosen comments. He told Marshall Dann, a writer from the *Detroit Free Press*, "We're along for the ride. [We have] everything to win and nothing to lose. The burden is on the mighty Red Wings—and what a disgrace it would be if they should lose."[2] Indeed, if Detroit did not think an upset could occur, the players merely had to look back two seasons to the 1949 Stanley Cup finals. That was when fourth-place Toronto—a sub-.500 team—swept the top-of-the-heap Red Wings in a thoroughly startling result.

Further hampering the Canadiens was a youthful and somewhat patched-up lineup that featured seven players with zero experience in the Stanley Cup playoffs. "I'm the most optimistic man in the world," declared the cheerful Irvin. "Sure, these are only kids, but we have hustle, spirit, legs, and ability. These kids aren't going to run off the rink in fear of the great record of the mighty Wings."[3]

Dann gave credit to Montreal where it was due. He noted,

> It would seem that Irvin was thinking about the team, which from March 6 to 17, vaulted from a solid hold on fifth place past New York and Boston, into third place and the playoffs. That club had all the qualities Irvin described, as it won six and tied two of nine games in a sparkling stretch drive.[4]

On Tuesday, March 27, a sellout crowd of 13,246 spectators packed Detroit's Olympia Stadium to watch the hometown Red Wings square off against the Montreal Canadiens in Game One. Among the spectators was NHL president Clarence Campbell. He and everyone else certainly got more than their money's worth of hockey excitement. In fact, the paying customers saw the equivalent of two games—and then some—as the outcome was not yet decided after six periods of sustained action. "It was one of the greatest of all playoff games," Dink Carroll opined in his report for the *Montreal Gazette*, "with both teams maintaining unbelievable pace throughout [it]."[5]

The final score was 3–2 for the underdogs from Montreal. Maurice Richard scored the winning goal 1:09 into the *fourth* overtime period to secure a surprise win for the visiting Habs. The decisive moment in the game came when Richard stole the puck from blond, leg-weary Detroit defenseman Leo Reise. The Rocket advanced on the Detroit net and swiftly fired an accurate shot past a surprised Terry Sawchuk into the left corner of the goal.

The March 28 edition of the *Montreal Star* reported Richard's tally and its aftermath this way: "Charging like a wild mustang, [Richard] shifted by defenseman Leo Reise for the winning goal. His delirious teammates almost bore him into the ice. They [then] rushed after little Gerry McNeil [and] lugged him shoulder-high into the dressing room."

What was left of the crowd seemed stunned by the outcome, as Detroit had outshot the Habs by a 62–42 margin over the course of the long night at the Olympia and probably deserved to be the winners. Detroit coach Tommy Ivan certainly thought so. Montreal goalie Gerry McNeil was as much of a hero for the visitors as Maurice Richard—arguably more so. Detroit general manager Jack Adams said after the game that his talented team had not previously encountered any goaltending comparable to the what McNeil displayed, especially during the long overtime. He likened it to a baseball team running into "one-hit pitching."[6] The Montreal goaltender had faced more shots during the four extra periods (33) than he had in the 60 minutes of regulation time (29) preceding them.

The overtime marker represented the only time the Canadiens possessed the lead during the arduous game. In his coverage for the *Montreal Gazette*, Dink Carroll reported that Habs coach Dick Irvin had told his troops prior to the opening faceoff, "If we ever get a goal ahead of them, we'll win." Carroll cheekily added, "He was right."[7] It had been the longest game ever played in the history of Olympia Stadium. That arena first opened for NHL hockey in October 1927.

The result was certainly an aberration. Detroit had only lost three of their 35 home games during the 1950–51 NHL regular season. Montreal had only managed one win and one tie in the seven games they had played at the Olympia.

"Sawchuk and Montreal netminder Gerry McNeil were phenomenal as they stopped shot after shot in the hectic endurance contest,"[8] wrote an unnamed United Press correspondent. The same scribe noted that the enormous crowd at the Olympia had shrunk considerably as the overtime periods mounted with no end to the marathon game in sight. Depending upon which newspaper one read, Richard's winning tally came at either 1:10 or 1:11 a.m. The opening faceoff had taken place at 8:30 p.m. One Detroit broadsheet carried the headline, "Detroit Sleeps While Red Wings Lose." There would not be another quadruple overtime game in the Stanley Cup playoffs until 1996.

The UP scribe reported, "The playoff opener was a defensive battle royal from start to finish and gave indications that despite winning three straight [regular season] league titles, the Red Wings are in for a rough time from Montreal in the best-of-seven series."[9]

Detroit twice held a one-goal edge in the hard-fought game, but the stubborn Habs refused to capitulate. Twice they levelled the score, forced the multiple overtime sessions, and eventually prevailed well past the midnight hour.

2. Semifinal Series "A"

The Red Wings began fast and dominated play in the early going, but youthful Montreal goalie McNeil was up to the challenge and kept the home team off the scoresheet for the first half of the period. Detroit's Gordie Howe finally opened Game One's scoring on a scrambly play. The NHL's newest scoring champion got the hometown Red Wings a 1–0 lead on a close-in shot that deflected into the net off McNeil's skate. Montreal reporter Dink Carroll, showing a hint of bias, described Detroit first goal as "a lucky backhander."[10] The time of the Howe tally was 12:15 of the first period.

Detroit's lead was a short-lived one, however. Less than two minutes later, Montreal found an equalizer from the stick of Émile (Butch) Bouchard who flipped in a screen shot past Sawchuk who never saw the puck until it was behind him in the cage. The official time of Bouchard's first-period goal was 13:55. The Red Wings' lead had lasted 100 seconds.

No goals were scored in the second frame. Detroit took the lead on a Leo Reise goal in the third period. He knocked home a pass from Sid Abel at 1:10 of what is normally the final 20 minutes of a hockey game. Bert Olmstead of the Canadiens erased the home team's advantage with an accurate backhand shot that eluded Sawchuk about eight minutes later. The time of that goal was 9:08. The score remained knotted at two goals apiece until Richard's overtime heroics more than two hours later.

The game had been a cleanly contested affair. No penalties had been called in the third period of regulation play, nor in any of the overtime stanzas. There were only five handed out during the entire game, with all of them coming in the first 40 minutes of play. The penalty timekeeper was a lonely fellow after the second period.

The *Montreal Gazette* reported that the Red Wings had been listed as 5:3 betting favorites to win the semifinal series by bookmakers, but Dink Carroll figured those odds would surely narrow after the Habs' marathon victory in Game One.

Despite losing the opening game, Detroit goaltender Terry Sawchuk was better off financially than he was when the game began. He learned he was to get a $1,000 windfall from team owner Jim Norris. Al Rollins of the Maple Leafs had won the Vezina Trophy, but Norris magnanimously decided to pay Sawchuk the specified bonus mentioned in his contract as if his talented goaltender had won the award instead of the Toronto netminder.

Remarkably, Game Two at the Olympia on March 29 was another drawn-out affair that again lasted beyond midnight. This time the game ended at 2:20 of the *third* overtime period with Montreal prevailing by a 1–0 score. Again, it was the stick of Maurice Richard that eventually provided the winning goal for the surprising visitors from Quebec. According to the time-of-day clock at the arena, this climax came at 12:40 a.m. The 0–0 tie was broken when Richard was fed a clever pass by teammate Billy Reay. Richard collected the puck and swooped in on Terry Sawchuk, beating him with a powerful backhand shot to an open corner of the net.

An unnamed United Press reporter's description of the 28-year-old Richard's second overtime goal appeared in the March 30 edition of the *Boston Globe*:

> The whirlwind scoring play ... started out with [Jim] McPherson capturing the disc at mid-ice and quickly firing it to Reay at the right side of the goal. Reay then feinted goalie Terry Sawchuk with a fake shot that turned into a blistering pass to Richard who was blazing in from the left.
>
> Richard had an open corner to shoot at. He let loose with a terrific blast that nearly tore a hole in the meshes.[11]

According to the Canadian Press, the news agency believed the combined amount of play in Games One and Two of Series "A"—223 minutes and 29 seconds—had established a record for the longest duration of two consecutive Stanley Cup playoff contests in history.

Of course, both Sawchuk and Montreal netminder Gerry McNeil were outstanding performers in such a nerve-racking contest where one small error could be potentially fatal for whichever team had committed it. One statistic undoubtedly proved how evenly Game Two was contested from its beginning to its end: Before Richard iced the triumph for his club with his second sudden-death marker in two games, both goalies had faced—and stopped—exactly the same total of 42 shots.

Dink Carroll praised the quality of the two teams and the generally clean play on display during the six periods. He wrote in his game report for the *Montreal Gazette*, "Again it was a rugged, close-checking contest, but it was comparatively clean. Referee Red Storey meted out only six minor penalties, four of them going to the Canadiens. The players are so careful they just don't risk penalties."[12]

However, Carroll said Game One was the superior battle of the two playoff clashes contested at the Olympia. He opined, "[Game Two] was a game in which defense was stressed over offense. It lacked the thrills of the opener."[13]

Carroll figured the heavily favored Red Wings had to be a thoroughly demoralized bunch after dropping two games at the Olympia where they had seldom suffered setbacks throughout their wildly successful, 101-point 1950–51 regular season. With the series now moving to Montreal for the next two contests, Carroll now boldly predicted the Canadiens would advance to the Stanley Cup final with a spectacular four-game sweep of the mighty men from Detroit.

2. Semifinal Series "A"

One of coach Dick Irvin's promising newcomers for the Canadiens was the very promising Bernie (Boom Boom) Geoffrion. Despite the exciting Montreal victory, the rookie did not enjoy participating in the Stanley Cup playoff action very much. Geoffrion suffered a broken nose during Game Two.

Clarence Campbell nearly missed the game at the Olympia. The NHL's president had been in Toronto the previous day to watch the Bruins-Leafs playoff clash at Maple Leaf Gardens. His travel arrangements to Detroit via Buffalo went slightly awry, however. By the time he arrived in Detroit for Game Two of the Habs-Wings semifinal series and taken his seat among the sellout crowd, the game was well underway. Of course, he had missed no scoring plays as defense was the order of the day.

While many hockey writers assigned to the Detroit-Montreal semifinal series were lamenting the length of the games—and the very real problem of meeting deadlines for their stories to run in the next day's morning newspapers—others were having fun with it. In his sidebar column for the *Montreal Gazette*, Dink Carroll reported this amusing comment made by one clever Detroit scribe, "Counting the overtimes, the teams have played what amounts to four games. The Canadiens only won two, so the series must be tied, right?"[14]

With Montreal and Boston both holding surprising leads in their respective playoff series, the situation inspired the following commentary from Baz O'Meara in his daily sports column for the *Montreal Star* on Friday, March 30:

> So, as it stands, it is entirely possible that the Canadiens and Boston will wind up in the Stanley Cup finals—and won't that kipper your herrings. Anybody even mentioning such a thing just a month ago would have been considered a fair subject for the queer house, and rightly so.

Having been beaten twice on overtime goals by Maurice Richard, Red Wings coach Tommy Ivan learned his lesson well. For Game Three, 23-year-old checking specialist Marty Pavelich was assigned the tedious but important task of shadowing the Rocket for most of the night. It worked. Richard seldom had a decent scoring opportunity all game. On those rare occasions when the Rocket managed to break free from Pavelich's tight checking, Sawchuk proved to be an unbeatable foe on this night.

The four-game Montreal sweep predicted by Dink Carroll was not to be. The real Red Wings finally showed up for Game Three at the Forum. At least they were the Wings who knew how to win hockey games. Victory was not without a mighty struggle, however. The visitors, in a virtual must-win scenario for them, beat Montreal by a 2–0 count on March 31.

The Saturday night game was played before a crowd of 14, 417 disappointed spectators. Some of the patrons had paid the inflated price of $15 per ticket to speculators stationed outside the Forum's doors.

"The Red Wings looked more like the team in this game that had such a big edge on every club during the regular schedule," candidly wrote Dink Carroll in the April 1 edition of the *Montreal Gazette*. "They were in full drive and hustled on every attack and were very tough defensively." In contrast, Carroll described the home team as having "lost the zip and spirit that carried them to two unexpected victories in the first two games [of the semifinal series in Detroit]."[15]

Following the established practice of Game Two, goals were again a scarce commodity in Game Three for both sides. The two teams nearly went into the third period without either club managing to trigger the red light. However, the drought was finally broken by Gordie Howe at 18:23 of the second period.

The NHL's reigning scoring champion happened to be celebrating his 23rd birthday that very day. Unexpectedly, he was given something akin to a wonderful present by the Canadiens. A bad line change by the hometown Habs somehow left Howe uncovered. He was spotted alone on his wing by teammate Bob Goldham, who wasted no time delivering a perfect cross-ice pass to him. Carroll wrote, "[Howe] waltzed right in on Gerry McNeil and faked a shot, forcing McNeil to make the first move." Howe deftly maneuvered the puck around the helpless Montreal goalie and coolly flipped it into the unguarded cage with a casual, artistic flair. It was the first Detroit goal since the third period of Game One—ending a drought of 218 minutes and 42 seconds. "That was it, to all intents and purposes," declared Carroll. "The Red Wings didn't make the mistake of trying to play defensive hockey. [For the remainder of the game] they had more of the puck than the Canadiens."[16] Afterward, Howe praised the accuracy and timing of Goldham's pass after the game. He also told the press that his goal was the best birthday present he had ever received. In the *Ottawa Journal*, it was noted that the previous year the youthful Howe had marked his 22nd birthday in a Detroit hospital fighting for his life after sustaining a serious head injury in the opening game of the Red Wings semifinal series versus Toronto.

Sid Abel added a deserved second goal for the vaunted visitors 13:45 into the third period. Abel alertly collected a loose puck in the Montreal zone and blasted a 30-foot shot that cleanly beat McNeil. Detroit had a 2–0 lead. Considering how well the visitors were playing, the two-goal edge held by the Red Wings looked like an insurmountable barrier for the Canadiens. It was. One Detroit journalist figured the result from Game Three would prompt the Red Wings to re-establish their regular-season form and prove that "class will tell."

Over the three periods, Detroit outshot Montreal by a 31:24 ratio. The Red Wings' goaltending was superb—and it needed to be that way. "Terry Sawchuk, of course, was unbeatable in the Detroit net," penned Carroll with a sense of admiration. "He had plenty of tough ones to stop from Bert Olmstead, Doug Harvey, Maurice Richard, Billy Reay, Paul Meger, and Floyd Curry."[17] Montreal defenseman Tom Johnson was also singled out by Carroll for his excellent two-way play. Howe, according to Carroll, was the best player on the ice for either side in Game Three.

It was reported that Red Wings boss Jack Adams was so nervous during the third period that he had to leave the building. He only returned after a cab driver parked outside the Forum, who was listening to a radio broadcast of the game, informed the Detroit general manager that his club had won. This coping tactic was nothing new to Adams. The previous spring, Adams similarly absented himself from the Olympia during the overtime in Game #7 of the 1950 Stanley Cup final. He thus missed seeing Pete Babando score one of the NHL's most dramatic goals against the New York Rangers that gave his Wings the series and the championship.

Terry Sawchuk received high praise from other scribes for his flawless work in the Detroit net. A United Press journalist glowingly wrote, "When Montreal forwards did break into scoring position, Sawchuk ... was there to rob them of what appeared to be certain goals time and again."[18]

With the Red Wings unexpectedly fighting for their playoff lives, interest in the series had measurably grown in Detroit. The *Montreal Gazette* reported that a dozen media people (both print and radio) from the Motor City had been granted press credentials for Games Three and Four. They were being shepherded *en masse* around Montreal by Fred Huber, the Red Wings knowledgeable publicity director, who apparently knew the city quite well.

Dink Carroll, who after Game Two optimistically declared he expected the Habs to engineer a sweep of Detroit, was more philosophical in his musings after Game Three was in the books. He wrote, "The Red Wings were the outstanding club in the league over the regular schedule. The Canadiens certainly didn't figure to knock them off in straight games. If they can do it in seven, they should be happy."[19]

Detroit coach Tommy Ivan was pleased with his team's first win of the series, of course, but he thought his Red Wings deserved to be up 3–0 in the best-of-seven affair. "At least we got the breaks tonight," he told Baz O'Meara of the *Montreal Star*. "We should be three up in this series, but that's the way it goes. Now don't get me wrong," he continued, "I'm not trying to alibi those two losses at home. But the Canadiens did get the breaks in both of them when we should have won them in regulation time."

Ivan felt compelled to add the following individual tribute to an opponent, "That kid beat us [twice] and he was still plenty hot out there tonight. He is playing brilliantly."[20] The "kid" whom Ivan was referring to was Montreal goaltender Gerry McNeil, who, on April 17, would turn 25 years old.

The *Windsor Daily Star* reported that the Red Wings, staying in a secluded spot in Granby, Quebec between their two games at the Forum, were certainly a relaxed bunch prior to the fourth game of their semifinal series with the Habs. While not practicing, the Detroit players amused themselves with billiards, bowling and table tennis. With Detroit located immediately across the Ontario-Michigan border, the Red Wings were very much considered the home team by NHL fans who resided in the Windsor area.

That same newspaper's sports editor, Doug Vaughan, was appalled by the stories and photographic evidence of continuous violence and mayhem coming from the Toronto-Boston semifinal series. (Toronto's Ted Kennedy was pictured in that day's edition sitting in the Leaf dressing room, leisurely quaffing a bottled beverage while sporting two huge bandages on his face.) Vaughan contrasted the rough stuff to the pacific goings-on in the Montreal-Detroit confrontation:

> At no time in the series thus far between the Wings and the Canadiens has there been any semblance of such violent outbursts of stick-swinging and fist-throwing as has highlighted the games between Boston and Toronto.
>
> Every Detroit-Montreal game has seen the players on both teams sticking strictly to hockey. There is no guarantee, of course that this is the pattern which will be followed the rest of the way, but at least it has been pliantly different....[21]

Edward MacCabe, the sports editor of the *Ottawa Journal*, had an interesting take on the series in his April 2 column. MacCabe figured Detroit's victory in Game Three in Montreal was huge from not just a hockey standpoint, but also from a financial standpoint. He suspected the Red Wings would have faced a heavy backlash at the Olympia's turnstiles in 1951–52 had they bowed out weakly to the Habs in four straight games after running roughshod over most of the league during the 1950–51 regular season. "Fortunately for them and for the NHL," he penned, "it appears [Detroit] will make a battle of it, and the Wings still stand a good chance of taking it all."

Game Four, played on April 3, was also a Detroit victory—remarkably making it four games out of four in Series "A" in which the home team failed to record a win. This time it was a solid 4–1 triumph for the Red Wings at the Montreal Forum. The favorites from Michigan were now level in the best-of-seven series after a disappointing and disastrous beginning at home.

2. Semifinal Series "A"

In Game Four, the Red Wings struck twice in the first period, getting goals from Leo Reise and Metro Prystai just 90 seconds apart, to assume a lead they would not relinquish. (Prystai had missed the first two games of the semifinal series while recuperating from a fractured leg.) Elmer Lach halved the Detroit advantage with a second-period power-play tally, but that was the extent of the home team's offensive output in Game Four. Detroit responded with two third-period tallies to put the game out of reach for the Habs. Those goals were scored by Gerry Couture and Sid Abel less than three minutes apart.

"The Canadiens looked bewildered in the first period and tired and listless in the third," wrote a correspondent from United Press. "Elmer Lach's goal, which came at 14:28 of the second period, fired the club up considerably, but the fuel did not last."[22]

The same UP scribed praised Leo Reise of the Red Wings, declaring he "led Detroit both offensively and defensively in one of the finest one-man performances seen here this winter. The blond defensive stalwart scored the first Wing goal and assisted on two others."[23]

Referee Bill Chadwick called 11 penalties in the game as it turned nasty on occasion. The most flagrant example occurred in the second period when Ted Lindsay knocked down Montreal goaltender Gerry McNeil from behind. The Habs top defensemen, Doug Harvey, retaliated by levelling Lindsay with a vicious cross-check.

With the series tied at two games apiece, the resurgent Red Wings were suddenly a very optimistic bunch—and so were their supporters. Harold Atkins of the *Montreal Star* wrote, "Detroit's entourage, which had been crying that the breaks will decide the Stanley Cup semifinal series with the Canadiens, were convinced to a man after last night's win that it is only a matter of time before they bury the Habs for another season."[24]

Game Five at the Detroit Olympia proved to be the pivotal contest for the whole series. The Red Wings, riding the momentum of two victories at the Montreal Forum, returned home re-established as the favorites. They jumped out two a 2–0 first-period lead—and then badly squandered away their advantage. To the shock of the overflow Olympia crowd of 14,221 Wings' supporters—which included about 2,000 standees—Montreal roared back to take Game Five, 5–2, despite not having scored during the first period.

"The surprising Canadiens did it again here [in Detroit] tonight," cackled Dink Carroll in his report for the *Montreal Gazette*, "upsetting the favored Red Wings on their own ice ... to go ahead in the best-of-seven Stanley Cup semifinal series. They now lead the series three games to two and will be favored to close out the playoff when they meet the Detroiters in Montreal on Saturday night."[25]

Remarkably, the home team had lost all five games played thus far in Series "A." That was a fact duly noted by Carroll. "It is odd [the Habs] have played their best games here in the Olympia, winning all three on the Red Wings' ice," he wrote, "While the latter have notched their two wins in the Forum."[26] In the space of just eight days, the powerful Detroit Red Wings had lost as many games at home as they had during the whole 1950–51 regular season. It was utterly startling to their supporters.

"They beat us; we have no alibis," Detroit general manager Jack Adams ruefully told the press after his Red Wings shockingly were handed their third home loss of the series by the Canadiens. He added, "They will be hard to beat at home."[27]

The Canadiens did not start out Game Five playing well. They fell behind the home side 2–0 thanks to first-period goals by Sid Abel just 69 seconds after the opening faceoff, and Gordie Howe at the 14:27 mark. "It was a great win for the Habitants because they had to do it the hard way," insisted Carroll. "They came back from a two-goal deficit to down the powerful Red Wings."[28]

Detroit's second scoring play had a comical aspect to it: Two Montreal players (Elmer Lach and Maurice Richard) not only ran into each other behind the Canadiens' blue line, they also flattened referee George Gravel with their mishap too! Their collision allowed three Red Wings easy and unimpeded access to the Montreal net where Howe gave the Red Wings what turned out to be their final goal of the game.

"The Canadiens had plenty of spirit and drive tonight," penned the enthused Carroll. Those qualities showed 4:04 into the second frame when the turning point of the contest occurred. It came from the stick of Montreal's Billy Reay, who got the first goal for the visitors while Montreal was playing shorthanded. (Richard was sitting out a major penalty for fighting.) Reay's strike cut the Red Wings' lead in half and palpably shifted the game's momentum. "This seemed to give the Canadiens the vinegar they needed,"[29] Carroll opined.

Author Brian McFarlane claims there was a different turning point in the game. He wrote in his book, *The Lively World of Hockey*, that the momentum of the series changed late in the first period when Maurice Richard flattened Ted Lindsay with a single punch. Lindsay was widely regarded as the toughest man in the NHL in 1951. That was when Richard was handed a major penalty, but Detroit seemed deflated by the humbling incident.

Later in the second period, a power-play goal by Bert Olmstead at 11:48 (who deflected a Richard shot past Terry Sawchuk) and an even-strength tally by newcomer Bernie Geoffrion at 17:51 sent the feisty visitors to their dressing room now holding a 3–2 advantage over favored Detroit. The Red

Wings were unable to muster a response. A United Press reporter labeled the Wings "a dazed and unaggressive club"[30] from that point forward.

The only goals in the third period were scored by Montreal players when Detroit was forced to take more chances in their pursuit of goals that never came. Maurice Richard, sent in alone on Sawchuk, got one of them at 14:45 to extend the Habs' lead to 4–2. Calum MacKay put the game absolutely out of reach by knocking home a juicy rebound past Sawchuk at 18.07. It was MacKay's first NHL playoff goal—and it completed the scoring in Montreal's 5–2 thumping of the regular-season champs.

Montreal goaltender Gerry McNeil played well for the victorious visitors, definitely outshining Sawchuk who had a rare, subpar game for Detroit. After a shaky start, McNeil stopped 26 of 28 Red Wing shots. Montreal's third line of Reay, Geoffrion, and Paul Meger earned special plaudits from the Montreal writers, although Meger had missed an open net for the Habs in the first period.

Compared to the first two games contested at Olympia Stadium, Game Five was a short one. This contrast did not go unnoticed by the hockey writers. "It was pleasant that there was no overtime," wrote Baz O'Meara in his *Montreal Star* column. "Incidentally, [NHL president] Clarence Campbell is on record as being favorable to a move for next year that would allow a maximum of 20 minutes of overtime."[31]

Game Six was at the Montreal Forum on April 7. It was a thriller, but for some unknown reason it is rarely discussed today. Sadly, it appears that the passage of time has eroded this game from even the memories of hardcore Habs fans who ought to cherish and celebrate it. Montreal secured the series-clincher that Saturday night, by a tight 3–2 score.

The thrilling finale saw all five goals in the game scored in the final 20 minutes. "A roaring crowd of 14,448 kept the Montreal forum in a bedlam throughout the third period," declared an Associated Press scribe. "Pent-up tension of players and fans alike through two scoreless periods broke out in the third with excitement crammed into every minute."[32] He was right. Dink Carroll of the *Montreal Gazette* confirmed it. He wrote, "The last period provided 20 minutes of the most exciting hockey ever played anywhere. It was an example of hockey at its spine-tingling best."[33]

Billy Reay, Maurice Richard, and Ken Mosdell scored the three Montreal goals. Sid Abel and Ted Lindsay (perhaps) replied for the visiting Red Wings. Two goals—one from each club—were scored in the first eight minutes of the third period.

The first one occurred when Billy Reay tipped a long shot from teammate Bernie Geoffrion past Terry Sawchuk at 6:49. (Whether or not Reay's timely redirection was intentional or accidental was debatable. Opinions varied.) The crowd was still in an uproar when Sid Abel leveled the game at a goal apiece at the 7:31 mark. It came on a close-range shot made possible by a shot on goal fired by Gordie Howe that Habs goalie Gerry McNeil skillfully saved. Abel, however, was positioned perfectly to fire home the rebound.

Just over two minutes later, Maurice Richard accepted an Elmer Lach pass behind the Detroit net and scored on a wraparound play in which Montreal's #9 came around the net and stuffed the puck between Sawchuk's goalie pads. The puck dramatically rolled along the goal line—and Sawchuk may have pushed it into the net with a desperate lunge to make the save. The Habs were back in front, 2–1, and the Forum faithful rocked with delight.

"The Wings fought back furiously and gambled on chances,"[34] wrote the unnamed AP reporter. Montreal's Ken Mosdell took advantage of the Red Wings sacrificing defense for offense. He took a Floyd Curry pass at his own blue line and had no Wings defenders to impede his advance on Sawchuk. Mosdell's clean breakaway resulted in an important insurance goal at 15:45 for the home team. Mosdell's shot never left the ice. Montreal now held a huge two-goal advantage.

The valiant Wings got one of those goals back when a shot by Gordie Howe, through traffic, was deflected into the Montreal net, allegedly by Ted Lindsay. (It would later—much later—be credited to Howe.) With Montreal's edge sliced to just 3–2, there were 45 seconds left on the Forum clock for one final Detroit effort to level the contest. With Sawchuk having been lifted for an extra attacker in the game's last 30 seconds, Detroit put extreme pressure on the defensive-minded Habs. A final faceoff with six seconds remaining pitted Elmer Lach and Sid Abel against each other. Neither team controlled the puck from the draw, but Montreal's Doug Harvey got to it first and bounced it off the boards. It went safely out of the Habs' defensive zone as the half-dozen seconds ticked away.

The final buzzer sounded. Finally, a home team had managed to win a game in Series "A" after five futile attempts. The startling upset was complete. Gerry McNeil joyfully tossed his heavy goalie's stick recklessly into the air; it missed landing on referee Bill Chadwick's head by mere inches. The Hab goaltender was mobbed by equally happy teammates. The unfashionable Montreal Canadiens—who had lost five more games than they had won during the 1950–51 regular season—had unexpectedly booked their passage to the Stanley Cup finals. It marked the first time the Habs had won a playoff series since 1947—and the first time they had ever knocked out Detroit in postseason play.

On the other side of the coin, Detroit's superb 101-point regular season meant nothing at all when the Red Wings began postseason play with the highest of expectations. After making the sportsmanlike gesture of congratulating the Canadiens—Sid Abel actually embraced Maurice Richard—the Wings left the ice a disappointed crew. "It's unbelievable, but it's true,"[35] said a crestfallen Jack Adams to reporters after the upset had been completed and his team had been shockingly ousted from the playoffs. The Red Wings were not the first NHL team to succumb to the allurement that their regular season excellence would automatically take them to the Stanley Cup championship. Nor would they be the last.

It had been a thrilling game. Referee Bill Chadwick had had an easy night and "handled the game superbly,"[36] according to Carroll. No penalties were called throughout the exciting and swift-moving 60 minutes of playoff hockey at its best. Detroit outshot Montreal by a 29:26 ratio but came up one critical goal shy.

"Detroit's Production Line of Howe, Lindsay and Abel carried the burden of the Red Wings' attack," declared the AP reporter, "and fought [the team's] great effort into the final minutes." The same writer gave high praise to Montreal goaltender Gerry McNeil, whom he described as "sensational all the way."[37] He did, however, concede that Maurice Richard had been the game's overall outstanding performer.

Dink Carroll thought the series had truly been won in Game Five by Montreal. That was when the Habs rallied to turn an early two-goal deficit against Detroit at the Olympia into a comfortable 5–2 victory. When semifinal Series "A" ended, the *Montreal Gazette* scribe humorously wrote, "When the Red Wings took a two-goal lead in the opening period of the fifth game, a small boy could have bought the Canadiens' chances with what he had in his piggy bank."[38]

A Canadian Press article that appeared in the *Calgary Herald* said the Red Wings lost not only a chance to play for the Stanley Cup with the team's upset loss to the Canadiens, but also something intangible too. It claimed, "The Montreal victory ... meant the favored Red Wings not only lost the best-of-seven series 4–2 on games but considerable prestige in the process." The same article also humorously noted, "A gala hockey bandwagon labeled 'Montreal Canadiens' had a surprising lot of fast climbers today."[39]

Decades later, a retrospective article about the 1951 postseason on the website of TheHockeyWriters.com noted, "The Cup favorite Red Wings were quickly reminded how playoff hockey is far more intense than the regular season. The Canadiens reached another gear and defeated Detroit."[40]

Next up for the Habs would be the survivor of the Boston-Toronto clash. It was settled decisively the following night, with the Leafs routing Boston, 6–0, to win Series "B." Jack Koffman wrote in the *Ottawa Citizen* the next day, "The Toronto Maple Leafs did the expected in running the Boston Bruins out of the hunt [for the Stanley Cup], but the Canadiens, expected to play the role of dead ducks against the Detroit Red Wings, are liable to throw the Cup finals into a panic."[41]

Semifinal "A" Results
Game #1 at Detroit: Montreal wins, 3–2 (quadruple overtime)
Game #2 at Detroit: Montreal wins, 1–0 (triple overtime)
Game #3 at Montreal: Detroit wins, 2–0
Game #4 at Montreal: Detroit wins, 4–1
Game #5 at Detroit: Montreal wins, 5–2
Game #6 at Montreal: Montreal wins, 3–2
Montreal wins the series four games to two.

3

Semifinal Series "B"
Boston vs. Toronto

"These postseason parties—particularly those involving the Bruins and Leafs—are always vigorously prosecuted."[1]
—Tom Fitzgerald, *Boston Globe*

Going into their 1951 playoff series, the Boston Bruins and Toronto Maple Leafs were not exactly postseason strangers. The upcoming clash would be their ninth matchup in Stanley Cup play. History showed that the Leafs had won six of the teams' previous eight Stanley Cup series; the first four and the most recent two. The Bruins' pair of triumphs (1939 and 1941) occurred in years when they captured Lord Stanley's prized trophy.

The second semifinal of the 1951 Stanley Cup playoffs—officially called Series "B" by the NHL—opened at Maple Leaf Gardens in Toronto on Wednesday, March 28. Although they finished the regular season with seven straight triumphs, and were overwhelming favorites to defeat the seemingly overmatched Boston Bruins in their best-of-seven semifinal, the Toronto Maple Leafs entered the series with a serious injury to a key player. Harry Watson, Toronto's star left winger, was hobbled with a shoulder separation he had suffered four days earlier in the Leafs' final home game of the regular season. Coincidentally, it occurred versus those same Boston Bruins. Toronto had finished 33 points clear of Boston in the NHL standings and had recorded 10 wins and two ties against the Bruins in the 14 regular season games the two clubs had contested in 1950–51. Even with the injury to Watson, playoff Series "B" had the strong potential to be a rout for Conn Smythe's mighty Maple Leafs.

Nevertheless, there were harbingers of positivity for the overmatched Bruins. The Watson injury was cited as one example. "The Boston Bruins' chances of survival in their Stanley Cup series with the favored Toronto Maple Leafs were raised today," commented Tom Fitzgerald in the March 28 edition of the *Boston Globe*. "Harry Watson will be sidelined for at least the opener. He will be replaced by capable rookie Danny Lewicki, who has recovered from last weekend's leg injury received at Boston Garden."[2] The Bruins had staggered to the finish line with just a single win and a tie in their final six games of the regular season.

Tom Fitzgerald noted in his pre-series report for the *Globe* that the Bruins were at least a relatively fit and healthy crew as they headed northward to Maple Leaf Gardens to contest Game One that evening. "The Bruins are in comparatively good shape," he penned. "The only Boston man out of the starting lineup will be Murray Henderson. He is at his home in Toronto with a cracked rib. Steve Kraftcheck has been recalled from Indianapolis to fill in the vacant position." Fitzgerald also noted that Milt Schmidt's gimpy knee was "considerably improved."[3] Defenseman Bill Quackenbush, who had just turned 29, was going to be a key man for Boston. He told writer Fitzgerald he expected a heavy workload from coach Lynn Patrick. Specifically, he figured to be on the ice for about two-thirds of Game One. The noticeably trim Quackenbush estimated his weight had dropped by about 10 pounds since the previous season. He said he felt better than he had in years. After beginning his NHL career with seven campaigns in Detroit, this was Quackenbush's second season as a Bruin.

Fitzgerald forecasted a cautiously played semifinal between the Leafs and Bruins. He wrote, "The hockey on display in the playoffs generally is a combination of ferocity and conservatism. Teams are not inclined to take daring chances in a short series that would be rated as sound, calculated risks during the 70-game campaign. The Bruins are not going in for abnormal, close-to-the-vest tactics."[4]

Boston coach Lynn Patrick figured the Maple Leafs would try to rough up the Bruins—especially in the first two games in Toronto to start the series. "I suppose they'll really try to give it to us up there," he told the *Boston Globe*. "Milt [Schmidt] will be a marked man."[5] Patrick recalled that the final regular season game of the 1950–51 season, contested between the two clubs at Boston Garden, saw Schmidt specifically targeted by Toronto's Fern Flaman, Bill Barilko, and Bill Juzda. Patrick fully expected more of the same once the puck was dropped at Maple Leaf Gardens on Wednesday.

The Canadian Press' preview story on Series "B" said Boston's chances rode mostly on the aging legs of veteran Milt Schmidt, who was still a formidable competitor at age 33. "He goes into the series with a shaky knee," wrote the unnamed CP scribe. "That is small comfort to the Leafs who have seen him play bruising playoff hockey before now despite painful injuries."[6]

Interest in Game One was high. It was reported by the Canadian Press that about 150 determined fans had lined up overnight outside

Maple Leaf Gardens to make sure they would be among the first patrons to have the chance to buy the few remaining available seats for the first Boston-Toronto clash. Cold weather did not make it a pleasant night for the dedicated hockey diehards waiting in the queue.

To the great surprise of most NHL followers, the Bruins marched into Maple Leaf Gardens for Game One and shut out the hometown Maple Leafs by a 2–0 score. Rookie Lorne Ferguson, age 20, got the opening Boston goal at 15:58 of the first period by beating Rollins to a rebound. No goals were scored in the second frame, but Woody Dumart got an insurance tally for the B's 1:12 into the third period. As fate would have it, both Boston goals were scored from very close range. Boston hockey writer Tom Fitzgerald described the two Bruin tallies as mere "goalmouth flips."

Twenty-six-year-old goaltender Jack Gelineau—a decorated war hero for his service in Europe in 1944—picked up a well-earned shutout for the victorious visitors. Furthermore, the unbeatable Bruin netminder was clearly the star of the game, according to the account published in the next day's *Boston Globe*. "Gelineau Great as Bruins Upset Leafs, 2–0" roared the headline atop the *Globe*'s March 29 sports section.

Fitzgerald wrote that the close score actually flattered the favored but defeated home team. He penned, "The B's obviously amazed the 12,919 patrons as they outhit, outplayed and outsmarted the second-place Leafs to dispel a couple of jinxes that had bedeviled the team and coach Lynn Patrick for quite a spell."[7] In their seven trips to Maple Leaf Gardens during the regular season, the Bruins had been a thoroughly dismal bunch, managing just one tie and six losses. Coach Patrick—including his tenure as coach of the New York Rangers—had failed to win a game in Toronto in his previous 17 tries. That personal luckless streak was now mercifully over for Boston's bench boss.

A Canadian Press article penned by Gerald Lougheed praised the effort of the underdog Bruins—who were 3:1 betting long shots to take the opening game of the semifinal series in Toronto against the mighty Maple Leafs. "The Bruins may turn out to be the surprise package of the NHL playoffs," he wrote. "Their win was convincing. They outhustled the Leafs from the opening whistle."[8]

Toronto not only lost Game One, they lost their first-string goaltender. Al Rollins hurt himself in a violent collision with Boston's Pete Horeck, who was storming the Maple Leaf cage on a shorthanded breakaway. The incident occurred with slightly more than three minutes left in the first period. Boston was holding a 1–0 lead and had Paul Ronty sitting in the sin bin serving a minor penalty for holding. Despite being a man down, Boston left winger Horeck found a loose puck and headed with it speedily toward the Toronto goal. Rollins, the Vezina Trophy winner, opted to charge out of the net at the advancing Bruin.

Something had to give—and it did. The resulting collision resulted in what was first diagnosed as bruised ligaments in the goaltender's left knee. One of Rollins' goalie pads fared worse than he did: A large gash was ripped into it, presumably by one of Horeck's skates, and much sawdust spilled onto the Maple Leaf Gardens ice surface, delaying the resumption of the action while attendants armed with shovels did the clean-up duty. In the following days, Horeck received some criticism by the Leafs and the Toronto media for being reckless in his aggressive charge toward the Leafs' net. It was a thinly veiled charge that Horeck had deliberately planned to hurt the Toronto netminder. Horeck and the Bruins' management strongly denied the accusation.

At first, Rollins was only concerned with his damaged equipment. Then a more urgent problem surfaced. Only after his goalie pad was adequately refilled and repaired did he realize his knee was not functioning as it should. After receiving some medical attention, Rollins courageously tried to return to the game, but he realized he would not be able to do so when he was given a few soft warmup shots to handle by teammates. Further medical examination found that the ligaments in Rollins' knee were torn—not just bruised. It was little wonder why he was unable to continue in the game.

An intermission was called after which 36-year-old veteran and fan favorite Walter (Turk) Broda relieved his fallen teammate in the Toronto goal. Broda's last game had been 17 days ago, against the same Boston Bruins on March 11—a contest the Bruins won, 3–1, at Boston Garden. On this night Broda literally had to be summoned from the stands at Maple Leaf Gardens to replace the injured Rollins.

Toronto's team physician opined that Rollins would likely miss the rest of the semifinal series while he recuperated. "This doesn't cripple the Leafs," declared Fitzgerald. "Broda is noted as a 'money goaltender.'"[9] Fraser MacDougall, writing for the Canadian Press, basically penned the same thing in predicting the Leafs would be without Rollins' services for 10 days, but the aging Broda was a more-than-capable backup goaltender to rescue his team.

Despite the short notice, Broda played well for the Maple Leafs in his unexpected relief role in the opening game of Series "B." He was beaten just once, the third-period goal notched by Boston's Woody Dumart, but Toronto could muster no response at all in the final 18½ minutes of Game One. No goals got past Gelineau, who was magnificent for the visitors as the shoutout proved. He had blocked all 24 Toronto shots that came his way. It was Gelineau's first whitewash of the favored Maple Leafs all season. In playing in all 70 of the Bruins' regular-season games, Gelineau had recorded just four shutouts in 1950–51.

Game One was also a terrific team effort by the underdog Bruins as a whole. "The Bruins played a rugged, bruising game right from the start," according to the praiseful MacDougall. "Veteran Milt Schmidt, playing despite a knee injury, led the forward brigade. Bill Quackenbush topped the defensive formation in front of Gelineau."[10]

Boston only mustered 12 shots versus the Maple Leafs over the course of the entire game. Three were aimed at the Toronto net when Rollins was on the ice and nine when Broda took over the Leafs' goaltending duties. "But the Boston team was sharper twice when it counted around the net,"[11] noted the CP correspondent.

Game Two, also played at Maple Leaf Gardens, was oddly inconclusive. It was also a very rough affair. The contest ended in a 1–1 tie due to a strictly enforced Sunday curfew law, the federal Lord's Day Act, that was on the books in Toronto—and all of Ontario in some form in 1951. It was the first playoff game to end in a deadlock since the NHL discontinued its total-goals-in-two-games format after the 1935–36 season.

The tie was entirely due to a religious-based provincial ordinance stating that no professional sports event could be scheduled for a Sunday—or extend past 11:45 p.m. on Saturday night. (The venue was supposed to be cleared of spectators and participants by midnight. That was a hopeful bit of legislation.) Game Two was played on March 31—a Saturday night. It was level, at 1–1, after regulation time. With the game at serious risk of lasting past 11:45 p.m. if a second overtime began, the decision was made by the NHL and its on-ice officials to simply terminate it without a winner emerging. If necessary, the suspended game would be replayed in its entirety in Toronto, basically as an eighth game of the best-of-seven series. Game Two's statistics counted, however. Thus, Series "B" of the 1951 Stanley Cup playoffs turned into a quirky best-of-eight struggle. Thirty-seven years would pass before there was another unfinished Stanley Cup playoff game. The Boston Bruins were involved in that one too—when the electricity at Boston Garden abruptly shut off during the second period of a 1988 Cup finals game versus the Edmonton Oilers.

With Canada's governor-general Viscount Harold Alexander making a special trip from Ottawa to be among the spectators at Maple Leaf Gardens for Game Two, defenseman Bill Barilko opened the scoring for the home side early in the first period on a 50-foot blast that was the result of sloppy play by Boston in their own zone. Thanks to a giveaway, the home team finally found a weak spot in goaltender Jack Gelineau's armor. (The Bruin netminder had been screened on the play and did not see Barilko's shot sail past him.) Johnny Peirson equalized for the feisty visitors in the second stanza with a 20-foot backhander that eluded Turk Broda. Neither team managed to create a goal in the third period nor in the 20 minutes of overtime that was permitted before the midnight hour approached.

"The tie left the Bruins in a fairly comfortable position as they head back to Boston," wrote the optimistic Tom Fitzgerald in the Sunday edition of the *Boston Globe*. "They already hold an edge in Series B by virtue of their 2–0 victory here on Wednesday. They hope to bolster that advantage in their games at [Boston] Garden on [Sunday] and Tuesday night."[12]

Apart from the curfew issue, the major story of the game was its extremely rough play and the resulting casualties. The *Ottawa Journal*'s headline atop its coverage of Game Two said "Blood and Stream of Penalties Feature in 1–1 Tie in Toronto." Toronto's *Globe & Mail* was blunt in its assessment of the rough contest, referring to the game as "vicious." Its report on Game Two claimed, "Actual hockey was of secondary importance as players of opposing teams skated out but with one thought in mind: to soften the other fellow up." Among Toronto's walking wounded was captain Ted Kennedy, who suffered a five-inch cut over his eye courtesy of an unapologetic Milt Schmidt. "We were both high-sticking," said Schmidt afterward. "I admit I cut him, but I got a five-minute penalty for it. It was either him or me and I happened to get him. What are they crying about?"[13]

But Boston got the worst of the blood-letting by far. An Associated Press story that appeared in the April 2 *Fitchburg Sentinel* said, "The Boston Bruins may be in a bad way Tuesday night when they again oppose the Toronto Maple Leafs." That was putting things mildly. In the *Boston Globe*, Herb Ralby went into all the gory details. He wrote, "The Bruins' dressing room looked like a battlefront first aid station. Johnny Peirson, who scored the Bruins' only goal, sustained a fractured right cheek bone when he was checked heavily into the glass backboards by Jimmy Thomson in the overtime."[14] Peirson was the worst injured of the bunch of battered B's—which was saying something. In no shape to travel back to Boston with the rest of his club, he was left behind at Toronto General Hospital to heal. Peirson was so thoroughly dazed by his injury that he had to have his uniform removed by two teammates. He would certainly be unavailable to play in Game Three at Boston Garden. (According to a story in the *Ottawa Journal*, Peirson did send a telegram to his Bruin teammates, wishing them good luck in Game Three.) Boston's Pete Horeck was another casualty. He received a 10-stitch souvenir over his left eye when he came out second-best in a stick duel with Bill Barilko. The Fitchburg newspaper noted that the Bruins would not be practicing on Monday but would instead focus on recuperation.

Indeed, Barilko seemed to be firmly in the center of the mayhem.

Canadian Press staff writer Gerry Lougheed commented that the man nicknamed Bashing Bill "was almost a permanent part of the penalty box with a total of 21 minutes in penance"[15]—which included a 10-minute misconduct for disagreeing too heartily with referee Red Storey. Earlier in the sudden-death frame, about seven minutes into it, Boston's Dunc Fisher was, according to Tom Fitzgerald, "hoisted heartily into the fence by Barilko and taken off the ice on a stretcher after an examination by [Bruins team physician] Dr. Tom Kelley."[16] Fisher, who was knocked unconscious, ended up bleeding from a 12-inch gash in his scalp. Barilko was handed a major penalty by referee Storey for what was deemed to be an illegal hit—a decision that so angered Toronto owner Conn Smythe that he rushed toward ice level to berate NHL referee-in-chief Carl Voss. (Born in Chelsea, MA, the 44-year-old Voss was a former NHL player. In his eight seasons in the league, he had remarkably been on the rosters of eight different teams! Four of them were now defunct: The New York Americans, St. Louis Eagles, Montreal Maroons, and Ottawa Senators.) Smythe was not the only non-player who tried to enter the fray. At one point in the game, enraged Boston coach Lynn Patrick leaned over the boards and punched Toronto's Jim Thomson in the face! Smythe later attempted to downplay the violence of Game Two by saying that no team that opted to play rough against his feisty Maple Leafs could ever hope to win a playoff game against them.

The Bruins failed to capitalize on their lengthy power play, however. Their offensive impotence in that stretch was typical of the game. Outplayed, Boston was having trouble generating much sustained offense in Game Two. The visitors managed only 17 shots on Turk Broda in 80 minutes. On balance, Toronto was clearly the better club that Saturday night. Yet, Boston hung tough against the favored Maple Leafs, and returned to their home ice holding an unusual one-game edge after two games in a playoff series. It had been a spirited encounter.

The inconclusive ending of Game Two prompted much discussion among NHL followers. Some hopeful ticketholders wondered if they were entitled to the equivalent of a raincheck because the game produced no winner. The answer to that query was clearly no, considering they saw four full periods of playoff action. Secondly, there was some confusion about whether the NHL had erred in its enforcement of the puritanical "blue law" prohibiting Sunday sports in Ontario. Toronto had passed a special municipal law, which apparently usurped provincial legislation on the matter, to allow for Sunday sporting events—as long as they were contested in the four and a half hours between 1:30 p.m. and 6 p.m. The provincial curfew of 11:45 p.m. on Saturday still applied to all sports events—even the Stanley Cup playoffs—so the NHL and local law enforcement indeed made the correct decision to halt the game after the first overtime period expired. It was the right one, but it was certainly not very popular with the fans. By the time the series was nearly completed, Massachusetts governor Paul A. Dever announced that a new law had been passed in the legislature to legally permit sporting events to go beyond 11 p.m. in his state. That was news to many Bostonians who were unaware there had been any such restriction on the books—until the Bruins announced prior to Game Three that play would cease at the 23rd hour that Sunday if the game was still tied, in accordance with a generally forgotten (or ignored) Massachusetts statute.

Paul A. Dever is pictured here. A sports fan and the 58th governor of Massachusetts, he did not want a repeat of the terminated playoff game in Toronto under his watch, so his administration rescinded previous legislation barring curfews on professional sporting events in his state (courtesy Boston Public Library, Leslie Jones Collection).

Overtime was not an issue at all in Game Three. The following evening in Boston, the hockey game was a bit more civilized than in Game Two—but not much more. Twenty penalties were called by referee Bill Chadwick. Fifteen of them were whistled in the first period of what Tom Fitzgerald called "an old-fashioned roughhouse that kept 13,768 spectators in the Garden shouting through long stretches."[17]

Before the largest hockey crowd to see a game in Boston during the 1950–51 season, the Maple Leafs skated to a comfortable 3–0 victory to level the series at 1-1-1. Their goal scorers were Max Bentley, Cal Gardner, and Fern Flaman. Flaman had been on the Bruins' roster at the

3. Semifinal Series "B"

beginning of the season. He had been dealt to Toronto in a six-player deal on November 16. On that Thursday, Flaman, Leo Boivin, Phil Maloney and Ken Smith were dispatched to Toronto in exchange for Vic Lynn and Bill Ezinicki. The latter had greatly fallen out of favor with both the Maple Leafs' management and the team's fans. Ezinicki seemed to hold grudges against his ex-teammates in Game Three. Boston was handed seven penalties in the opening period. Ezinicki got four of them. He had five before the contest had ended.

Conn Smythe, of course, was delighted by the game's outcome. "It was stormy weather for a while," the Leafs owner told the *Boston Globe* with a mariner's analogy. "The Bruins came out to rough it up with us and for a while it looked bad. The storm seems to have cleared and now they are dropping back."[18]

Toronto coach Joe Primeau called Game Three a must-win situation for his club—and they came through with the necessary triumph in front of a hostile Boston crowd. "We were up for this game. We had to be," he insisted. "It was a tough game and the players were tired near the end of it. Maybe the Bruins had less left than we did and that's what won it for us."[19]

Red Burnett of the *Toronto Star* was appalled by the constant rough play that was on display in Series "B." He wrote, "If the boys keep making with the high sticks, elbows, punches, boards checks, etc., they're liable to leave the series survivors weak and wobbly for the finals. At times it has been a Tong war as they charge around using sticks as hatchets."[20]

Boston coach Lynn Patrick took his team's defeat in stride. He said, "I'm not worried. We're even with them, aren't we? Let them worry. Two of the next three games are here [in Boston]. I'm more concerned with our injuries than this one game."[21]

Indeed, it had been a costly outing for the Bruins. Over the course of the game, the 33-year-old Milt Schmidt somehow managed to injure *both* of his knees. His right one was hurt in a collision with ex-teammate Fern Flaman. Some observers believed Flaman had deliberately kneed the Bruins' captain. After the game, Schmidt had considerable difficulty straightening out that leg especially. Compounding the B's troubles, Boston's rookie defenseman Steve Kraftcheck worsened a problem with his ailing knee and Max Quackenbush oddly injured both of his wrists. The Bruins were indeed a battered bunch.

Patrick confirmed Primeau's theory about the fitness of the two teams. "We tired quicker than they did because we were short of men," he agreed. "Dunc Fisher had a dizzy spell after a first-period check. I didn't dare use him again. Vic Lynn played with a charley horse. Peirson was out with a fractured cheekbone. That broke up all our lines and reduced our effectiveness."[22]

Turk Broda recorded the shutout for the Maple Leafs—the twelfth one he had attained in Stanley Cup play since 1937. He was only required to make 16 saves as the Boston offense continued to sputter. It was also Broda's hundredth NHL playoff game. Al Rollins, as expected, was still sidelined with the knee injury he suffered in the spectacular Game One collision with Boston's Pete Horeck.

There was no scoring in the opening period as the checking was tight from both clubs. Cal Gardner's goal at 3:02 of the second period was described as "freakish" by the unnamed Canadian Press reporter who offered this description of it:

> [Gardner] picked up the disk in his own zone, skated through center, and was apparently checked only a few feet in front of the [Boston] net by Bill Quackenbush and Murray Henderson.
> As Gardner fell, however, he gave the rubber a slight shove. It slid between goalkeeper Jack Gelineau's feet as Eddie Sandford skated across the cage in a vain effort to clear.[23]

In contrast, Fern Flaman's goal, also occurring in the second period, was a whistling shot accurately launched from about six feet inside he Boston blue line. It sailed cleanly over Gelineau's shoulder and into the top of the cage to give the visitors a 2–0 edge. It was a power-play marker coming at 13:11 with Boston's Pete Horeck sitting out a minor infraction for high-sticking. The third Toronto marker was added in the final period by Max Bentley at the 5:30 mark. His 30-foot shot cleanly beat Gelineau. It sealed the 3–0 victory for the Maple Leafs, who had 32 shots on the Boston goal—twice as many shots as the outgunned Bruins fired at Turk Broda in the Toronto cage.

Before the fourth game of the series, NHL president Clarence Campbell announced what the league would do with the gate receipts from the inconclusive second game. His answer was basically "business as usual." Apart from the game not counting in the best-of-seven series, the money would be handled as it would in any of the first four playoff games in a series, with the lion's share going to the players and to their pension fund. The pension allotment comes from the increase in ticket prices applied to all NHL postseason games. There had been some grumbling about what was to become of Game Two's cash, with some fans and writers calling for it to be donated to a worthy charity due to no winner being declared.

Game Four was played two nights later at Boston Garden. The Maple Leafs won again, 3–1, making it four straight games in this quirky playoff series in which the home team had thus far failed to post a victory. Defensive stalwart Bill Barilko was the game's outstanding performer, this time as an offensive threat. The next day's *Toronto Telegram* affirmed it by blaring, "Barilko, top Toronto man tonight and most other nights in this series, is the top Leaf scorer with two goals."[24]

Tom Fitzgerald of the *Boston Globe* noted that while the near-sellout crowd of 13,154 patrons may have left Boston Garden disappointed, at least they had seen a fast, cleanly played hockey game compared to the roughness of Game Three. Fitzgerald cited the lack of a parade to the penalty box as evidence. "This time referee George Gravel handed out only six penalties in the 60 minutes compared to 20 [that were assessed] in the Sabbath brawl,"[25] he wrote. The headline in the *Ottawa Citizen* concurred. It read, "Bruins Bow in Clean Game, 3-1." Still, there was a bit of nastiness in how the game was played. Milt Schmidt opened up a cut on Bill Barilko's face with a high stick early in the first period.

Despite their team still missing Johnny Peirson's services, the B's jumped out to the lead in this match—the first time the Bruins had held an advantage on the scoreboard since Game One. The goal scorer was Dunc Fisher, who beat Turk Broda at 7:50 of the first period with a backhand shot from close in that flew over the sprawled Toronto goalie. Fisher had been well positioned to knock home the rebound from Dave Creighton's deflection. The goal injected extra life in the Boston rooters who, until Fisher's tally lit the goal light behind Broda, had yet to see their team score a playoff goal at home.

The Bruins' one-goal lead lasted for more than a period. Toronto's first goal came on the power play at 12:17 of the second period. Sid Smith equalized with Max Bentley and Jimmy Thomson each picking up an assist while Boston's Bill Ezinicki was sitting out a minor high-sticking infraction. Shortly thereafter, Max Bentley put the Maple Leafs up 2-1 with an unassisted marker at 14:33. The tide of the game had suddenly and irreversibly turned in favor of Toronto. Bill Barilko added an insurance goal for the visitors at 8:02 of the third period. The *Toronto Telegram* noted in its coverage of Game Four that it was Barilko's second tally of the series—putting him unexpectedly in the lead in that offensive category. No other Leaf or Bruin had two goals thus far in the Stanley Cup playoffs.

The series moved back to Toronto for Game Five with the home team clearly possessing all the momentum garnered from the two victories at Boston Garden. A long rest was built into the series' schedule. Game Five would not be played until the night of Saturday, April 7.

Lynn Patrick made an odd roster maneuver for his Bruins to start Game Five at Maple Leaf Gardens. Conspicuous by his absence was Boston goaltender Jack Gelineau who had played every minute of every Boston game in 1950-51—including the first four playoff games. In his place was Gordon (Red) Henry—so nicknamed because of his distinct hair color. It was a pure gamble on Patrick's part, considering that no one had accused

Gelineau of playing badly in any of the first four series games. However, during the regular season, according to *Boston Globe* scribe Tom Fitzgerald, the Bruins had been occasionally demoralized by some soft goals that eluded Gelineau. Patrick firmly believed that elevating Red Henry from the minors to the parent club would bolster the Bruins' confidence in Game Five. The decision to bench Gelineau raised some eyebrows across the NHL. Fitzgerald claimed a team switching goalies during a Stanley Cup playoffs series for any reason other than an injury was unprecedented.

A story in the April 7 edition of the *Boston Globe* said Lynn Patrick had called up a total of four players from the minor league Hershey Bears to fill in the gaps caused by the injuries to his regulars. "What a difference from last Sunday in Boston," beamed the happy Bruins coach. "I had to scrape the bottom of the barrel to get enough players for that game. Now I have more than enough."[26]

Of course, one such player was Red Henry, a promising 25-year-old goaltender from Owen Sound, Ontario. Henry did not have much of an NHL résumé, having played in only three big-league games for Boston spread over two seasons—neither of which was the current one. His record in those contests was a mediocre one win and two losses. Still, he was generally considered the top goaltender in the American League. With Hershey having been knocked out of the AHL playoffs, he could be used by the Bruins in the Stanley Cup playoffs, if the Bruins so chose. They did.

In other Bruins news, the team confirmed the speculation that Johnny Peirson, who had notched 19 goals for the Bruins during the 1950–51 regular season, was lost to the squad for the rest of whatever hockey the club had left to play in the postseason. No one would see him on the ice again until the 1951–52 season's training camp. Peirson's eye was still shut from the broken right cheekbone he received in the overtime in Game Two. Still, Patrick remained upbeat about his team's chances for an upset victory over the favored Maple Leafs. "We're not as cocky as we were when we had a one-game lead or when the series was even," Patrick noted the day before Game Five, "but we're still confident."[27]

The Boston coach's confidence in his club before Game Five turned out to be ill-founded. The headline atop the sports section of April 8 Sunday *Boston Globe* said it all: "Leafs Outclass Bruins, 4–1, Lead Series 3 Games to 1." In the accompanying story, Tom Fitzgerald wrote that it was the first time in the semifinal series where the Bruins looked to be truly overwhelmed by the favored Maple Leafs. He further commented that the score did not truly reflect the dominance the Leafs showed over Boston for the game's entirety. It should have been more lopsided than just a three-goal margin.

Just before game time, Lynn Patrick opted to play Red Henry in

3. Semifinal Series "B"

net—marking the first time all season that Jack Gelineau was not guarding the pipes for the Bruins. [Red] Henry played well, but, as Fitzpatrick noted, "he could not have been blamed had he sued his mates for non-support."[28] Indeed, a subheading in the *Globe*'s coverage read, "No help for Henry." The red-headed goalie stopped 41 of 45 Toronto shots aimed toward his net.

The hero of the Toronto triumph was blond-haired Joe Klukay. He figured in three of the Leafs' goals, scoring two of them—the first and third for the home team. Klukay—called "Kluke" by his teammates—also had an assist on the second Leaf tally, a goal by Fleming Mackell. Ted Kennedy had the fourth Toronto goal. The Maple Leafs held a 1–0 lead after 20 minutes, a 2–0 lead after 40 minutes, and padded their advantage to 4–0 before the halfway mark of the third period. Bill Ezinicki got one back for Boston just 38 seconds after Kennedy's goal. It came on a pretty, three-way passing play involving Milt Schmidt and Woody Dumart, but it mattered little to the game's eventual outcome. It did spoil Turk Broda's bid for another playoff shutout, however. An apparent fifth Toronto goal in the game's dying seconds was eventually disallowed by referee George Gravel. He ruled the puck had not entered the Boston net, despite the goal judge signaling otherwise.

Along with goaltender Henry, the Bruins also employed two other Hershey call-ups in Game Five. They were Jack (Moose) McIntyre and another player named Red—George (Red) Sullivan. "It wasn't the fault of this trio that the Bruins suffered their worst defeat of the series," Fitzgerald explained. "The Bruins' defense, which had been unusually sound in the four previous games, picked tonight to crack."[29] Lynn Patrick had to agree ... and he did. "The team played one of its worst games of the season. The defense played particularly badly,"[30] the Boston coach opined.

Toronto's first goal of Game Five may have been the backbreaker. It came in the final minute of the first period while the Maple Leafs were playing shorthanded. With Howie Meeker sitting out a tripping penalty, Klukay intercepted a terribly errant Bill Quackenbush pass directly in front of the Boston net and beat Red Henry on a quick shot that definitely surprised the Bruin goaltender. Quackenbush was normally a very reliable Bruin who seldom made silly mistakes, but his cavalier pass in his own zone was clearly one instance of poor judgment. All the other Leaf tallies resulted from Toronto hustling to rebounds after Henry saves and converting the second chances into goals.

Their easy victory was doubly good for the Maple Leafs as they learned that Montreal had upset the mighty Detroit Red Wings in Game Six of Semifinal A at the Forum that that same evening. Another triumph over the Bruins the following night at Boston Garden would advance

Toronto into the Stanley Cup finals where they would be the clear favorites to capture the trophy.

Game Six was an absolute rout. With Red Kennedy again in net for the home side, the Maple Leafs romped to a 6–0 win at Boston Garden, continuing their dominance from the previous game—only more so. The contest was played before only about 10,600 fans, a few thousand ticketholders shy of the arena's capacity for hockey. It was the fourth consecutive win for Toronto after beginning their playoff series with the Bruins at Maple Leaf Gardens by surprisingly dropping the opener and playing to an unsatisfactory draw in Game Two thanks to the local and provincial curfew laws.

In the end, the overall superiority of the Leafs' roster was just too much for the underdog and injury-plagued Bruins to endure. The better team had prevailed. An unnamed Canadian Press reporter agreed, stating, "The Bruins could not match the visitors last night."[31] The best Bruins may have been the call-ups from Hershey, Red Sullivan and Jack McIntyre, whose play was described as "sprightly" by *Globe* sports journalist Tom Fitzgerald. The fans certainly took a shine to them. Fitzgerald noted, "Some of the customers disapproved when the youngsters were pulled off [the ice] after a short turn, but they saw plenty of action throughout the evening."[32]

There was a bit of controversy early on. Toronto's first goal, scored at 10:16 of the opening period, featured what the Bruins thought to be Ted Kennedy wrongly using his hand to play the puck. In a goalmouth scramble near Boston goalie Red Henry, Kennedy, who was sprawled on the ice, used his fist to knock the puck forward to his own stick—which he then used to knock the puck into the Boston net. As long as Kennedy did not pass the puck to a teammate by that method, or grasp the puck, or push into the goal with his hand, the play was legal. Referee Bill Chadwick correctly allowed Kennedy's goal to stand. Toronto was off and running and would not be stopped as they rolled to an easy 6–0 whitewash. One disgruntled home fan thought his Bruins had gotten a raw deal on the play. He angrily flung a fedora from the upper seats that landed in the visitors' bench.

Repeating his Game Four efforts, Joe Klukay scored twice for the winners. The other four Toronto goals were credited to Sid Smith, Fleming Mackell, Teeder Kennedy and Tod Sloan. The score was 3–0 after the first period. No goals were scored in the second frame. Toronto got three more in the third stanza to complete the shellacking of the hometown B's. Even though a photo in the *Boston Globe*'s sports section showed a large melee of players on both teams apparently preparing to do battle, no penalties were called by referee Chadwick throughout the mild-mannered game. (Chadwick had been the official who whistled 20 penalties in Game

Three.) By the time the final horn sounded, many of the Garden patrons were not present to hear its echo. They had already departed the venue in stony silence. Their Bruins had provided them with precious little to cheer about in Game Six.

Toronto's Turk Broda only had to handle 16 Boston shots to earn his shutout. Broda had allowed just four Boston goals in 283 minutes of play since replacing the injured Al Rollins partway through Game One. *Globe* sports journalist Tom Fitzgerald claimed, "The guy who got most of the bear hugs from his mates at the brief victory to-do at the game's end was Broda. The 36-year-old veteran with the expanding waistline had an easy time compiling his second shutout of the series."[33]

In the Boston goal, Red Henry made stops on 23 of 29 Maple Leaf shots. Fitzgerald said the Hershey goaltender "was off his showing from Saturday night, but the Bruins did not throw a very tight defense in front of him."[34]

All in all, Fitzgerald seemed to be disgusted by Boston's showing in the semifinal series. He wrote, "The Bruins continued another fruitless quest for the Stanley Cup last night when the Toronto Maple Leafs blasted them out of the playoffs by a 6–0 count at the Garden."[35] In their three playoff home games versus Toronto, the Bruins went 0–3 and scored just one measly goal in 180 minutes.

At least Boston showed outward indications of confidence prior to Game Six. An optimistic sign was posted in the home team's dressing room advising the Bruin players that the train they would be boarding for Toronto for the next game would leave on Monday at 4:30 p.m. Of course, Boston's one-sided loss to the Maple Leafs made that planned trip to southern Ontario completely unnecessary.

Defeated Boston coach Lynn was gracious with his compliments to the victors. He said the Maple Leafs had effectively whacked Milt Schmidt and Johnny Peirson into submission, depriving the B's of their two best scoring threats. (He meant the remark as praise.) Patrick continued with his analysis of why Toronto won:

> Jim Thomson did most of the heavy work for them, but they've got a bruising defense. Guys like Bill Barilko, Bill Juzda, and Fernie Flaman can hurt you if they get a good shot at you. Gus Mortson is no Little Lord Fauntleroy. Barilko was just about their best man in the series—and he didn't do a thing against us all season. We hardly noticed him, but it always seems to happen like that [in Stanley Cup play].[36]

Lynn also admitted that replacing Jack Gelineau in net was pure a gamble that simply did not pay dividends for the desperate Bruins. Nevertheless, Lynn felt that Jim Henry had played satisfactorily in the two contests in which he guarded the Boston goal against Toronto, despite the final game being a 6–0 shellacking in favor of the Maple Leafs. "We just didn't have a chance,"[37] Lynn lamented to the *Boston Globe*.

The better team had clearly emerged victorious in Semifinal "B." Boston was competitive in the first two games, but slowly and surely the overall depth and quality of the Maple Leafs became obvious as the series progressed. The Bruins averaged less than a goal per game in their six matches versus Toronto. They had scored just twice in the final four games. This included two shutout defeats at Boston Garden.

Once Game Six had concluded that Sunday evening, it assured a Toronto-Montreal Stanley Cup matchup for the 1951 finals as the Habs had completed a major upset in eliminating Detroit in Series "A" the previous night at the Montreal Forum. The Habs' surprise series win was a result that undoubtedly pleased Toronto's players and fans. Shortly afterward, NHL president Clarence Campbell announced the schedule for the first five games of the best-of-seven, all–Canadian championship round. As Toronto had finished higher than the Canadiens in the regular-season standings, the Maple Leafs would be the beneficiaries of home-ice advantage. They would host four of the seven games (One, Two, Five and Seven) if the series went the distance. Game One would take place on Wednesday, April 11 at Maple Leaf Gardens. The Leafs would attempt to win Lord Stanley's holy grail of hockey for the fourth time in five seasons.

In his April 9 column in the *Ottawa Citizen*, sports editor Jack Koffman wrote, "The two best-drawing clubs in hockey this winter are prepared to lock horns in the Stanley Cup finals, and it could be a series to end all series."[38] Hockey fans certainly hoped Koffman's hunch was an accurate one.

Semifinal "B" Results

Game #1 at Toronto: Boston wins, 2–0
Game #2 at Toronto: Tie game, 1–1 (game terminated by curfew law)
Game #3 at Boston: Toronto wins, 3–0
Game #4 at Boston: Toronto wins, 3–1
Game #5 at Toronto: Toronto wins, 4–1
Game #6 at Boston: Toronto wins, 6–0
Toronto wins the series four games to one (with one tie game).

4

Montreal vs. Toronto

Their Histories and Rivalry

The Montreal Canadiens are the only current National Hockey League team whose history predates the circuit. The very early days of the Canadiens are challenging for dedicated hockey historians to totally grasp; they are even more tricky to comprehend by typical modern fans who are generally unschooled about the sport's formative years.

A hockey team known as Les Canadiens was established on December 4, 1909, by John Ambrose O'Brien. It seems to have had a loose, short-lived affiliation with a general sports organization located in Montreal, Le Club Athlétique Canadien, from which it borrowed the name. The hockey club was founded eight years before the NHL was formed. It came into existence as an amateur team, playing its first game on January 4, 1910, as a member of the Canadian Hockey Association. However, the Canadiens quickly jumped to the newly formed National Hockey Association, a professional circuit at a time when play-for-pay hockey was just beginning to emerge as a viable entity in Canada. They finished their inaugural season in last place. The Canadiens occupied the NHA's cellar in their next two seasons as well. Such are the humble origins of one of the most successful franchises in all North American team sports.

By 1914 the Canadiens had acquired their nickname, the Habs. Its brevity has certainly been a boon to headline writers over the succeeding 11 decades. The term seems to have originated from a local reporter's newspaper stories about them. It is an abbreviation for Les Habitants—a term for the seventeenth- and eighteenth-century land-owning settlers from the days when Quebec was New France—a French colony. In modern usage, the term "Habitant" is a pejorative among French-Canadians, meaning something akin to a country bumpkin. The term Habs, in terms of the NHL hockey team, however, has luckily escaped that negative connotation.

Things began to turn around by the 1915–16 campaign. That year the

Canadiens were a very strong club featuring star players such as Édouard (Newsy) Lalonde, Didier Pitre, Jack Laviolette and goaltender Georges Vézina. All four of them would eventually be enshrined in the Hockey Hall of Fame. The Habs finished first in the league standings with a 16–7–1 record to win a long-forgotten trophy called the O'Brien Cup. They also won the NHA crown in the playoffs that season, but that was not the same thing as winning the Stanley Cup. Between 1914 and 1926, the championship hockey club from eastern Canada had to win a playoff series against the best pro club from western Canada, the champions of the Pacific Coast Hockey Association (PCHA), to capture Lord Stanley's silver trophy. To minimize travel, the series was always played in one city, with the location alternating between western and eastern locales from year to year. In the even years, the Stanley Cup games were hosted by the eastern champions, so the 1916 series was played entirely at the Montreal Arena. Complicating matters was that two sides of the continent played hockey under different sets of rules. Most notably, PCHA games were contested with seven men on the ice at a time compared to the NHA's six. Of course, other minor rule differences also existed. For example, PCHA rules allowed players to freely kick the puck. This tactic was illegal in eastern hockey. The two Cup finalists alternated which rules were to be used on a game-by-game basis. It was a confusing time to be a fan of professional hockey.

The western representatives who traveled eastward to vie for the Stanley Cup in 1916 were the Portland Rosebuds. (The historically significant American-based club from the PCHA was the first non–Canadian team to play for the coveted trophy. Nobody seemed to mind very much, even though the deed to the Stanley Cup specifically said the trophy was to be awarded to "the championship hockey club of Canada.") In the best-of-five series, played between March 20 and March 30, the Canadiens eked out a narrow victory, three games to two, over the Rosebuds. Two Montreal victories in that series, including Game Five, were won by a single goal. It was the first of two dozen Stanley Cups won by the Habs over a span of 77 years.

Largely due to internal bickering—and huge loathing for Toronto owner Eddie Livingstone by his peers—the NHA folded after the 1916–17 campaign and was replaced in November by the new National Hockey League, a circuit that did not invite Livingstone to join. It was a four-team outfit—and the Montreal Canadiens were one of its founding members. When the NHL began play in November 1917, the Canadiens sported uniforms featuring a new crest. It was a stylized C with an H in its middle. Those letters in the crest symbolized the team's new official name: the Club de Hockey Canadien. The H in the famous logo stands for "hockey"—not "habitants"—as many Montreal fans wrongly believe.

The Habs, led by superstar Howie Morenz, won the Stanley Cup again by defeating the Calgary Tigers in 1924—their second and final championship before the NHL's modern era began. (Interestingly, the final game of that best-of-three series was hastily moved to Ottawa on March 25 where artificial ice was available; Montreal Arena's natural ice surface had started to turn slushy in the early days of spring.) The Canadiens also hold the dubious distinction of being the last NHL team to lose to a western team when they fell three games to one to the Victoria Cougars in British Columbia in the 1925 Stanley Cup final. No hockey team located west of the Mississippi River would win the Stanley Cup again until 1984. In the 13 times there was an east-west battle for the Cup between 1914 and 1926, only three times did a western club win the cherished chalice.

At 2313 Saint-Catherine Street West, the famous Montreal Forum was opened in time for the beginning of the 1924–25 NHL season—but not necessarily for the use of the Canadiens, however. An NHL expansion team, the Montreal Maroons, were intended to be the prime inhabitants of the modern new arena (featuring artificial ice!), but the Canadiens quickly joined them as co-tenants. When the city had those two NHL clubs, the Maroons were perceived as the team that was supported by Montreal's anglophones while the Canadiens were, of course, the favorites of the city's francophones.

With the demise of major professional hockey in western Canada, the NHL took sole possession of the Stanley Cup beginning with the 1926–27 season, thus beginning the league's "modern era" which included sizeable expansion to employ all the western players who were suddenly without clubs. By the start of the 1930s, the NHL was a 10-team operation. Six of those clubs were located in American cities—something that was probably unthinkable a decade earlier. The Canadiens won back-to-back Stanley Cups in 1930 and 1931 but then the club fell on hard times during the Great Depression. Canadien teams that were mediocre or worse combined with the severe economic woes of the era almost drove the team into bankruptcy. The Montreal Maroons did not survive despite winning the Stanley Cup as late as 1935. The two-time Stanley Cup champions quietly folded after the 1937–38 season. Their demise made the Canadiens the Forum's only NHL tenant.

The Second World War turned out to be an enormous boon to the struggling Habs franchise. Most of the English-speaking stars of the NHL willingly enlisted in Canada's armed forces, while most of the French-Canadians did not. Even when military conscription became the law in Canada, French-Canadians could use a loophole that allowed them to be in the equivalent of a home guard, remain in Canada, and still play professional hockey. While the rest of the six-team NHL searched frantically for players to fill their rosters who were either too young, too old or too infirmed for military service, the Montreal roster was hardly affected. By 1944, the end result was the decimation of the two best prewar NHL teams—the Boston Bruins and New York Rangers—and the sudden ascension of the Montreal Canadiens. The Habs lost just five of 50 games in the regular season in 1943–44 as they cruised to their first Stanley Cup in 13 years. "Les Canadiens sont là," echoed through the Forum when the Cup was presented. The English translation is, "The Canadiens are here." Yes, they certainly were. And they were not going away.

The Canadiens were also the biggest beneficiaries of an NHL policy that granted territorial rights to teams regarding the signing of amateur players. In the days before the NHL draft, the six NHL teams, in order to foster wider "local interest" in their clubs, were granted the first opportunity to sign a promising youngster to a C-form as early as age 14, provided they lived within 50 miles of their home arenas. (The C stood for commitment; once it was signed, it bound that player to that specific team even if the player was legally a minor.) It was a rule specifically designed to help the struggling Canadiens acquire the best francophone players and generate greater gate receipts. This system worked out wonderfully for the Habs, almost as well for the Toronto Maple Leafs and, to a lesser extent, the Detroit Red Wings. The other three NHL clubs (Chicago, Boston and New York) seldom cultivated any home-grown prospects because more than 90 percent of NHL players at the time were Canadians. Sometimes the percentage was close to 100. For more than a generation, the best NHL hockey players from Quebec were almost always on the roster of the Montreal Canadiens. Some excellent francophones managed to elude the grasp of the Habs (such as Rod Gilbert, Jean Ratelle, Pit Martin and Marcel Pronovost), but not very many. After missing the playoffs in 1948, Montreal qualified for the postseason every season for the next 21 years. Most of the time it was without much difficulty.

When the NHL was founded on November 26, 1917, with Frank Calder as its president, Toronto was one of the tiny circuit's four teams. That squad was boringly called the Arenas. Officially, the club had no nickname at all, but journalists sometimes referred to them as the Arenas because they were technically a temporary NHL team operated by the Toronto Arena Gardens. They managed to win their league's championship in 1917–18 and defeat the western challengers, the Vancouver Millionaires, three games to two to win the Stanley Cup. As 1918 was an even year, every game in the championship series was played in Toronto. The last one was a 2–1 squeaker. One of Toronto's players was Jack Adams who would achieve great fame in later years with the Detroit Red Wings as the club's coach and general manager. Oddly, the Arenas did not bother to have their victory engraved on the Cup—a perquisite of being its holder. It was only done in 1948–30 years after the fact—when a new "collar" was designed for the trophy.

After a disastrous 1918–19 season the Arenas were sold to the Toronto St. Patricks Amateur Hockey Association and adopted the Irish nickname for the team's third NHL season. The St. Pats won the Stanley Cup in 1922. Again, the opponents were the Vancouver Millionaires. Again, all the games were played in Toronto. Again, the home team narrowly won the best-of-five Cup series three games to two. Again, Jack Adams was a player—but this time he was on the Vancouver roster. Babe Dye, a future Hall of Famer, scored nine of the 16 goals the St. Patricks netted in the championship series.

A full decade would go by before a Toronto team threatened to win another Stanley Cup. In the interim, the St. Patricks were sold in the middle of the 1926–27 season for $160,000 to an ownership group led by Conn Smythe. A higher bid was made from a group in Philadelphia who wanted to move the club to Pennsylvania, but Smythe argued that having an NHL team in Toronto was a source of civic pride more important than money. Apparently, that argument convinced the St. Pats owners to sell Smythe and his associates the team—which he kept in Toronto. On February 14, 1927, the team was renamed the Maple Leafs—the national symbol of Canada—and played its first game under that name on February 17. (For legal reasons, the team was still officially listed with the NHL as the Toronto St. Patricks for another year and a half until the name change was formally approved by the league governors in September 1928.) Be that as it may, it was a 4–1 victory for the home side over the New York Americans. The Leafs wore a green leaf on their jerseys that first night, but they eventually sported blue and white uniforms. They were the same colors used on the fleet of sand and gravel trucks that Smythe owned, which was likely no coincidence. They were also the school colors of the University of Toronto, of which Smythe was a proud alumnus.

Within a very short time, the Maple Leafs became enormously popular, thanks to *Hockey Night in Canada*'s radio broadcasts that began on the Canadian Broadcasting Corporation (CBC) in 1929. The old Arena Gardens, renamed the Mutual Street Arena, with its seating capacity of just 8,000, was simply too small to hold everyone who wanted to see Smythe's popular team play. Games quickly sold out; 2,000 standees were common. Toronto's passion for hockey could not be stifled even by the tough economic times of the 1930s. During the height of the Depression, Smythe financed the construction of spacious Maple Leaf Gardens. (When cash ran short for the project, some laborers accepted 20 percent of their payment in arena stock. That turned out to be a terrific deal for them.) The

(From left) Syl Apps, Dick Irvin, Conn Smythe and Gordie Drillon at a Leafs practice at Boston Garden circa 1938. Drillon was the NHL scoring champion in 1937–38 (courtesy Boston Public Library, Leslie Jones Collection).

building was completed in less than a year and was ready for opening night of the 1931–32 NHL season on November 12. The Leafs lost that opener to the Chicago Black Hawks, 2–1, and did not register a win until their sixth game, but they won the Stanley Cup at season's end.

For the next decade Toronto remained consistently competitive, but seemed to be snakebit in the Stanley Cup playoffs once they got to the championship round. The Leafs lost in the finals six times in a span of eight years (in 1933, 1935, 1936, 1938, 1939 and 1940) without winning the trophy even once. The 1942 Stanley Cup finals appeared to be another disappointment as the Maple Leafs fell behind the Detroit Red Wings three games to zero in the best-of-seven series. Remarkably Toronto rallied to win four straight games and capture the Stanley Cup. Thirty-three NHL seasons would pass before another club—the 1975 New York Islanders—duplicated that playoff comeback in a seven-game series. That was in a quarterfinal series. As of 2023, no other team has ever rallied in such a manner in the Cup finals.

Toronto won the Stanley Cup three years later in 1945, again beating the Detroit Red Wings in seven games. This time, though, the Maple Leafs almost suffered a reversal of 1942. They roared out to a 3–0 series lead in which Toronto goaltender Frank McCool surrendered no goals to the Wings. That daunting advantage was squandered as the Red Wings rallied to win the fourth, fifth and sixth games of the Cup finals. Somehow Toronto managed to avoid what would have been a catastrophic collapse to win Game Seven, 2–1, at the Detroit Olympia.

Toronto was clearly the class of the NHL in the late 1940s, winning the Stanley Cup three consecutive times. Although coach Hap Day considered his 1947–48 Maple Leafs to be the best team he ever coached—in a 1963 interview, Day proclaimed them the best NHL team ever assembled—the club's 1948–49 triumph may have been the most impressive of the three. The Leafs struggled throughout the regular season, never winning more than two games in succession. They finished their schedule with a sub-.500 record before catching fire in the playoffs. The fourth-place Maple Leafs knocked off the top two seeds (Detroit and Boston) by winning eight of nine playoff games. In the finals, top-seeded Detroit was shockingly swept. In each game Toronto scored exactly three goals—but that was enough. The scores were 3–2, 3–1, 3–1 and 3–1. Even oxygen tanks on the Detroit bench paid no dividends for the favorites. If not for the outstanding goaltending of Detroit's Harry Lumley, the results surely would have been more one-sided. Since the advent of professionals competing for the Stanley Cup in 1910, no club had won the trophy three straight times before the Maple Leafs achieved the feat in 1947, 1948 and 1949. One had to go back to the days of the famous Ottawa Silver Seven in the sport's amateur era in the first decade of the 20th century to find similar Cup dominance. Despite covering the Red Wings on a regular basis, Doug Vaughan of the *Windsor Daily Star* had nothing but enormous respect for the triple Cup winners. He penned,

> It is not without justification that they call the Toronto Maple Leafs' brain trust of general manager Conn Smythe and coach Clarence (Hap) Day "the greatest team in hockey." The record of these two over the past nine years speaks for itself. They have won five Stanley Cup championships, the last three of them in a row. Of all their Cup triumphs, the one just completed probably gives them the most satisfaction.[1]

In 1950, the Maple Leafs' championship streak ended with a tough seven-game loss to the Red Wings in the semifinals. Game Seven was a 1–0 overtime defeat at the Detroit Olympia, with Leo Reise firing the winning goal past Turk Broda eight and a half minutes into overtime on a 35-foot shot. (Reise had also tallied an overtime game-winner for the Red Wings in the fourth game of that series.) Wrote Vaughan, "Reise put the finishing touch to a great seven-game duel between a pair of clubs that were just about as evenly matched as any pair of rivals you will ever see in any sport."[2] Toronto owner Conn Smythe was disappointed but philosophical about the narrow defeat when he noted to the press, "It has been a long reign."[3]

The thrills of the 1950 Stanley Cup playoffs extended to the finals where the Red Wings ousted the New York Rangers in seven games—with the climactic contest going into a second overtime before Detroit's Pete Babando won the game with his timely goal. Despite the Maple Leafs' absence, Toronto still played a part in the Cup finals. In what would seem inconceivable today, Maple Leaf Gardens hosted Games Two and Three—they were technically New York Rangers' home games—while a circus occupied Madison Square Garden! The other five games were played at the Detroit Olympia, certainly a terrific advantage for the Red Wings. Detroit won three of them, two of which were Game Six and Seven.

The 1951 championship series would be just the second instance in NHL history that Toronto had met the Canadiens in the Stanley Cup finals. The lone previous time was in the spring of 1947. The Maple Leafs won that tilt in six games—and did so as mild underdogs. Montreal had finished atop the NHL standings in 1946–47 with 78 points in 60 games. Toronto ended up in second spot, not too far in arrears, with 72 points. Yet somehow Montreal was largely perceived by hockey writers and fair-minded fans alike as the far better team. A 6–0 Montreal rout in the opener seemed to prove the experts right, but it was followed by three straight Toronto wins. Game Five went to the Habs, 3–1, at the Forum. Undaunted, Toronto won Game Six to capture the Cup on home ice, 2–1. Ted Kennedy scored the decisive goal for the Maple Leafs with about five and a half minutes left in the third period. Journalist Doug Vaughan complimented the victors by describing them as "a brash brigade of warriors with more bounce than a rubber ball and more spirit than a fighting rooster."[4]

Overall, the 1951 get-together would be the sixth postseason meeting between Canada's two NHL teams. Toronto had won three of the five previous playoff encounters with the Habs. Two of the clashes occurred prior to the NHL's "modern era" which hockey historians generally agree began with the 1926–27 season. The first Montreal-Toronto playoff series dated back to the league's inaugural campaign, in the 1917–18 season, the lone year when the Toronto club was called the Arenas. In that year's postseason, the two teams split a home-and-home series, but Toronto won 10–7 on total goals scored. Seven years later, in 1925, now dubbed the St. Patricks, Toronto lost to Montreal in another two-game, total-goals affair, 5–2.

In both 1944 and 1945 the two rival teams faced off against each other in best-of-seven semifinal series. Montreal won the first one in five games;

Toronto won the latter in six games. Toronto's victory in 1945 was considered an enormous upset as the Canadiens had finished well ahead of the Leafs—by 28 points—in the NHL standings. Toronto captain Ted Kennedy would often say that surprise win was the highlight of his Hall of Fame career. The Leafs' 3–2 victory in the last game at Maple Leaf Gardens was especially tension-packed. Coach Hap Day told reporters afterward, "Those last two minutes seemed like a lifetime."[5] He was likely correct. In the final minute of play alone, Montreal forced four faceoffs in the Toronto zone but came up empty in their frenzied attempts for a tying goal. The visitors were "battling like demons," according to *Montreal Gazette* sports editor Dink Carroll, "but the Habitants did not get the breaks that had aided the Leafs in similar situations."[6]

The two clubs' next meeting was the aforementioned 1947 Stanley Cup finals, a thoroughly captivating series that again featured a Toronto upset victory over the favored Habs.

"The Leafs and Canadiens are old rivals," penned Jack Koffman in his *Ottawa Citizen* column two days before the 1951 Cup final series began. "People in both Montreal and Toronto will be fighting each other for tickets for as long as the series lasts. The crowds in these two Canadian cities have been nothing short of sensational this season—in a year when the American clubs, apart from Detroit, were playing in front of small turnouts."[7]

Hockey fans across North America hoped for tremendous excitement from the two storied franchises when they battled for the Stanley Cup to conclude the 1950–51 NHL season. Their hopes would be fulfilled—and then some.

5

The 1951 Stanley Cup Finals
The Anticipation

"If the inspired hockey remains a part of the Habs' efforts in the next series, the Leafs will have plenty of trouble on their hands. The Canadiens, it seems, never hit their true stride until the playoffs [begin], as the Red Wings found out."[1]—Jack Koffman, *Ottawa Citizen* sports editor

The Toronto Maple Leafs entered the 1951 Stanley Cup finals as the solid favorites to walk off with the trophy in the best-of-seven tussle. This was a fact, not just an opinion, widely shared by diehard or biased Leaf rooters.

Toronto had pretty much manhandled the Canadiens all season long, losing just twice to the Habs in their 14 regular-season meetings during the 1950–51 campaign. Before Game One, bookmakers listed the odds on a Toronto series triumph at 5:7, meaning that one had to wager $7 on Joe Primeau's club to win $5. Some hockey writers figured that ratio was quite generous to the underdogs in the red, white and blue Montreal jerseys. A Canadian Press article that appeared in the *Montreal Star* without a byline on April 11—the same day the Cup finals began—said as much. It noted, "Montreal's poor regular-season record against Toronto would seem to be grounds for wider odds, but the Canadiens rate respect for their good showing against the power-packed Detroit Red Wings."

The Canadiens had also lost more games than they had won during the 70-game regular season. Only two teams in NHL history had overcome that stigma to win the Stanley Cup. They were the 1938 Chicago Black Hawks and the very recent 1949 Toronto Maple Leafs.

Even Dink Carroll, the sports editor of the *Montreal Gazette*, openly acknowledged that his beloved hometown NHL club would be hard-pressed to pull off another playoff upset and upend the vaunted powerhouse club from southern Ontario. Despite the Habs having shocked

5. The 1951 Stanley Cup Finals

the Detroit Red Wings in their semifinal series, the 51-year-old Carroll thought the second-place Leafs would present an even more formidable obstacle for the Habs than the first-place club from Michigan had. Writing from Toronto on the day of Game One, Carroll admired the Leafs as a team and appreciated how talented and efficient they were throughout their 70-game schedule. Toronto's .679 winning percentage was their best in club history. More than seven decades later, it still is.

Carroll was not alone in his praise. Boston coach Lynn Patrick had made the trip to Maple Leaf Gardens to see the opening two games of the championship series for his own amusement. Patrick had nothing but positive things to say about the team that had thumped his Bruins in the semifinals.

"Lynn hadn't seen the Canadiens play in a few weeks, so he didn't know how to rate them in this series" noted Carroll, "but he'd seen more than enough of the Leafs."[2]

"They [Toronto] were flying against us after the first two games," the Bruin coach recalled with a slightly awestruck tone. "I never saw them look better than in the last game of the series where they beat us, 6–0. They looked like a perfect hockey machine that night." Patrick then oddly added with a chuckle, "I'm glad it's all over for us this year. Now I can stand in one of the runways at Maple Leaf Gardens, eat peanuts, and watch [Dick] Irvin and [Joe] Primeau sweat. I'll bet Irvin is up pacing in the corral right now."[3]

Be that as it may, some Toronto-based hockey writers were expressing concerns that the Habs were being greatly underrated as a serious threat to the local NHL team they covered passionately each day. One such scribe was James (Red) Burnett of the *Toronto Star*. He cautiously informed his readers,

> A month ago, we'd have picked the Leafs in four straight games. However, this collection of Habs isn't the same band of misfits that was flattened consistently by the Leafs all season. This is a fighting unit, a group that has caught fire. They've won or tied all the "must" games in a stretch drive that carried them from fifth spot to third place and then past the mighty Detroit Red Wings into the finals.[4]

Burnett predicted Toronto and Montreal would engage in what he called "a long, tough wrangle"[5] for the Stanley Cup championship.

A similar sentiment was expressed by the esteemed Ted Reeve, who had covered all the games of the Montreal-Detroit semifinal series and had been duly impressed by the showing of the surprising victors from Quebec. In his *Toronto Telegram* column, Reeve penned, almost apologetically,

> We are not trying to be alarmists. We think the sturdy Leafs can wallop Montreal if they work at it with their usual playoff spirit. Only remember that

after tying the Leafs on February 15, the Canadiens lost a game in Detroit and another in Chicago. [They recorded] seven victories and three ties in their last 13 league games. Add their four-and-two record in the [first round of the] playoffs and you will realize that something new has been added.[6]

Carroll likened the present version of the Habs to the Maple Leafs club of four years before—a team that had completed a surprise upset in the Stanley Cup finals. Carroll commented, "It has occurred to one and all that the Canadiens right now are something like the Leafs of 1947. That spring, Happy Day had a hungry band of young Leafs who upset the experienced and heavily favored [sic] Canadiens in the Stanley Cup finals. There are still fellows on the Canadiens with long memories [such as] Elmer Lach, Butch Bouchard, Kenny Mosdell, and Maurice Richard who would like nothing better than to get even for that 1947 debacle."[7]

Jack Koffman of the *Ottawa Citizen* foresaw the 1951 Stanley Cup finals as a tremendous goaltending battle, one for the ages—both figuratively and literally. "The series offers one of the league's rookie goaltenders in Gerry McNeil and, the daddy of them all, Turk Broda. The latter appears to be getting better every time out. The Bruins found this out."[8] he wrote.

Baz O'Meara, the sports editor of the *Montreal Star*, also foresaw the Canadiens having problems with the Maple Leafs, especially if the games became chippy. He wrote in his column the day of Game One, "Dick [Irvin] knows this is going to be a tough series. He doesn't expect the Leafs to be gentle, so he is hopeful the teams will draw the Number One Man to handle the game tonight."

In case O'Meara's readers could not decipher whom he was referring to, the scribe elaborated. "The Number One Man, of course, is [referee] Bill Chadwick who came up with two classy displays [of officiating] in the Wings-Habs series. When Chadwick operated as he did in the last game, he is a standout. He moves fast and fearlessly against rough stuff."[9] O'Meara, in fairness, tempered his plaudits slightly by noting that while Chadwick had worked three of the Wings-Habs games, he was only at the top of his form in two of them. Chadwick (who acquired the amusing nickname "The Big Whistle" later as a broadcaster) was the first American-born referee employed by the NHL. He was the man who introduced the now-familiar hand signals to indicate various penalties and other infractions so players, coaches, spectators and broadcasters could understand immediately what he was calling. Those signals were officially adopted by the NHL in 1956. Chadwick would eventually work 42 games in the Stanley Cup finals over his fine career—the most by any referee in NHL history. Thirteen of those games were Cup-deciders.

Montreal Coach Dick Irvin had previously held the same position in Toronto during the Maple Leafs' early glory years of the 1930s. After a storied amateur career as a player and a pro career that was cut short by a fractured skull, Irvin had begun his NHL coaching career with the Chicago Black Hawks in 1930–31 and led the club to the 1931 Stanley Cup finals. They fell one game short of winning the most prized trophy in the sport—losing to the Montreal Canadiens. For reasons best known to the Hawks' management, Irvin was fired in September 1931 just before the 1931–32 season was about to begin.

He was out of hockey only for a short time. The Toronto Maple Leafs—who were winless in their first five games of 1931–32 under coach Art Duncan—hired Irvin in desperation to right the ship. He did so spectacularly by winning the Stanley Cup that spring. The Leafs would advance to six more Cup finals under Irvin's guidance, but not win another championship for their likeable bench boss. After the 1939–40 season, another in which Toronto got to the Cup finals and lost—Toronto owner Conn Smythe figured Irvin had taken the Leafs as far as he could. He also questioned the mild-mannered coach's ability to keep players under control.

Dick Irvin (left) and Conn Smythe tour Boston Garden circa 1939. Irvin had coached the Maple Leafs to success during the 1930s. In the 1951 Stanley Cup finals, Irvin was behind the bench of the Montreal Canadiens (courtesy Boston Public Library, Leslie Jones Collection).

Smythe replaced Irvin with Hap Day. Day, as a player, had been the former captain of the Maple Leafs.

Smythe and Irvin obviously remained on good terms despite the former dismissing the latter. Irvin was still under contract to the Leafs, but Smythe suggested the woebegone Montreal Canadiens hire him as their new coach. Montreal had won just 10 of their 48 games during the trying 1939–40 season, finishing at the bottom of the seven-team NHL's standings. The club was also in financial difficulties as attendance at the Forum dipped to dangerously low levels. An arrangement was made for Irvin to go to Montreal to try to literally salvage one of the NHL's original teams from 1917.

He succeeded beyond anyone's expectations. During the war years, the Canadiens became an NHL powerhouse. They rolled to the Stanley Cup in 1944. Two years later, in 1946, they did it again, albeit with a bit more difficulty.

Maurice Smith, the sports editor of the *Winnipeg Free Press* reminded his readers about Irvin's long tenure in the NHL. Praising the Habs coach, he wrote in his April 11 column,

> Irvin has made a successful career out of hockey. True, he did not make a great deal out of the game as a player ... but he has always had a lucrative coaching job since he gave up playing.
>
> In comparison to Dick Irvin, all of today's coaches in the NHL are youngsters. The coach of the Montreal Canadiens is currently making his 21st appearance in Stanley Cup playoff competition.[10]

Both teams in 1951 had several players who had played in that title-deciding series four years earlier. Dick Irvin, the Habs' present coach, held that same position in 1947. That series had been a particularly rough one. Fiery Maurice Richard was suspended for one game after a pair of particularly bad high-sticking incidents in which two Maple Leafs (Vic Lynn and Bill Ezinicki) had been knocked unconscious. The widely traveled Lynn—known to hockey trivia buffs as the only man to play for every NHL team when it was a mere six-team circuit—had briefly been a teammate of Richard's the previous season. Richard was fined $250 by Clarence Campbell for those dangerous transgressions. Passions were running so high in the stands between rival supporters that when the series ended in Maple Leaf Gardens, Campbell chose not to present the Cup publicly to the home team, fearing that the simple ceremony might antagonize the visiting fans from Montreal! It was presented without fanfare to Toronto captain Syl Apps in the home team's dressing room instead.

Nobody was expecting anything of that sort to occur during the 1951 Stanley Cup finals, but there was always a palpable quality of edginess

5. The 1951 Stanley Cup Finals 75

whenever Toronto and Montreal tangled. Decades later, Harry Watson of the Maple Leafs remembered, "The Canadiens were our biggest rivals back then. We hated them—especially Maurice Richard. There were other teams we wouldn't get as 'up' for—but Richard's Canadiens, we were always ready for them."[11]

Both teams were doing their best to underestimate their chances of winning the Stanley Cup so as not to appear arrogant. Dick Irvin had that tactic mastered. He was especially eager to foster an illusion of vulnerability and hopelessness for his club. "We'll try to win a game," he pitifully told a Canadian Press scribe. "Our club considers it an honor to be playing against the great Maple Leafs for the Cup. Look at their super scorers and the way they breezed through Boston." Nevertheless, Irvin insisted his Canadiens were confident and were riding the emotional high from their surprise semifinal win over Detroit. "Maybe by Wednesday they'll get around to thinking about the Toronto series,"[12] he said with a straight face.

Jack Koffman was thoroughly tired of that sort of typical, insincere, pre-series palaver. He mockingly wrote in his *Ottawa Citizen* column that ran on the day of Game One,

> [It's] nice to know the series is actually going to take place. On Monday night, it seemed neither [the Maple Leafs] nor the Canadiens might bother showing up.
>
> Conn Smythe announced ... [the] Leafs would be underdogs ... [as] the Canadiens were too hot.
>
> From Montreal [there was a] report that Doug Harvey and Boom Boom Geoffrion might [miss the] series opener because of knee injuries.
>
> Pregame injuries provide an interesting study. When the game starts, the "cripples" are on the ice ... and are [its] stars. Geoffrion and Harvey ... have shaken off their serious ailments.[13]

Knowledgeable NHL fans fully realized that regular-season results often meant nothing when ownership of the Stanley Cup was suddenly at stake. Despite the defeatist public proclamations of their clever coach, the Montreal Canadiens were preparing to give the heavily favored Toronto Maple Leafs a battle for the championship of professional hockey that would be captivatingly unique in how it unfolded. The classic 1951 Stanley Cup finals were about to begin.

6

Game One

Sid Smith Settles Matters

"The Canadiens did not have the same sharpness in the opening game of the Stanley Cup series that marked their initial win against Detroit. At that, it took all the Leafs' capacity to subdue them in five minutes and 51 seconds of overtime"[1]—Baz O'Meara, sports editor of the *Montreal Star*

Game One of the 1951 Stanley Cup finals was played at Toronto's Maple Leaf Gardens on Wednesday, April 11. The overflow crowd witnessed a close, hard-fought, and thrilling affair. Toronto's Harry Watson later said in hindsight, "Everyone knew the series was going to be close. I don't think anyone had any idea it was going to be as tight as it was."[2]

Aging but thoroughly reliable Turk Broda was again the Toronto goaltender. The younger but injured Al Rollins was still hobbling. He had not been able to don the pads for the Maple Leafs since being injured in the first game of the semifinal series versus Boston.

Excitement came early for the home team's supporters. Toronto's Sid Smith, a 30-goal man in the regular season, opened the scoring for the Maple Leafs just 15 seconds into the first period. Many ticketholders were still filing into Maple Leaf Gardens when the red light flashed behind the Hab goalie. Smith coolly snared a pass from Tod Sloan at the side of the Montreal net and beat Gerry McNeil with a short, rising shot. It was the first shot on goal of the 1951 Cup finals—and it had given Toronto a fast 1–0 lead.

"The fans were still going to their seats when the Leafs scored the first goal in the opening period," reported Dink Carroll of the *Montreal Gazette*. "Sid Smith was the sniper. Gerry McNeil had a piece of the puck, but it got away from him and trickled over the red [goal] line."[3]

6. Game One

The home team's one-goal lead held up for slightly longer than 15 minutes. At 15:27, Maurice Richard evened the contest at 1–1 with a pretty, unassisted goal off a terrific individual effort. Leaf blueliner Bill Barilko attempted to make a pass to fellow defenseman Fern Flaman from inside the Toronto zone. The puck was a few inches off the ice, but an alert Richard skillfully knocked it down with his stick, and quickly corralled it before Flaman did. The Montreal superstar then maneuvered deftly around Barilko who looked bad on the play, and then beat a surprised Turk Broda with a low, off-balance shot that found a corner of the net. Even the fans at Maple Leaf Gardens gasped at Richard's creativity and skill level. A few Toronto supporters even applauded the artistry of the game-tying goal. It was the fifth tally of the 1951 playoffs for Richard.

The game stayed tied for a mere quarter of a minute. A go-ahead goal by Toronto's Tod Sloan put the Maple Leafs in the lead, 2–1, before the first period had expired. Sloan received an accurate pass from teammate Gus Mortson inside the Montreal zone. His high, 15-foot shot cleanly beat Hab netminder Gerry McNeil at 15:42.

The Habs fought back in the middle period, however. The only goal of the second frame was notched by Montreal rookie Paul Masnick on a shot from the point. Teammate Billy Reay won a faceoff in the Toronto zone and sent a pass back to Masnick at the blue line. Broda seemed thoroughly surprised that Masnick decided to launch a shot from long distance, but the puck sailed past the Toronto goalkeeper and bulged the twine. The Canadian Press story claimed Broda had been screened on the play and was therefore helpless to block Masnick's drive. Broda scoffed at the idea. He said the puck just rose faster than he expected—and he had simply failed to get his shoulder in front of the shot. Be that as it may, the scoreboard at Maple Leaf Gardens now showed two goals for each club.

Late in the second period, Toronto's Fern Flaman likely prevented a Montreal goal when he hauled down Calum MacKay when the latter was about to get an excellent scoring opportunity on Broda's doorstep. As MacKay did not yet possess the puck, Flaman was whistled for an interference penalty, but his timely takedown of MacKay kept the score deadlocked.

No goals were scored in the final 20 minutes of regulation play. However, that did not mean there were no scoring opportunities. Paul Masnick had a chance to be Montreal's hero for the second time in the game, but he was foiled when Broda bravely charged out of his net and slid into the advancing Hab to spoil his shot before it could be released. Overtime would be needed to settle matters in Game One.

The fourth period was jammed with excitement in the short time it lasted. Both Elmer Lach and Maurice Richard had good scoring chances in the overtime session for the visitors. "Broda was too good for them,"[4] Carroll succinctly commented. However, Leaf defenseman Bill Barilko was the true hero when Richard's chance went for naught. Toronto's #5 slid in front of Richard's drive and tipped the puck over the open Toronto net with his stick. According to the next day's *Toronto Star*, "If the diving Barilko hadn't reached that scorcher, it was home."[5]

Years later, Toronto's Harry Watson explained why Richard was such a feared goal-scorer during his long and illustrious career with the Canadiens. "He would circle ... just trying to get some daylight," Watson recalled. "Then ... he would dart toward the net like an arrow. He had a great shot. He'd hardly ever miss [the net]."[6] Throughout Game One, the worried Toronto fans constantly shouted, "Hit that Richard!" whenever the Rocket got anywhere near the puck.

The Hockey News also praised Barilko for his timely defensive plays for the home team in Game One, describing the curly-haired defenseman as "a tower of strength. He's thrown himself in front of several hard shots that might have slipped into the Toronto goal."[7]

Gerry McNeil also showed his goalkeeping mettle by making good stops on three Leafs: Cal Gardner, Fleming Mackell, and Gus Mortson. "But Gerry couldn't stop them all," Carroll ruefully penned, "and the payoff goal by Sid Smith followed."[8]

Carroll described Smith's winning score. "The end came suddenly," he wrote, "to send the 13,939 [fans] into a paroxysm of joy. A pass by Tod Sloan to Sid Smith deep in the Montreal defensive zone gave Smith plenty of room to stickhandle. He weaved over in front of the net and beat Gerry McNeil with a blistering shot just inside the post for the clincher."[9] The Canadian Press noted that Smith was promptly mobbed by his teammates, quite a usual occurrence when one scores an overtime goal in the Stanley Cup finals. The time of Smith's goal was 5:51. More overtimes would follow in this series, but Game One's would be the longest.

Even the pool of reporters from the *Montreal Gazette* believed the more deserving team had won Game One. The headline atop its April 12 sports section read, "Leafs Outplay Habs but Need Overtime to Win 3–2." Sports editor Dink Carroll provided more details to back up that assertion. He wrote, "The Leafs had quite a margin on the night's play and a lot more of the puck than the Canadiens. They outshot the Canadiens 39 to 22 and controlled the play except in the second period when the Canadiens braced."[10]

The Canadian Press readily concurred with the Montreal journalist. In a game report published in the *Ottawa Citizen*, its correspondent wrote,

6. Game One

"The Canadiens, fresh from their upset victory over the Detroit Red Wings in the semifinal round, were outplayed throughout much of the match. The Maple Leafs were full value for their win."[11]

Toronto looked especially effective in killing off penalties. During one sequence when Ted Kennedy was sitting in the penalty box late in the second period for a slashing infraction, not only did the visitors from Montreal fail to get a shot on Broda, they also failed to advance the puck past the red line for the first 90 seconds of their man advantage.

Given the importance of the game and both teams having the ability to mix things up, it had been a relatively clean contest. Referee Bill Chadwick called nine penalties—five against Montreal and four against Toronto—which seemed to be about the right amount. "Contrary to expectations, it wasn't a rough game, though the checking was close and rugged."[12] Carroll noted. Tempers flared once: Bert Olmstead and Tod Sloan squared off in a third-period scuffle and were both given fighting majors by Chadwick, but neither team scored during the five minutes when each club was playing with a man sitting in the penalty box. There were no power-play goals scored by either team in the game.

Referee Chadwick disallowed two goals during the course of the hard-fought game. There was not much dispute about either of the chief official's decisions, however. In the second period, Montreal's Paul Meger had a goal taken away from him when the play was ruled offside. In the third period, Toronto's Gus Mortson had a goal nullified when Cal Gardner was ruled to have been illegally stationed in McNeil's goal crease when the puck entered the Montreal net.

Montreal coach Dick Irvin failed to be impressed by the team that had just defeated his club. He boldly told Fraser MacDougall of the Canadian Press, "If that's the best they can do, they're not so hot. We can beat them right in their own back yard."[13] Irvin thought his Habs had been unlucky to lose Game One. As evidence, he noted that Floyd Curry had cleanly beaten Turk Broda with a shot in the overtime period only to have it clang off the goalpost and deflect out of harm's way. Smith's game-winner for Toronto occurred about a minute later.

Habs captain Émile (Butch) Bouchard fully agreed with Irvin's general assessment of how things went for the visitors in Game One. "We didn't play a good game," he said, "and they only beat us by that one goal. We had a tough break when Curry's shot hit the post." Bouchard confidently added, "We can beat them."[14]

Turk Broda's Game One victory was his sixtieth career win in Stanley Cup play. No one could have foreseen that it was also his last one. In fact, Broda would never win another NHL game in the regular season, either.

After the Toronto triumph, a bus transported the jubilant Maple Leafs some 35 miles away to a hotel in St. Catharines, Ontario where they were staying in seclusion until Game Two on Saturday night. The visiting Habs had simply booked lodgings at a Toronto hotel instead of returning home.

In his column the following day, Jack Koffman of the *Ottawa Citizen* praised the Maple Leafs for their continuing excellence that had extended into postseason play versus both Boston and Montreal. While conceding that Montreal did well as underdogs to take the Game One into a fourth period, Koffman penned,

> The Leafs are proceeding to polish off the Habitants as they did all winter. Dick Irvin's crew made [Game One] close. They thought they'd won when Floyd Curry [struck] the goalpost. But the Canadiens find themselves one [game] down. [Toronto] could take a stranglehold on the Cup ... with a Saturday night triumph.
>
> The Leafs ... are very much like [baseball's New York] Yankees. Put the chips on the line and.... Conn Smythe's gang are tough to beat. They always play like pros when championships are at stake.[15]

In peripheral and unrelated NHL matters, several news outlets reported that Art Ross, the esteemed general manager of the Boston Bruins, was going to present three rule-change proposals to the NHL's board of governors during the offseason. They were wildly different. The first one was very liberal-minded: It would eliminate the center red line to allow for long passes from the defensive zone to the opposition's blue line. The second one was, in contrast, ultra-conservative. It would require any puck carrier to not only enter the opponents' zone before any teammate, but to continue that way too, thus preventing jam-ups in front of the goalie. The third change would require all empty net goals to be scored from inside the offensive blue line. Doug Vaughan of the *Windsor Daily Star* offered no personal opinions about Ross' ideas, but he did state the following: "Knowing from bitter experience how slow his fellow league governors are to react to anyone's suggestions, Ross figures he'll be lucky if he gets even one of his three [proposed ideas] adopted for next season."[16] The NHL did adopt Ross' first one—for the 2002–03 season.

Earlier that same day, Maurice Richard learned he had been named by the Associated Press as the "pro athlete of the month for March" as part of the year-long competition for the news agency's Hickok Award. In the voting, the Rocket finished ahead of golfer Joe Ferrier, heavyweight boxing contenders Rex Layne and Harry Matthews, basketball player George Mikan, and several others. It was a very close decision at the top between the top four vote-getters. Richard got 124 points in the poll to finish atop Ferrier's runner-up total of 116. (Matthews had 90 points while Layne received 84 for third and fourth places, respectively.) The AP explained that Richard got the nod for his sensational play in Montreal's Stanley Cup

6. Game One

semifinal triumph over the Detroit Red Wings. This was just the second year that the Hickok Award was up for grabs. Closely resembling a boxing championship belt, it was created by the Hickok Company, a belt manufacturer headquartered in Rochester, New York.

In case anyone doubted Richard's credentials as the rightful winner, he would certainly prove he deserved that award with his outstanding play in Game Two of the 1951 Stanley Cup finals.

Game One Scoring Summary
Montreal 2 at Toronto 3 (OT)
April 11, 1951

First Period
1. TOR Sid Smith (Ted Kennedy, Tod Sloan) 0:15
2. MTL Maurice Richard (unassisted) 15:27
3. TOR Tod Sloan (Gus Motson) 15:42

Second Period
4. MTL Paul Masnick (Billy Reay) 4:02

Third Period
No scoring

Overtime
5. TOR Sid Smith (Tod Sloan) 5:51

7

Game Two
Rocket Richard Responds

"They have been calling Maurice (The Rocket) Richard the Babe Ruth of hockey—and in at least one respect the Rocket does resemble the baseball immortal. He has a flair for the dramatic which enables him to rise to the big situation."[1]
—Dink Carroll, sports editor of the *Montreal Gazette*

"Toronto fans thought the game here on Wednesday was the best of the season," declared Dink Carroll in his *Montreal Gazette* column two days after the fact, "but there were at least three games in the [Montreal-Detroit semifinal] series that were better." He continued, "Games like those will pack them in anywhere, even in Panama. That banging, charging style might cause momentary excitement, but over the long run it is speed and finesse that draws the customers."[2]

Following Game One, the Canadiens were quick to honestly admit that they did not play well enough to win the first game of the 1951 Stanley Cup finals. However, the visiting Habs also believed that had the breaks gone their way a little more often, they might have stolen a victory at Maple Leaf Gardens. Overtime losses tend to make hockey teams moan about small differences. The Habs were doing just that when discussing the opener with various reporters. Still, they remained an optimistic but somewhat fatalistic crew, at least based on Émile (Butch) Bouchard's comments to Dink Carroll. "We've got to win one game here [in Toronto] if we are going to win the series," he noted, "and we'd better win the next one on Saturday."[3]

The general consensus from the reporters who covered Game One was that only about half a dozen Canadiens played up to their expected form. Those praiseworthy Habs were Bouchard, Gerry McNeil, Billy Reay, Paul Masnick, Floyd Curry and Maurice Richard. Montreal journalists agreed that goaltender McNeil had played as well as he had in the semifinal series versus Detroit, so he could not be faulted for Montreal's loss to Toronto in Game One. Doug Harvey, Montreal's best defenseman, was thought to have played below his usual excellent standards, however. Jack Adams, the Detroit general manager who was unexpectedly reduced to a mere spectator for the 1951 Cup finals, agreed with the Montreal scribes about Harvey's lackluster performance in Game One of the Cup finals. Dink Carroll quipped, "Adams, who has recovered enough to discuss that first series analytically, said that Harvey was magnificent against his Wings, but he was something less than that against the Leafs in the first game."[4]

A little bit surprising was that Montreal's best line in Game One was their third offensive unit, with Billy Reay at center, flanked by Bernie (Boom Boom) Geoffrion and Paul Meger. Geoffrion was slightly hobbled by a sore leg from the sixth game of the Habs' semifinal versus Detroit, but his two linemates picked up the slack. Paul Masnick took quite a few of the gimpy Geoffrion's shifts—and excelled in the extra work. "It's amazing how much Masnick has improved," Carroll opined. "It's odd that you think of him as little Paul Masnick, but he isn't little. He seems to have grown since the first of the season."[5] Even Conn Smythe was generous enough to give Masnick a compliment, calling him "quite a hockey player."[6] For what it was worth, Smythe, in his opinion, also declared ex-employee Dick Irvin to be the NHL's Coach of the Year.

Montreal's Paul Meger was the only notable casualty from Game One. He suffered a cut on his neck in an entanglement with Toronto defenseman Bill Barilko. He was sufficiently patched up and expected to be in the Montreal lineup for Game Two with no lasting ill effects.

One stat that should worry the Habs, according to Carroll, was shots on goal for both clubs. In Game One they were indicative of how much of the play truly favored Toronto. New York Rangers general manager Frank Boucher was also at Maple Leaf Gardens to watch the first game of the Cup finals. He left the building impressed by the home team's apparent dominance despite only winning by the smallest of margins on Sid Smith's overtime tally. Boucher told Carroll, "I thought the Canadiens had a good chance going into this series, but I've changed my mind after watching that game. The Leafs looked a lot sharper and outhustled the [Habs]."[7]

Sid Smith's tactics about covering Maurice Richard—or the lack thereof—were questioned by the inhabitants of the press box, but they worked well for him in Game One as Smith scored twice for Toronto to Richard's single goal for Montreal. The Toronto newspaper writers were amused that Sid's primary job was supposed to be preventing Richard from doing too much offensive damage versus the Maple Leafs, yet he managed to get a pair of tallies himself. Scoring goals was thought to be a secondary task for Smith. Carroll issued this warning for Smith, however.

It is true that Smith did not hound the Rocket like most of his opposite numbers—fellows like Tony Leswick and Marty Pavelich—do. He went out for goals and left the Rocket pretty much alone, as if to say, "Let the Rocket check me for a change!" It worked out alright for Smith on Wednesday, but we would say it's a pretty dangerous practice if he continues it.[8]

Dick Irvin made some interesting comments to reporters between games, hinting that the ice surface at Maple Leaf Gardens was deliberately tampered with to make it unusually slow! It was an accusation that elicited howls of derision and merriment from the Toronto press corps.

On Friday, the day before Game Two, the Canadiens held a spirited practice on Gardens ice—one that left coach Dick Irvin smiling. Carroll figured that was an omen that the Habs would rebound with a victory in Game Two and send the Cup finals back to Montreal with the series deadlocked at one win apiece. He wrote, "The Leafs were expected to win the opening game of the series—and they won it. But as long as Gerry McNeil stays hot, the Habitants are going to be right in it. Don't be surprised if they return home on Sunday on even terms with the Leafs."[9]

With Game Two scheduled for Saturday, April 14, the two Stanley Cup finalists had two full days off before meeting for the second time at Maple Leaf Gardens. The usual full house was present at the famed arena that dominated Toronto's Carleton Street. Again, both teams battled fiercely throughout 60 minutes of regulation play with no winner decided. For the second time, the game ended with a 3–2 score, but this time it was the visiting Canadiens who came out on top thanks to an overtime tally.

Dink Carroll reminded his *Montreal Gazette* readers about the importance of a Habs road win in the grand scheme of things. "The Canadiens knew they had to win one game in Toronto to win the Stanley Cup—and this was it. They return to the Forum for the next two games with the series all tied up at one win apiece."[10]

Much like the fast start the Maple Leafs had in Game One, Montreal jumped out front in Game Two with a quick goal this time. Youthful Paul Masnick—lauded by Carroll in his newspaper column the day before—scored just 3:44 into the first period to give the Habs their first lead of the 1951 Stanley Cup finals. It was something of a present to himself. Masnick was celebrating his twentieth birthday that night. The first 20 minutes of play ended with Montreal holding onto that slim one-goal advantage.

Montreal's chances of evening the series took a great leap forward when they got a second goal. This time the marksman was Billy Reay, who was having an excellent and productive postseason for the Habs. His goal came at 9:24 of the middle period. Bert Olmstead and Maurice Richard picked up assists on the play. Reay, who was stationed in the slot, accurately fired the puck into the corner of the net after receiving a horizontal pass from Olmstead along the boards. Olmstead was the recipient of a pass from Richard, who had picked up a loose puck behind the Maple Leaf goal.

Toronto lost a valuable player in the second period when defenseman Fern Flaman left the ice with a painful groin injury. Immediately following Game Two, the Maple Leafs issued a notice to members of the press informing them that the injury was indeed a significant one to the 24-year-old blueliner: Early reports stated that Flaman would be sidelined for the rest of the championship series. At least that was the team's initial indication regarding Flaman's fitness.

Things were looking grim for the hometown hockey team. However, penalties would become a factor in the game. A pair of Leaf goals, both of them coming when the home team was enjoying a man-advantage situation, leveled Game Two at 2–2. The first Toronto marker occurred before the second period expired, at 15:31. It came from the stick of Sid Smith while Montreal's Bud MacPherson was banished from the ice for two minutes for tripping Toronto's Joe Klukay. Max Bentley and Ted Kennedy were credited with assists on Smith's power-play goal. The Montreal lead had been narrowed to 2–1 with plenty of time left in the game—and the Leafs were a rejuvenated bunch.

Referee George Gravel became the center of controversy on the Maple Leafs' tying goal in the third period with Maurice Richard sitting out another Montreal minor penalty for tripping. It came on a rebound at 8:16. Tod Sloan took a pass from Ted Kennedy. Sloan's shot struck McNeil's leg. The puck caromed high off his goalie pad ... and then bounced off Ted Kennedy's knee and into the net!

While the home team celebrated, the Montreal players collectively insisted the puck had been directed into the Montreal goal by Kennedy with an illegal kicking motion. Gravel said no. The referee declared Kennedy had not deliberately kicked the puck across the goal line; it had just struck his leg. Montreal sports writers took note that the usually unflappable McNeil was livid with Gravel's decision. (However, Bill Tobin, the NHL supervisor assigned to the game made a point of telling reporters that Gravel's call, in his opinion, had been the right one.) Meanwhile, on the very same play, linesman Sam Babcock was pursued by an angry Doug Harvey for an entirely different reason. Harvey maintained the play should have been whistled down for a Toronto offside infraction long before the puck ended up in the net behind McNeil. "As usual," Carroll commented wryly, "the officials won the arguments."[11] There certainly was plenty of confusion and uncertainty surrounding the second Leaf goal, as it was originally credited to Sloan when it was first announced over the Maple Leaf Gardens public-address system. Not too long afterward, however, it was correctly reassigned to Kennedy, the Leaf captain.

Having rallied from a two-goal deficit, Toronto's seemed poised to complete the comeback and take a daunting 2–0 series lead with them to Montreal. There was no further scoring in the third period, but the Maple Leafs clearly had momentum on their side. Even though an overtime period would be required to settle matters in Game Two, the home team still looked to be the favorites to win another 3–2 tussle. But it was not to be. Montreal's fabulous #9 put an emphatic stop to the Toronto charge with a spectacular finishing play.

Against the run of play, Maurice Richard, halted the Leafs with a terrific, climactic, sudden-death goal. Richard, the 29-year-old who had scored two overtime game-winners in Detroit against the favored Red Wings in the semifinals, this time performed the same dramatic feat against the Maple Leafs in their home building. Dink Carroll realized Richard's extra-time heroics had come at a critical juncture in the Cup finals. He wrote, "The Rocket's clincher came at a time when the Leafs looked as though they would come from behind to grab the verdict and take a commanding lead in the series."[12]

Carroll colorfully described Richard's overtime winner in a fawning manner, a goal that came 2:55 into the fourth stanza. He penned,

> It was a beautiful goal. It came on a pass from Doug Harvey, who was a doubtful starter because of a wrenched knee. Harvey's long pass put The Rocket a half-step ahead of Gus Mortson, the Leafs' defenseman. He shifted into high, pulled away from Mortson, raced in on Turk Broda, faked the latter into a pretzel shape, and flipped the puck into the empty net.[13]

Richard would tell reporters afterward that Broda had erred in coming too far out of his net to challenge him. Broda disagreed. He told the members of the Fifth Estate that he had missed dislodging the puck from Richard's possession by two or three inches. (Broda illustrated his point by separating his hands ever so slightly as if he were telling a fish story to the reporters.) Be that as it may, the dramatic, game-ending play was allowed to develop to the Habs' advantage largely because of an ill-timed and sloppy line change by Toronto. Harvey, completely unpressured, had ample time to feed Richard with a perfect pass to set up Montreal's winning goal.

Writing for Canadian Press, Fraser MacDougall commented, "The Rocket's stunning, game-ending score spoiled a battling comeback for the Leafs, who had rallied after a slow start for two goals to wind up the regulation 60 minutes of play with a 2–2 tie."[14]

It was Richard's third overtime goal of these playoffs (and his sixth goal overall), equaling the feat of Mel (Sudden Death) Hill who got three overtime goals in the 1939 playoffs for the Boston Bruins—but all of Hill's tallies came in a single best-of-seven series versus the New York Rangers that spring. After noting that all three of Richard's overtime goals in the 1951 Stanley Cup playoffs had been scored on hostile ice, Carroll commented, "If these things had happened in the Forum, the fans would probably have torn the building down."[15]

MacDougall reported that Richard's goal gave him 61 points in Stanley Cup play over his career that began during the Second World War. That sum was just one point shy of the NHL record held by retired Hector (Toe) Blake. He had retired from the NHL following the 1947–48 season after 14 years as a player—all but one of those was as a member of the Habs. Blake was a Hall of Fame-caliber player (elected in 1966), but he became best known to hockey fans as the man who would eventually succeed Dick Irvin as the coach of the Canadiens and lead the club to lofty heights.

Jack Koffman of the *Ottawa Citizen* added to the heaps of praise liberally being piled upon Richard. He commented, "One of these days, some member of the Montreal cast other than Maurice Richard will contribute a dramatic, game-winning goal and a federal investigation will promptly be launched. Particularly if [the goal] occurs in overtime."[16]

Some fans and Toronto writers sought to place blame on Toronto defenseman Gus Mortson for allowing Richard to elude him for the decisive score. One knowledgeable observer did not see it that way at all. Thirty-four-year-old Jack Crawford, recently retired after playing 13 seasons with the Boston Bruins from 1937 to 1938 to 1949–50, could not find any fault at all with Mortson on Richard's fabulous game-ending play. Instead, he praised the excellent pass by Doug Harvey to create the perfect scoring opportunity for Richard. Crawford offered his opinion to Dink Carroll. The ex–Bruin said,

> Harvey was watching Richard. When he saw him get into position to take a pass, he [Harvey] took a couple of steps over [his own] blue line and let the puck go. It was a beautiful pass. Richard took it on the fly and was half a step ahead of Mortson when he got it. That half-step is enough. Nobody is going to stop The Rocket if he has a half-step advantage.[17]

Detroit general manager Jack Adams was prominently in attendance at Maple Leaf Gardens for both Game One and Game Two. He also told Carroll that Doug Harvey was the key man on the final play of the game and that no Leaf could rightfully be faulted on it. Adams added that he believed Montreal's chances of winning the Stanley Cup depended heavily upon the state of Harvey's health over the remainder of the series. Adams commented, "I thought he was terrific against us; he can be the difference again in this series. He was tonight."[18]

Though defeated on this night, Toronto owner Conn Smythe sang the praises of Richard when he was asked to rank him against the newest claimant for the best player in the NHL. "There's no comparison between the Rocket and Gordie Howe," Smythe insisted. "Howe will probably get the right-wing slot on the All-Star team, but he shouldn't. Richard is the best in the game today."[19]

A praiseful Doug Vaughan of the *Windsor Daily Star* opined,

> Honestly, we believe that every person in the jam-packed capacity crowd realized that this was the finish when they saw Richard wheel all by himself at the Toronto blue line to take Doug Harvey's pass. Within two strides he was in full flight. Broda need offer no alibis. It wasn't his fault [that Richard scored against him]. Put Richard face-to-face against any goalie and we'll wager he'll beat him 90 times out of 100.[20]

Gerry McNeil again performed admirably in goal for the visiting Habs. This time his efforts were kindly rewarded with a deserved win. Dink Carroll called McNeil a "standout" in stopping 34 of 36 Toronto shots in the three-plus periods. "Many of them were tougher than the ones Turk was called upon to stop," he opined. Broda had a much quieter night. He faced just 24 Montreal shots in the four periods of action, and he stopped 21 of them. "Gerry was at his best and saved the game for his team time and time again,"[21] Carroll insisted.

Carroll's opinion was heartily seconded by Vaughan. He wrote,

> The Leafs could have easily won within regulation time. The reason [why the Maple Leafs lost Game Two] was the little guy who guards the Montreal net, Gerry McNeil. He saved the Habs so many times in the last period and a half [of regulation play] that all Toronto knows by now that it wasn't eyewash that was written about his feats of puck-tending in the series against Detroit.[22]

Indeed, Montreal had outshot Toronto by a 10:6 ratio in the first period, but Toronto rebounded to outshoot the Habs in the second and third frames by sizable margins. Each team had managed exactly three shots on goal during the short overtime period. "After the Reay goal," wrote Fraser MacDougall, "the Leafs commanded the territorial play and let loose a blaze of shots at Gerry McNeil in the Montreal goal, but the diminutive goalie yielded goals only twice."[23]

In a sidebar column in the *Montreal Gazette*, Carroll wrote that McNeil, who was officially an NHL rookie despite being in his mid-twenties, had clearly earned the full respect of his Montreal teammates with his solid play—and it was showing. "The Canadiens are playing with great confidence in front of Gerry and leaving him alone frequently, but if Gerry continues to be as good as he has been since the playoffs started, they aren't making a mistake. He will keep them in every game."[24]

7. Game Two

Referee George Gravel had "ruled with a light hand, calling only six penalties, three to each team," declared the United Press report on Game Two that appeared in the *Boston Globe* the next day. The comment was not meant as a compliment, but rather a verbal jab at the official. The UP story, which ran without a byline, continued, "The game threatened to get out of hand in the second period, however, as tempers flared."[25]

The Canadiens were a happy and melodious bunch in the visitors' dressing room. They had a right to be in a celebratory mood. They had just broken the club's embarrassingly long losing streak in Toronto. Montreal had not won a game at Maple Leaf Gardens during the 1950–51 season—losing all seven of their regular-season appearances along with Game One of the finals! (The most recent Montreal victory in Toronto had occurred on March 22, 1950, their last visit of the 1949–50 campaign, when they eked out a 2–1 squeaker.) Dick Irvin happily chortled to a bevy of reporters that although the Leafs had finished well ahead of the Habs in the regular-season standings, "they're no better than we are now."[26]

The visitors from Montreal had impressed *Toronto Star* scribe Red Burnett with their victory. Sounding more like a fawning theater critic than a hardened sports journalist, Burnett wrote in his coverage of Game Two, "The Canadiens proved to a jury of 14,567 thrilled fans that they are quite a hockey team as they tamed the Leafs in this smash hit, a contest that reeked of box-office appeal."[27]

In their dressing room, the high-spirited Montreal players loudly and jauntily sang several choruses of the familiar French folk song "Alouette" as they changed into their civilian clothes to prepare for their train trip back to Montreal. The next two games of the Stanley Cup finals would be played on Tuesday and Thursday nights, April 17 and 19, at the Montreal Forum.

Boarding that homebound train proved to be a bit of an adventure for a handful of the victorious Habs, namely Elmer Lach, Floyd Curry, Gerry McNeil, Kenny Mosdell, and Maurice Richard. They were all running slightly behind schedule in leaving the arena. All five dawdling players managed to squeeze into a single cab that happened to be parked right outside the front door of Maple Leaf Gardens. They instructed the driver to take them to Union Station with all possible haste. They had not traveled very far when they were pulled over by a diligent traffic cop who noticed that the cabbie was driving an out-of-town vehicle that was not licensed for taxi service in Toronto. Apparently, this was a major municipal transgression on the driver's part. The policeman summarily went to work. The first thing he did was order the five tardy Montreal players to get out of the cab because, by local ordinance, it could only drop off passengers; it was not legally permitted to pick up new passengers within Toronto's city limits.

"But we are Canadien hockey players," one of them pleaded passionately to the officer, "and we don't want to miss the Montreal train!"

Utterly unmoved by the Montreal quintet's travel troubles, the lawman tersely replied, "Then get another cab because you can't ride in this one. That's for sure."[28]

The Leafs-Canadiens battle was not the only hockey attraction at Maple Leaf Gardens that Saturday. Insatiable hockey fans could get an extra fix by going to an important junior game that very afternoon—and more than 14,000 curious people did just that. It was the first game of the eastern Canada Memorial Cup championship series between the visiting Quebec Citadelles and the Barrie Flyers. The Flyers had decided to use Toronto's huge building for one of their home games to accommodate the tremendous fan interest the series was generating. Most of the excitement and hype was because of the presence of one Citadelle player in particular. The champions of Quebec featured 19-year-old Jean Béliveau, the most talked-about hockey player not presently employed in the NHL. As was the case with most of the promising French-Canadian puck chasers, Béliveau's professional rights were, not surprisingly, owned by the Montreal Canadiens.

"Right now, young Béliveau handles himself like a pro," wrote Doug Vaughan, who decided on a whim to take in the junior game to see what all the hype was about. The scribe left the building impressed. "He [Béliveau] skates with the long, effortless stride that reminds you of Syl Apps. He is a fine stick-handler, gives and receives passes well, and possesses a terrific and accurate shot. He is cool and cagey under fire. If there is anything lacking, we didn't catch it."[29] Similarly, Jack Koffman, the sports editor of the *Ottawa Citizen* caught the matinee game. He favorably reported, "The Great Béliveau resembles Boston Bruins ace Milt Schmidt with that wide, easy skating stride. Schmidt, of course, isn't a newcomer, and he's proven himself in the big time. Béliveau still has to make good in professional hockey, but he isn't overrated and he has everything in his favor."[30]

Béliveau was being talked about before the real 1950–51 season even began. He was elevated to play for the senior amateur Quebec Aces in a preseason exhibition game versus the Chicago Black Hawks. Veteran Gus Bodnar, a center with the Hawks, could scarcely believe the skill and hockey smarts that the teenager casually displayed against older, longtime professional opponents that night before an enormous crowd in Quebec City. The 27-year-old Bodnar was happy to predict to anyone who wanted to talk hockey with him that the teenage Béliveau was going to be a dominant force in the NHL in the not-too-distant future. A flattering article published in *The Hocky News* in March claimed that Béliveau was already better than half the centers presently employed in the six-team NHL.

Béliveau was reputedly earning $8,500 for playing junior hockey in 1950–51—more than a great many NHLers were taking in that year. He had also just received a new car as a gift from his legions of fans in Quebec at the final Citadelles home game of the regular season. (His teammates got mere wristwatches, a disparity which many writers found amusing.) Béliveau was called up to play in a pair of games with Montreal during the 1950–51 regular season—by rule two was the maximum number of games an "amateur" could play in the NHL at the time and still retain his eligibility for junior hockey. He certainly did not seem to be in awe of the NHL competition. In those two contests, Béliveau recorded a goal and an assist. In the series-opener against Barrie, however, Béliveau only managed a single assist. The Flyers won the opening game of that best-of-seven series, 6–2. "Béliveau may be the logical successor to the Rocket," wrote one cautious CP scribe, "but in the eyes of the Barrie Flyers, he was just a common garden variety of hockey player."[31]

Dink Carroll also reported on an impromptu and heart-warming incident that transpired shortly after Maurice Richard had notched his dramatic overtime goal to win Game Two. "The Rocket seems to have acquired a following among the fans at Maple Leaf Gardens," the scribe surprisingly wrote in his *Montreal Gazette* game summary. He went on to explain why he made that seemingly odd statement.

> After Richard scored his winning goal, he skated over to one side of the rink to present his stick to a spectator who was giving it to an invalid child. [Afterward] he had to skate to the other side of the rink to get to [the Montreal] dressing room. As he did so, the crowd rose and gave him a big ovation.

"You had to pinch yourself to make sure where you were,"[32] the impressed scribe from Montreal noted as an afterthought.

Writing in the *Windsor Daily Star* two days later, the newspaper's veteran sports editor, Doug Vaughan, exclaimed, "If Montreal wants to give Maurice Richard all the keys to the city and throw in Mount Royal as well, it's no more than 14,567 Toronto hockey fans think he deserves."[33]

Jack Koffman concurred. The Ottawa hockey scribe declared, "The Rocket has done more to ruin the Canadiens' opposition in these playoff games than the other hired hands of Frank Selke combined. The man is nothing short of sensational. Put him in an overtime period and he'll murder you."[34]

Game Two Scoring Summary
Montreal 3 at Toronto 2 (OT)
April 14, 1951

First Period
1. MTL Paul Masnick (Paul Meger) 3:44

Second Period
2. MTL Billy Reay (Bert Olmstead, Maurice Richard) 9:24
3. TOR Sid Smith (Max Bentley, Ted Kennedy) 15:31

Third Period
4. TOR Ted Kennedy (Tod Sloan) 7:27

Overtime
5. MTL Maurice Richard (Doug Harvey) 2:55

8

Game Three

Ted Kennedy Gives the Leafs the Edge

"It was Canadiens netminder Gerry McNeil's 25th birthday. Toronto ruined the celebration with a 2-1 win."[1]—Kevin Shea, Bill Barilko biographer

"[Ted] Kennedy not only won this struggle before 14,443 hoarse-voiced fans after 4:47 of overtime, but he saved it about 50 seconds before that by scooting in behind Al Rollins to clear a puck that lay on the Leaf goal line."[2]—Red Burnett, *Toronto Star*

On April, 17, on the day Game Three of the 1951 Stanley Cup finals would be played, the big news coming out of Montreal was a strong rumor from the visitors' camp that Al Rollins would be back in goal for the Toronto Maple Leafs instead of old, reliable Turk Broda.

The hot news item, first reported by Al Nickleson of the Toronto *Globe & Mail*, was startling in that Broda, who had not played badly in the first two contests, was being pushed aside in favor of the more youthful Rollins. Somewhat unkindly, Dink Carroll of the *Montreal Gazette* commented in his daily column that the Toronto goaltending change "recalls the fundamental truth that in sport you can be a hero today [but] a bum tomorrow."[3]

True, Broda had appeared to be overmatched on the final goal of Game Two in which Maurice Richard deked the onrushing Toronto netminder out of position and neatly deposited the puck into the gaping net for the overtime winner. (A photo of Richard tucking the puck into the vacant net with Broda looking helplessly backward at the situation appeared in many Canadian newspapers on Monday.) "It's doubtful if any goaltender in hockey could have stopped the Rocket from scoring," Carroll opined. "Certainly, Terry Sawchuk didn't in the Detroit-Canadiens series under the exact same circumstances."[4] Still, it looked like Broda was unfairly being slotted into the role of the fall guy for Toronto's 3–2 defeat at Maple Leaf Gardens on Saturday night.

"We don't know why we limit it to sport," Carroll continued in a more generous tone about the capriciousness of heroism. "It's true of any phase of human activity. Only it seems to happen more frequently and be so noticeable in sport where there is so much sentiment among the fans, if not among the bosses. Broda has been quite a guy over the years for the Leafs, but time and the management are beginning to run out on the Turk."[5]

It had been a rough and strangely trying season for Broda—something he had never experienced in Toronto since he first arrived there to join the club in 1936. He had begun the 1950–51 season, as usual, as the Maple Leafs' starting goaltender when the 70-game campaign began. Shortly thereafter, however, coach Joe Primeau boldly opted to elevate rookie Al Rollins to the starting position. When Rollins had a few questionable outings in the Toronto goal, it looked like Broda would reclaim his position as the team's primary netminder. Rollins, to his credit, showed great poise and did not buckle under the pressure that his job carried. To Leaf followers, there was little doubt that Rollins was being groomed to replace Broda permanently. Broda would be relegated to Rollins' stand-in—a virtual ostracism in the days when NHL teams only carried one full-time goaltender. This development was rough on the likeable and jovial Broda. Hockey journalists easily sensed that the unexpected demotion had affected the veteran's usual cheery mood. It was sad to witness for many reasons.

Carroll recalled encountering Broda in February during a train stopover in Montreal when the Leafs were heading home from a road game in Boston. The scribe recalled the demeanor of the famous pudgy Toronto netminder:

> He seemed disconsolate. It wasn't anything he said, but something almost indefinable in his attitude. How does a man feel who has once been a big shot and has [now] slipped several notches from that rating? [He] suffers a loss of confidence until he becomes accustomed to the idea. It came as no surprise when we later read ... that Turk had announced his intention to retire [at season's end]. No one wants to hang around after he has outlived his usefulness....[6]

Early in the 1950–51 NHL season, *Maclean's*, a prominent Canadian news magazine, featured a highly laudatory article about Broda. Unfortunately, by the time the piece was published, most everyone knew that Rollins had usurped Broda as the Maple Leafs' starting netminder. "It wasn't anybody's fault," acknowledged Carroll. "The mechanics of the publishing business required the piece to be written six weeks in advance."[7]

Still the realization that he was being phased out of his prominent hockey job must have greatly stung the proud Broda. "[Turk] had been a great workman over the years," Carroll commented, "a fellow so noted for his play in the clutches that he was called 'Big-Game Broda.' When the Leafs reached the playoffs year after year, they were conceded an edge because he was on their side. Other netminders might blow up because of the tension, but not the Turk."[8]

In his piece for the *Globe & Mail*, Al Nickleson presented a far less sentimental view of the Maple Leafs' goaltending situation. He accurately wrote, "It will be no disgrace to [Broda] if Angular Al does take over. It was Rollins' job in the first place. Only a leg injury in the first game of the semifinals against Boston brought the Turk out of a spectator seat he expected to be in for the rest of the playoffs."[9]

Despite the Stanley Cup finals being level at a game apiece, Montreal coach Dick Irvin now figured his underdog Canadiens now held the advantage in the series with home ice having shifted to the Habs' favor. "The edge is on our side," he announced to a scrum of reporters. "The series is now best-three-of-five. We have three of the possible five games right here at the Forum. That's our edge. We had to win one game in Toronto to put us in line for the Cup. We did."[10]

Irvin's optimism aside, Montreal fans were worried about the questionable health of defenseman Doug Harvey. It had been reported that the star defenseman had suffered a knee injury in the Habs' semifinal triumph over the Detroit Red Wings that he was doing his best to conceal from the Maple Leafs and the hockey media. Still, despite being in less than perfect shape according to the scuttlebutt, Harvey had made the key pass in overtime in Game Two that set up Maurice Richard's breakaway goal to win the contest for the plucky Canadiens.

Still, Harvey had been noticeably absent during Montreal's workout at the Forum two days after Game Two. "Harvey will be alright for [Tuesday] night," Irvin insisted the day before Game Three. "We had 20 men at the workout and I think we're all set. I've got Glen Harmon in behind Harvey as insurance, as well as Ross Lowe."[11]

Another hobbling Hab was rookie Bernie (Boom Boom) Geoffrion; he was also dealing with a bad knee. Irvin was unconcerned. "Geoffrion was going well in practice today." Emphasizing the plural, Irvin continued, "I expect more from him in our next games. [Elmer] Lach was skating well too. That's a good sign."[12]

As for his perception of the Maple Leafs' chances in what was left of the 1951 Stanley Cup finals, Irvin chose to be diplomatic in nature when speaking about them to the Montreal press. "I'm not taking the Leafs lightly," he strongly said. "They are a good road club. They have three well-balanced front lines and a good defense. This is an unusually close series, as shown by the two overtimes. Breaks may swing it one way or another."[13]

There was no goaltender drama within the Montreal Canadiens organization whatsoever, of course. Milt Dunnell of the *Toronto Star* was thoroughly impressed and surprised by what he has seen so far from diminutive Gerry McNeil. He wrote,

> The Maple Leafs have had a strange and baffling experience to date with the hitherto hapless Habs. The Leafs ... have the Vezina Trophy winner in [Al] Rollins and probably the best goalie in blue-chip competition over the years [Broda]. Yet, in the two games [thus far], they have been out-goaled [sic]. And by whom? By Gerry McNeil, a freshman backstop who allowed 184 goals through the regular season, as compared to 138 for Rollins and Broda [combined] in the Toronto cage.[14]

Frank Selke, the Montreal general manager, had a ready and simple explanation for what was puzzling the Toronto scribe. He told Dunnell that McNeil had not been given much help in some games early in the season when the Habs were clearly struggling badly. With the men in front of McNeil looking bad, he naturally looked bad too on occasion.

Dunnell was not quite sure about that theory, however. Considering how well McNeil had performed since the playoffs began, Dunnell responded, "Either this McNeil has more class than even his relatives suspected, or he's a hotshot in the big-bucks series."[15]

The Toronto writer also thought the result of Game Two was basically an outlier. Dunnell still liked his hometown club's chances to take Lord Stanley's silverware. Accordingly, Dunnell took the liberty of writing for both himself and all the other Toronto scribes covering the playoffs when he penned in his April 16 column, "We'll still take the Leafs for all the marbles again, even though they have blown one of their home games. They blew one to Boston, too, and tied another before they cleaned up in four straight [games versus the Bruins]. Over the season, the Leafs lost only two of 14 [games to Montreal] and outscored the Habitants 42 to 24."[16]

It was up to Toronto—as the visiting club for Games Three and Four at the Montreal Forum—to prove if they were worthy of such confidence.

Some writers who were used to covering the Habs continued with the theory that Game One had been played on an ice surface at Maple Leaf Gardens that had been deliberately "slowed" by the Leafs' management—meaning on the orders of Conn Smythe. Jack Koffman was among them. He wrote in the *Ottawa Citizen*,

> Conn Smythe has to shoulder some of the rap for the playoff-squaring victory recorded by the Canadiens on Saturday night. It would appear that Conn,

shaking with fright and thoroughly ashamed of himself, didn't dare "slow up" the ice for the second game of the Stanley Cup finals after Dick Irvin's accusations of last week. Once Dick's lads got a fast sheet of ice, the Canadiens took that overtime nod to tie [the series] up.[17]

Koffman also took a playful jab at Foster Hewitt, *Hockey Night in Canada*/beloved broadcaster who had been working Toronto games for more than two decades and was often accused of giving his descriptions of the goings-on a pro–Maple Leaf slant. "We were unable to catch Foster Hewitt's broadcast on Saturday," the Ottawa scribe wrote, "and thereby missed the roar which must have hit the airwaves when Foster cut loose on Toronto's tying goal in the third frame. If you've listened to him, you are probably aware of the fact that the man doesn't become too despondent over a tally by the Leafs."[18]

The schedule for the 1951 Stanley Cup finals provided another two-day rest between games as the two teams relocated to Montreal for the third and fourth games of what was becoming a delightfully competitive championship series. Game Two had been in Toronto on Saturday, April 14. Game Three was not held until the evening of Tuesday, April 17 at the Forum. The breather was much appreciated by the players who were still getting used to the long, arduous 70-game NHL regular season. As late as 1929, the NHL season was a compact one of 44 games per team, with the Stanley Cup awarded that year on March 29.

The big news from Game Three, as predicted in various Montreal and Toronto dailies, was who was guarding the pipes for the visiting Maple Leafs: It was the familiar presence of Al Rollins, apparently recovered well enough from his serious leg injury to resume his role as Toronto's number-one goaltender. It was not that Turk Broda had played badly in the first two games of the Cup finals for the Leafs—although some fans and media people criticized his decision to stray too far from his net to challenge Maurice Richard in Game Two's overtime period. It was simply a hunch by coach Joe Primeau to put Rollins back in the Toronto net. Rollins had last played in Game One of the Leafs' semifinal series versus Boston. Bruins coach Lynn Patrick had gambled by changing goalies in midstream of that series by replacing healthy Jack Gelineau with the untested Red Henry—a maneuver unheard of in Stanley Cup play. Patrick's gambit did not pay off for Boston. Primeau, however, had higher hopes that his Vezina Trophy holder would pick up precisely where he had left off in the 1950–51 regular season.

Indeed, Rollins needed to be in fine form for Game Three—and he was. During the opening period, Montreal applied heavy pressure on the visitors' defense but the Habs were only rewarded by a single goal in the first 20 minutes of play. Dink Carroll of the *Montreal Gazette* lamented,

"The Canadiens lost the game in the very first period when they might have scored three or four goals with a little more skill or luck around the goalmouth. They came out of that period with a one-goal lead, Maurice Richard being the marksman."[19] Rollins proved to be an absolutely unbeatable opponent for the Habs thereafter.

In keeping with the fast excitement of the first two games of the 1951 Stanley Cup finals, Richard's tally occurred early in the opening stanza. Coming just 2:18 into the first period, it was a power-play effort scored while Toronto's Tod Sloan was halfway through sitting out a minor penalty for holding. He had been assessed it at the 1:03 mark for impeding Montreal's Calum MacKay. Bert Olmstead picked up the only assist on Richard's goal. It came on a timely and fortuitous rebound for the hometown Habitants.

Carrying the puck across the Toronto blue line, Richard was sandwiched by a pair of Maple Leaf defensemen: Gus Mortson and Jimmy Thomson. Richard was temporarily taken out of the play by the legal, two-man check. However, Richard's alert teammate, Olmstead, picked up the puck and launched a shot toward Rollins. The Toronto netminder made a fairly routine save with his leg, but the rebound was alertly gathered by Richard who had swiftly risen from the ice and gotten himself back into the play. Without hesitation, Richard fired a drive toward the target. He beat Rollins with his quick shot. The Forum fans erupted with cheers.

That goal not only gave Montreal an early and valuable 1–0 lead, it also gave the Habs' fabulous #9 a total of 62 career points in Stanley Cup play, thus equaling the NHL's all-time record held by former teammate Toe Blake who had last played in the NHL in 1948. In just 57 playoff contests, the productive Blake had totaled 25 goals and 37 assists—an average of slightly more than a point per game. Richard preferred denting the twine rather than just accruing assists. Forty-one of Richard's postseason points had come on goals.

The two teams skated to their respective dressing rooms after 20 minutes with the home team retaining its small 1–0 lead.

Toronto's equalizer was notched by Sid Smith at 5:58 of the second period. It was somewhat controversial, to say the least, as the home team and its supporters strongly believed that Max Bentley of the visitors was clearly offside at the Montreal blue line. Bentley was credited with an assist on the goal. It occurred when the Maple Leafs were enjoying a man advantage thanks to a high-sticking penalty assessed to Doug Harvey. Dink Carroll certainly thought an offside had occurred. He wrote, "Max Bentley appeared to be over the blue line ahead of Sid Smith after dropping the puck back to Smith on the other side of the blue line. The spike-haired Smith then fired a shot, partially screened by Bentley, that landed just inside the post [behind Gerry McNeil]. The Canadiens hollered to no avail."[20] More than a couple of items littered the ice courtesy of the disgruntled paying customers seated inside the Forum. Controversial as it was, Smith's goal was the only one scored in the middle period, despite Toronto managing 13 shots on McNeil's net against Montreal's four on Rollins' cage. After 40 minutes of play, Game Three was tied at a goal apiece.

No goals came in the third period as caution prevailed. Carroll commented that the action in the final 20 minutes of regulation time noticeably "slowed down in the third period with both teams playing careful hockey. Elmer Lach and Billy Reay had the best scoring chances for the Canadiens, but Rollins turned their shots aside."[21]

The Canadiens emerged from their dressing room as an inspired group. They quickly moved to the offensive to start the fourth period, hoping to catch the Maple Leafs unprepared for a quick attack. Montreal had the better run of the play from the outset. Maurice Richard came very close to scoring his fourth overtime goal of the 1951 playoffs when he moved around Leaf defenseman Bill Barilko and forced Rollins to make a sprawling save. Bernie Geoffrion and Ken Mosdell both had scoring chances, but the Vezina Trophy winner from Toronto continued to stand tall and efficiently turn away the onrushing Habs. "The crowd was still in a hubbub," wrote W.R. Wheatley of the Canadian Press, "when the Leafs struck for the winning goal."[22]

Indeed, completely against the run of play in the frantic overtime, Ted Kennedy notched the decider for the visitors. The Associated Press report that appeared in the next day's *Boston Globe* described Kennedy's game-winning tally for Toronto this way:

> The winning goal came at 4:47 of the overtime. Kennedy took a pass from Tod Sloan well inside the Montreal defensive zone, and drilled a hard angle shot that whistled into the net past goalie Gerry McNeil.
> The home crowd of 14,443 was caught unprepared because only a short time before Maurice Richard and Ken Mosdell almost counted for the Canadiens in the wide-open battle for the winning sudden-death goal.[23]

What the AP's report failed to divulge was that Toronto's game-winning play began with an egregious and horribly costly error committed by Montreal's Calum MacKay in his defensive zone. He made a careless pass from behind his own goal that was happily intercepted by Tod Sloan of the Maple Leafs. Sloan, taking full advantage of MacKay's unexpected gift, promptly fed teammate Kennedy with an accurate pass. Captain Kennedy wasted no time in beating McNeil to suddenly end Game Three with a stunning Toronto triumph. A Canadian Press story printed in the

Calgary Herald said, "The puck, traveling no more than two feet above the ice, caught the net with a swish."[24]

With sudden swiftness, the Leafs had regained the momentum of the 1951 Stanley Cup finals. "The edge the Canadians held because of their split on foreign ice has now gone up in smoke,"[25] Jack Koffman correctly noted in his game report. Indeed, Toronto regained the home-ice advantage that they had squandered with their defeat at Maple leaf Gardens in Game Two. The headline in the *Calgary Herald*'s coverage of Game Three concurred. It read, "Leafs Win 2-1 in Overtime, Canadiens Again Underdogs." Montreal would have to win a second game in the series at Maple Leaf Gardens to capture the Stanley Cup—a tough task for any team in the 1950-51 NHL campaign.

Dink Carroll praised the work of both netminders in the tightly contested battle. He wrote in the next day's *Gazette*, "Rollins ... turned in a fine game, though he had nothing on little Gerry McNeil. The Leafs had the edge in shots on goal, 30 to 24, but the Canadiens had just as many good scoring chances."[26] Indeed, two of them came from Calum MacKay, the man whose blunder directly led to Ted Kennedy's game-winning goal. In the first frame, MacKay failed to capitalize on a glorious chance when he was sent in alone on Rollins. Later in that same period, a MacKay shot was partially stopped by the Toronto netminder but it trickled behind him. The puck slowly and dramatically rolled along the goal line as the partisan Forum crowd prematurely celebrated. Rollins, however, adroitly managed to snag it before it entered the net.

Bill Chadwick, as in Game One, was assigned the referee's duties for Game Three. Over the course of the contest, he whistled eight penalties, four per team. All were minor infractions—except for a 10-minute misconduct given to Toronto's Howie Meeker in the third period for verbal abuse of an official. (A Canadian Press writer said Meeker was penalized for too much back-talk.) Other than that transgression, Meeker was one of the outstanding players for the victors of Game Three. In his summary of the events, Dink Carroll declared, "Little Howie Meeker turned in a brisk game going both ways."[27]

Not only was Kennedy the offensive star of the game, he also shined in his specialty: winning faceoffs. The more important they were, the more likely Kennedy was to win them. Throughout the tense game, Maple Leaf coach Joe Primeau often put Kennedy on the ice solely to take faceoffs in the Toronto zone, especially when the Maple Leafs were playing shorthanded. After he had won the draw—which he did the vast majority of the time over his terrific career—Kennedy would quickly skate to the Toronto bench and be replaced by a teammate who was more skillful in killing penalties. This type of specialization and game micromanagement was quite uncommon, even at the NHL level, in the early 1950s.

Despite scoring Montreal's only goal of Game Three, Maurice Richard was angry at himself for missing later opportunities to increase the Habs' paltry goal total. "I threw away three good chances," he moaned to the gentlemen of the press. "I should have scored at least two more goals." After a long pause, Richard added, "Maybe I'll get some breaks in the next game."[28]

On that same topic of squandered opportunities, a Canadian Press correspondent believed the Habs were the authors of their own demise for failing to capitalize on their plentiful chances in regulation time. "The Montrealers," wrote the unnamed scribe, "helped to thwart their own efforts by gumming up plays when in scoring position. [Calum] MacKay missed one of their greatest chances when he skated in alone on Rollins and fired dead into the [Toronto] goalie's pads."[29]

Former Montreal goaltender Bill Durnan made a point of stopping by the home team's dressing room after Game Three concluded to offer a few consoling words to his replacement, Gerry McNeil. "It was a tough one to lose, kid," Durnan kindly informed him. "It's not your fault. You played a swell game."[30] The 34-year-old Durnan had abruptly retired the year before once the 1950 Stanley Cup playoffs had ended for the Habs. High-strung, the tension of being an NHL goaltender in the hockey hotbed of Montreal was apparently too much for Durnan. (In 1951, Durnan was now in the less stressful job of coaching the amateur Ottawa Senators of the Quebec Senior Hockey League.) In his seven-year NHL career, Durnan had remarkably won the Vezina Trophy six times.

Jack Koffman, the *Ottawa Citizen*'s sports editor, was not present at the Forum for Game Three, but he did offer these comments from afar the following day:

> You gather from reports that the Canadiens blew two or three red-hot chances in the overtime, short as it was, before Ted Kennedy broke it up. On the other hand, Gerry McNeil was nothing short of sensational in spots. He started to sizzle the first time the Habs met Detroit in the semifinals, and he hasn't cooled out as yet.[31]

A United Press correspondent, whose name did not merit a byline in the next day's early edition of the *Brooklyn Daily Eagle*, was not at all impressed with the style of play displayed by either club in Game Three. He penned, somewhat disgustedly, "It was one of those typical Toronto-Montreal tussles: Lots of high sticking and brutal slashing."

The contrasting postgame moods of the two coaches were the

opposite of what one might expect them to be. Joe Primeau, despite his Maple Leafs winning Game Three and taking the lead in the best-of-seven series, was sullen and worried. Dick Irvin, on the other hand, outwardly exuded confidence although his team had just lost a tough battle, thrown away its home ice advantage, and now trailed powerful Toronto two games to one. They both cited the fickle nature of the hockey's "breaks" for their respective attitudes.

"It's the breaks that count," stressed the optimistic Irvin. "We didn't get them [tonight] but we will before the series is over."[32]

"This is going to be a series of breaks,"[33] echoed Primeau, hinting that his club had gotten more than their fair share in Game Three. His boss, Conn Smythe, agreed. "We've got one game in the slot. That gives us a slight margin. But we can't forget what Montreal did to Detroit."[34] Diplomatically, Smythe predicted the Stanley Cup finals would go the full seven games.

The Canadian Press thought Montreal had indeed been supremely unlucky in the brief fourth period. One of that news agency's correspondents wrote, "The Canadiens supplied all the thrills for the 14,443 hometown fans early in the overtime when [both Maurice] Richard and Ken Mosdell came within a whisker of scoring."[35]

There was an odd occurrence in the second period of Game Three. A Canadiens fan, angry that Sid Smith's important goal was not ruled offside and allowed to stand, flung a deck of playing cards onto the ice during a stoppage in play. (It was anyone's guess why he used such curious things to vent his frustration.) Montreal's Elmer Lach eagerly and helpfully scooped up the cards. However, Lach then skated toward the visiting bench and he dumped all 52 of them directly into the lap of unsuspecting Toronto owner Conn Smythe who was sitting nearby! Unbothered by this action, Smythe stood and gracefully bowed in the direction of Lach. Next, he turned to face the Hab fans seated behind him and merrily waved his fedora, all the while displaying a huge smile on his face. According to the local press, Smythe was booed heartily and "given the raspberry" by thousands of ticketholders inside the Forum. "I can still win a popularity contest in Montreal,"[36] the Maple Leafs' top man kiddingly told a scrum of reporters after the game as he happily held court in the upbeat Toronto dressing room in the wake of Ted Kennedy's game-winning tally.

Dink Carroll reported that many Montreal fans were still angrily grumbling about Sid Smith's disputed goal in the second period as they departed the Forum to make their way home in the springtime darkness outside. Their collective mood matched the color of the midnight sky above the Forum.

Although absent, Jack Koffman of the *Ottawa Citizen* mixed a bit of humor and philosophy into his game report based on wire service reports from the Forum. With Major League Baseball's opening day now competing with the Stanley Cup finals for newspaper coverage—especially in Canada—the two sports' seasons were now blended together and dividing the attention of some sports fans. He noted that the intrusion of MLB into the sporting season was generally welcomed by Canadians as something different than what the saturation of their long winter game provided. He wrote, "Well, it has been something of a long [hockey] season, at that. Queer things are starting to happen, too, when Rocket Richard fails to score an overtime goal."[37]

A jersey worn by Toronto Maple Leaf captain Ted (Teeder) Kennedy, for the 1953–54 season. Kennedy was one of four Leafs to score an overtime goal during the 1951 Stanley Cup finals (photo by Carl T. Madden).

Game Three Scoring Summary
Toronto 2 at Montreal 1 (OT)
April 17, 1951

First Period
1. MTL Maurice Richard (Bert Olmstead) 2:18

Second Period
2. TOR Sid Smith (Max Bentley) 5:58

Third Period
No scoring

Overtime
3. TOR Ted Kennedy (Tod Sloan) 4:47

9

Game Four

Harry Watson's Goal Puts Toronto in Control

"Four Toronto thieves broke into the Canadiens' defense last night to help pilfer pucks that were in the possession of the Habs. As a result of their fast filching, the Canadiens are now down 3-1 in the Stanley Cup series."[1]—*Montreal Star* sports editor Baz O'Meara

Prior to Game Four, every hockey fan in Canada and beyond seemed to be talking about the big goal scored during Game Three—but not the one that won the pivotal contest for Toronto. Teeder Kennedy's overtime tally for the Maple Leafs ran a poor second in water-cooler conversations between the third and fourth games of the 1951 Stanley Cup finals. The main subject of discussion was Sid Smith's goal in the second period that tied the game, 1-1, for the visitors. The Canadiens figured they had been the victims of an untimely bad non-call. That seemed to be the prevailing sentiment among the ranks of the press too. Feelings ran especially high in Montreal, naturally.

Of course, in the pre-television days of the Stanley Cup playoffs, the only people who saw exactly what happened were those who were present in some capacity at the sold-out Forum for Game Three. Baz O'Meara, of the *Montreal Star* was certainly there. The esteemed scribe was typical of those who felt there had been a costly injustice done to the hometown Habs. He was quite definite about it. Two days afterward, O'Meara wrote in his April 19 *Star* column,

> Smith took a drop pass from [Max] Bentley that went back over the [blue] line. Smith came in and shot it between Bentley's legs [for a goal]. Dick Irvin and the Canadiens would like to see a movie of that play, not that it would do them any good because the verdict stands. Only a movie might show that linesman [Bill] Morrison was actually going to whistle the play as he had the tooter to his mouth.

Morrison's non-call certainly riled up the Canadiens' bench, especially coach Dick Irvin who was overly excitable even at the best of times. "Irvin, is a man who can get very bitter about things, and rightly so," continued O'Meara. "He is a person of high, competitive quality. He still insists, along with many others, that Smith's goal the other night was way offside. Dick was more than slightly incensed over the incident."[2]

Making things worse, Montreal netminder Gerry McNeil informed reporters that he had relaxed on the play, assuming a whistle from the linesman was forthcoming to stop the action. The implication was that McNeil had let his guard down when the important Toronto goal was scored against him.

Irvin was still bemoaning the overall lack of breaks his club was experiencing during the three games of the series already in the books. "If I was as lucky as the Maple Leafs, I'd be a millionaire," he gruffly told Dink Carroll of the *Montreal Gazette*. "None will disagree with him,"[3] replied the writer. Irvin said there were three instances in Game Three in which Rollins looked behind him into his own net to see if Montreal had scored. Each time, to his relief, the puck was not there.

In less controversial matters, it was announced that Montreal defenseman Calum MacKay would miss Game Four because of a nagging injury to his right ankle. He had clearly been hobbling in Game Three. MacKay was also notable for making the ill-advised pass in the direction of teammate Doug Harvey that was intercepted by the Maple Leafs and led to Ted Kennedy's overtime winner. ("There have been quite a few plays in this series that have not gone according to blueprints,"[4] noted Baz O'Meara with a little bit of understatement.) Coach Dick Irvin did stress to several reporters that MacKay was not being sidelined for the game-ending mistake; the roster move was wholly based on giving the ailing Hab defensemen some time to rest his weak ankle. That seemed to be an accurate statement, as MacKay did not participate in the Habs' Wednesday practice.

On the brighter side of the Montreal defense corps, young Tom Johnson was impressing veteran hockey observers. Jack Crawford, who played defense for the Boston Bruins for 13 seasons before retiring in 1950, said of the 23-year-old rookie blueliner, "I like him a lot. He's got a lot of zing and he doesn't make many mistakes."[5]

The Leafs opting to change goaltenders midway through the finals was still being widely discussed. Jack Koffman of the *Ottawa Citizen* was certain it was Conn Smythe's decision rather than coach Joe Primeau's. Accordingly, Koffman wrote in his column,

> Conn Smythe yanked Turk Broda in favor of Al Rollins for the third game. Broda has been an ace for the Leafs since Rollins was injured in the first playoff game [versus Boston], but he made a major mistake on Richard's

game-winning goal last Saturday. Major Smythe never has let sentiment interfere with his judgment, and apparently he isn't taking a new slant on life at this late date.[6]

The Hockey News announced there would be co-winners of its prestigious Player of the Year Award for the 1950–51 season. Gordie Howe and Maurice Richard shared the honors. Undoubtedly, this compromise created fuel for discussion about which one of the superstars was truly the best player in the NHL.

In some circles these NHL championship games were already being referred to as "The Overtime Series"—and rightly so, of course. On the day of Game Four, the *Windsor Star*'s headline atop its sports section amusingly stated, "Bring Lunch—Overtime Lads Go Again Tonight." Similarly, Jack Koffman wrote in his daily broadsheet, "It seems the Montreal Forum and Maple Leaf Gardens could advertise 'overtime guaranteed' with their Stanley Cup attractions these nights. The teams have gone into an extra period three times running, which is better than par for any three-game course."[7]

Game Four was definitely on for Thursday, April 19, at the Forum and Game Five was slated for two nights later in Toronto. The exact dates and times for Game Six and Game Seven were still somewhat up in the air. The NHL did announce, finally, that the sixth game of the series, if necessary, would be back at the Montreal Forum on Tuesday, April 24. The league also announced that Game Seven had been tentatively penciled in for Thursday, April 26—with the adverb "tentatively" heavily emphasized.

When not discussing the numerous things about the exciting 1951 Stanley Cup championship series, some sports journalists who were running short of ideas to fill the inches in their daily columns opted to pick on the woeful Chicago Black Hawks. Those Hawks, having missed the playoffs by 26 points, had dispersed and were long into their summer vacations. From the safety of his desk at the *Calgary Herald*, that publication's sports editor, Bob Mamini, took this not-so-subtle shot at the pitiful NHL hockey club from Illinois on April 19. He wrote, "Remember when the Chicago Black Hawks, managed by Tommy Gorman, won the Stanley Cup 17 years ago by defeating the Detroit Red Wings? It was the first Cup title for the Hawks who won the basin again in 1937–38. Honest! They really did."[8]

The Stanley Cup finals can be a tense affair for the players who contest it, the spectators and other fans who passionately follow it, and even the veteran scribes who cover it. Therefore, newspapers in Toronto had fun with the following light-hearted anecdote. As the Maple Leafs prepared to play Game Four, captain Ted Kennedy got his Toronto teammates' attention in the visitors' dressing room at the Forum to read them a message he had received earlier that day. It was an amusing telegram sent

9. Game Four

by an anonymous trio of Leaf fans allegedly enrolled at a hostile university located in Montreal. It humorously read, "As Stanley Cup hockey is reducing studying time for all important final examinations next week, request immediate elimination of unworthy opposition. Signed: Three hard-pressed McGill students."[9]

The Game Three loss by the Canadiens returned the home-ice advantage back to the favored Maple Leafs. If Montreal was to win the Stanley Cup, the best-case scenario would require them to win another game at Maple Leaf Gardens. A Montreal loss in Game Four on April 19 would require two triumphs for the Habs in Toronto—an unlikely prospect considering that wins for Montreal there had been a truly scarce commodity lately.

In the moments leading up to Game Four, a dignitary was honored at center ice by the Canadiens. Barbara Ann Scott, the 1948 Olympic women's figure skating champion from Ottawa, was given the red-carpet treatment at the Forum. Affectionately known as "Canada's Sweetheart," she dropped the puck in a ceremonial opening faceoff. A much-beloved person throughout the whole of the country, the 22-year-old Scott was given a tremendous ovation by the capacity crowd when her name was announced. She was the main attraction of a glitzy ice carnival that would occupy the Forum after Game Four.

The visiting Maple Leafs began the scoring not long after the real opening faceoff from the hand of referee George Gravel took place. Inside the first minute of play, the visitors had established a 1–0 lead to silence the partisan fans at the Forum. Writing in the *Montreal Star*, Baz O'Meara noted, "The Leafs, as is their habit, broke fast for the opening goal when Bud MacPherson failed to flag down [Ted] Kennedy when he twisted in for a pass to the inevitable [Sid] Smith. That goal only took 38 seconds and had an unsettling effect [on the Canadiens]."[10] The goal was the seventh notched by the productive Smith in the 1951 playoffs.

Montreal got on even terms with Toronto before the first period ended, however. Maurice Richard's eighth goal of the playoffs came at 14:41 with both Billy Reay and Doug Harvey earning assists on the equalizer. O'Meara wrote, "Richard, taking a looping pass from Harvey, on an almost impossible angle sent a shot through an inch aperture. The puck hit the post and slid into the back of the net." O'Meara, apparently forgetting the Rocket's sensational and plentiful overtime heroics, strangely commented, "Of all the goals [Richard] has scored this year, this was the most dramatic."[11]

The tying goal put Richard alone atop the NHL's all-time playoff scorers with 63 points, supplanting his ex-teammate, Toe Blake. According to O'Meara, Montreal's best-known player had played "a tremendous two-way game that dispelled all doubt about his all-around quality."[12]

As was the case in Game Three, there was another odd, midgame incident involving Leafs owner Conn Smythe. In the second period, Smythe became enraged at a call made by referee George Gravel that sent Toronto's Max Bentley to the penalty box for two minutes. Harold Atkins of the *Montreal Star* described what allegedly happened:

> Conn Smythe literally exploded out of his seat to make a very dramatic protest to NHL president Clarence Campbell over a play in last night's Canadiens-Leafs clash. In his usual bombastic style, Smythe waved his hands, gesticulated, and caught Campbell by the lapel to get a point across. The act caught fire like mad. Some folks had Smythe punching Campbell on the nose.... Boy was he really seething![13]

Neither Smythe nor Campbell would offer any comments to reporters about the incident. Atkins wrote, "After the game, the two principles in the rhubarb were as mum as one of those Egyptian crypt dwellers."[14]

Baz O'Meara was happy to put in his two cents' worth, however. He penned, "If a player does that with a league official, he is fined $500, but if a magnate does it, will he get away with it? In all these things it depends on whose ox is gored and how."[15]

Early in the second period, Toronto got their second goal of the game to restore a one-goal lead for the visitors. It was scored by Howie Meeker. It came off a faceoff in the Montreal zone. Harry Watson fed the puck to Meeker who slid the disc past McNeil. O'Meara said Meeker's tally was the result of "bad defensive coverage" by Montreal. The time of the goal was 1:27. There was no further scoring by either team in the second period of Game Four.

After more than 30 minutes of trying to mount some meaningful offense, Montreal got the important tying tally in the third period. "The Habs' ... avalanche of rushing finally paid off," declared O'Meara. "Butch Bouchard broke through at the left wing in the Toronto defensive zone, shot a pass across to the Rocket who did a complete turnaround as he shot [the puck toward the Toronto goal.] Elmer Lach cut to the left. The puck deflected off his stick and into the net."[16] The Forum erupted with cheers for the home team's creative goal. It came at 13:49 of the third period and tied the game 2–2. The final six minutes of the regulation 60 produced no goals. For the fourth straight time in the 1951 Stanley Cup finals, overtime would have to be played to determine a victor.

In the overtime period, there was a bit of confusion at the Toronto bench—and somehow it paid enormous dividends to the visitors. Years later, the game's hero for the Maple Leafs, Harry Watson, succinctly described what happened in the final seconds of the overtime period. It was more of an impromptu action than a great plan. "There was a line change coming up," he remembered. "I just jumped onto the ice because no one else was moving."[17] Max Bentley, who had deftly relieved Montreal's Bernie Geoffrion of the puck, fed a quick pass to Watson. His low and hard shot sailed past McNeil for the tally that won Game Four for the visitors by a 3–2 count—and put Toronto up three games to one heading back home to Maple Leaf Gardens. Baz O'Meara bluntly wrote in his report, "The weak-checking Geoffrion let the experienced Bentley steal the puck from him."[18]

Young Montreal prospect Bernie Geoffrion had a truly awful night for the home team in several respects. Not only did the 20-year-old's careless giveaway result in Harry Watson's game-winning goal for Toronto, the promising rookie also broke *five* sticks during the hard-fought game. In one instance, he accidentally skated over a fragment of one of the shattered pieces of lumber—and promptly fell headlong into the boards. The groggy Geoffrion had to be assisted off the Forum's ice surface by an escort crew of concerned teammates.

"The Canadiens came out of [Game Four] moaning about bad luck, breaks, unseen hands, invisible fingers, and stacked odds," declared Baz O'Meara in his lengthy report for the *Montreal Star*. "You couldn't blame them because twice in the overtime the Habs could have wrapped it up. Once [Bert] Olmstead, instead of passing to Richard, elected to shoot. [The other instance] was when [Billy] Reay, from a few feet out, was beaten by Rollins' extended foot." O'Meara further commented, "The Leafs appear to be better opportunists than the Canadiens. When a fellow like [Ted] Kennedy is on the loose, anything can happen, and usually does."[19]

"We just can't get a break,"[20] insisted Elmer Lach, proving O'Meara's point to be true.

Toronto had an excellent chance to win the game earlier in the fourth period. Danny Lewicki had been sent in alone on Montreal goalie Gerry McNeil, who had to make a fine stretching save to temporarily preserve the tie score. Lewicki, a 20-year-old rookie left winger from Fort William, Ontario, had scored 16 goals for Toronto during the 1950–51 regular season. He finished third in the Calder Trophy voting.

Red Burnett, a *Toronto Star* reporter assigned to cover the Stanley Cup finals, commented about Al Rollins' overall excellence in the Leaf net. "Rollins has outplayed [Gerry] McNeil in these two games in Montreal. He proved beyond a doubt he's a top major leaguer, a brilliant performer with the chips on the line." Burnett applauded the play of McNeil, too. He wrote, "McNeil has been anything but a slouch. He didn't have a chance on Harry Watson's screamer from 20 feet out."[21]

Burnett discussed the imperturbable temperament of the Leaf netminder. He wrote, "Al Rollins the daddy longlegs who guards the Leafs' twine, never thought at any time his side would lose, never so much as a strained blood vessel, when everyone, including Leaf boss Conn Smythe, was busting a gasket."[22] Rollins exemplified coolness under pressure. He told Burnett shortly after the game concluded, "Funny thing, but I was never in doubt of the result. Even when Billy Reay was taking dead aim in overtime, I was confident we'd win. I knew he'd go for that corner, and I turned his shot aside with my pad."[23]

Conn Smythe was thrilled by the Toronto triumph and their two-game lead in the series, but he refused to count Montreal out—at least not yet. "The Canadiens will still be tough," he told Baz O'Meara. "We are not counting ourselves in until we have wrapped up another game."[24]

O'Meara, and most every other sports journalist covering the Stanley Cup finals, was impressed with the play of Howie Meeker. A three-time Cup winner with Toronto, Meeker had won the NHL's Rookie of the Year award—the Calder Trophy—in 1947. The 28-year-old was probably at his skillful peak in 1951, but rumors had Meeker quitting hockey at the end of the playoffs to become the manager of the newly constructed Kitchener Memorial Auditorium. (Kitchener was the city in southwestern Ontario where Meeker was born in 1923.) It was expected that if he got the arena job he desired, he would also double as the hockey coach of the Kitchener Flying Dutchmen—a senior amateur team of great repute. O'Meara wrote, "For the Leafs, one of the outstanding players [of the fourth game] was little Howie Meeker. He scored a very decisive goal, and he stood up to heavy hammering in fine style. The Canadiens defense may have given him too much leeway. He was one of the most valuable invaders."[25]

The prominent Montreal scribe also combined both reporting and partisan commentary with this bitter quote about the Maple Leafs: "The Toronto defense was in tremendous form, battling, fighting, hooking, clutching, hauling, and doing all the effective things for which they have become noted."[26]

Another of Meeker's admirers, Milt Dunnell of the *Toronto Star*, doubted the skillful Leaf would be quitting the NHL anytime soon for any reason. He wrote, "He'll need to be released from his contract. The way Meeker has been going in his last couple of games, he'll need an Abraham Lincoln to get his freedom."[27]

Neither Meeker nor Harry Watson were presently on offensive hot streaks. In fact, neither of those noteworthy Maple Leaf players had notched a playoff goal in quite a while. Meeker's last postseason goal had been scored in 1949. Watson's dry spell was even lengthier: His last marker in Stanley Cup play had occurred in the 1948 playoffs. Milt Dunnell commented on this in his daily sport column on April 20:

> [His goal] was unexpected because it was the first time that Mr. Watson had lighted a bulb in a playoff fray in two seasons. He hadn't even managed an assist until he got a piece of last night's second Leaf goal by little Howie Meeker. His goal—scored in overtime, of course ... that's the only kind of games they have in this series—just about ended Montreal's hopes for the Cup.[28]

Writers were generally impressed with the play of Eddie Mazur of the Habs. The youngster from Winnipeg was making his NHL debut under the most trying of circumstances—the intense pressure of the Stanley Cup finals. O'Meara penned that the 21-year-old was "a big fellow who was highly recommended to the club by Babe Pratt."[29] Pratt was a former NHLer who was now toiling in the minors with the New Westminster Royals of the Pacific Coast Hockey League. Mazur was a flexible addition for the Habs. He could be slotted into both forward and defensive positions by coach Dick Irvin. Mazur would oddly play in three NHL postseasons before he ever played in a regular-season game for Montreal. O'Meara also tossed a bouquet to Paul Masnick, whom he described as "the surprise package of the series."[30]

Montreal had outshot Toronto 21–19 overall in the fourth game of the Stanley Cup finals. It was a surprisingly small combined total of 40 shots for a game that was wide open at times and played at a frantic pace by both teams.

Turk Broda, now resigned to being Al Rollins' emergency backup for the rest of the championship series, spent most of the contest sitting beside ex–Montreal goaltender Bill Durnan in the Forum's press box. The two men seemed to enjoy each other's company and were merrily chatting throughout Game Four, no doubt sharing "war stories" that only fellow goaltenders could appreciate.

The fourth consecutive overtime game between the Habs and the Maple Leafs established some esoteric NHL history. Never before had two teams in a single postseason series played so many consecutive extra-time tussles. The previous record was three straight overtime games. That occurred in the Boston-Toronto best-of-five series back in the spring of 1933. (That series featured overtime periods in Games One, Two and Three. No overtime was required to determine the winning team in Game Four, which Toronto captured, 5–3, in an atypical wide-open affair. The fifth game, however, was the famous six-overtime battle at Maple Leaf Gardens which the Leafs won, 1–0, on Ken Doraty's goal in the wee hours of the morning. Thus, the evenly matched Bruins and Leafs had contested four overtimes in five games in that memorable playoff clash.)

Before Game Four, the Canadiens announced that their coach, silver-haired Dick Irvin, had signed a contract to guide the club for two more seasons. The formal announcement was made by Montreal general manager Frank Selke. He praised Irvin's past successes and lauded him for the achievement of getting the underdog 1950–51 version of the Habs into the Stanley Cup final where they had been very competitive. "No one better pick us for last place next year,"[31] Selke sternly told *Montreal Star* reporter Harold Atkins. (Indeed, some hockey pundits, prior to the first puck of the 1950–51 season being dropped, had picked the Habs to occupy the six-team NHL's cellar.) Selke opined that Irvin's work in getting an underdog club to the Stanley Cup finals may have been the finest in his long career of service to the sport. Selke also suggested that additional personnel might help Irvin do his job better. According to a Canadian Press story, the general manager said he was considering hiring an assistant for their 58-year-old coach in order to give Irvin "the time to be the master coach of the Canadiens' hockey empire."[32]

The Habs were very confident about their young players soon maturing into stars, but they still searched for opportunities to bolster their club via trades. One rumor being bandied about in the press was the Canadiens being quite interested in acquiring defenseman Bill Barilko from Toronto for the 1951–52 NHL season. Baz O'Meara noted, somewhat negatively, in an April 20 sidebar column, "There is talk of Barilko coming this way. Of what has been seen [of him] in the playoffs, he isn't exactly essential to the Habs, but they could use another policeman on defense."[33]

Strangely, two stories about the already contested pair of semifinal series made news. The NHL announced the official records from Game Six of the Montreal-Detroit get-together had been amended to take a goal away from Ted Lindsay of the Red Wings. It was properly assigned to Gordie Howe. This was done based on statements by both players and numerous comments from media people insisting that Howe should have been credited with the goal. That tweak bumped Howe's goal total for the postseason from three to four. On the other side of the coin, Lindsay's tally sum dropped from one measly goal to zero. His offensive numbers in the semifinal were shockingly low: Lindsay had disappointingly only managed a single assist in his club's six-game loss to the Habs. During the 1950–51 regular season, the reliable Lindsay had recorded 24 goals and 35 assists for the mighty—and heavily favored—Detroit Red Wings.

The second story was a lingering debate about what should be done with the gate receipts from the inconclusive second contest between Toronto and Boston at Maple Leaf Gardens—the one that was halted with the score level at 1–1 as Sunday morning approached in adherence to the local Sabbath Day curfew laws. There was a similar precedent—but in baseball, not hockey. During the 1922 World Series, Game Two between the New York Yankees and New York Giants was controversially halted by chief umpire George Hildebrand due to "impending darkness" when the score was tied, 3–3, after 10 innings had been played. (Baseball journalists of the day widely insisted the game could have easily continued for at least another inning.) Embarrassed by the debacle, angry MLB commissioner Judge Kenesaw Mountain Landis ordered the entire gate receipts from that terminated contest—approximately $120,000—be donated to various war charities in New York City. (It was done to avoid the appearance of MLB trying to improperly extend the Fall Classic for financial gain.) It was both a wise and popular decision, one that brought baseball's czar much praise from fans and reporters alike. Nearly three decades later, a movement was afoot for something similar to happen to the cash received in ticket sales for that inconclusive Leafs-Bruins playoff game contested on Saturday, March 31. Writer Ted Heard had some fun with the ongoing discussion. He wryly offered the following zinger: "Why doesn't the NHL donate the receipts to some worthy charity … say the Chicago Black Hawks?"[34]

Game Four Scoring Summary
Toronto 3 at Montreal 2 (OT)
April 19, 1951

First Period
1. TOR Sid Smith (Ted Kennedy) 0:38
2. MTL Maurice Richard (Billy Reay, Doug Harvey) 14:41

Second Period
3. TOR Howie Meeker (Harry Watson) 1:27

Third Period
4. MTL Elmer Lach (Maurice Richard, Butch Bouchard) 13:49

Overtime
5. TOR Harry Watson (Max Bentley) 5:15

10

Game Five

Bill Barilko Becomes Famous

"All the excitement, all the thrills, and all the drama that can come out of a hockey game were crammed into the last three minutes and 24 seconds of this one. During that stretch there didn't seem to be a sane person amongst the 14,577 witnesses"[1]—*The Hockey News*

"This is quite a series for Montreal Canadiens goaltender Gerry McNeil: Four overtime games, [one in which] he celebrated a birthday. This morning his wife presented him with a baby girl. We hope his cup is full to overflowing—as long as it isn't the Stanley Cup."[2]—*Toronto Star* editorial, April 21, 1951

Toronto's victory in Game Four at the Montreal Forum on April 19 meant they were just a single win away from the Holy Grail of professional hockey: the Stanley Cup. Traditionally, the sport's most famous trophy was on hand for a potential series-clinching victory. However, it was reported that that might not be the case on Saturday, April 21. A superstition had set in among the Toronto management—especially owner Conn Smythe—that it was somehow bad luck to view the Cup before it had been won! The origin of this curious belief is rather murky and seems to have been lost over time. As of 1951, Toronto had never *not* won the Stanley Cup in a final series where they were one game away from winning it.

Accordingly, a rumor began to circulate that the silver trophy would be denied entry into Maple Leaf Gardens in advance of the game! Indeed, the *Toronto Star*'s Joe Perlove wrote in the April 21 edition of his newspaper, "The Cup was supposed to arrive at the Gardens sometime this morning. Whether it will be accepted and permitted into the building is something else again."[3] NHL president Clarence Campbell, certainly a no-nonsense type, was having none of that malarkey. He tersely informed

10. Game Five

Perlove, "Superstition or no superstition, the Cup goes to Toronto."[4] It was in the building and ready to be presented to the home team if the Maple Leafs were able to wrap up the Stanley Cup final in five games.

The Maple Leaf organization could remarkably win two major championships on Saturday, April 21. Their top farm club, the Pittsburgh Hornets, was playing Game Seven of the American Hockey League championship series versus the Cleveland Barons. Pittsburgh had trailed that series three games to one before rallying to win Games Five and Six to force a winner-take-all match in Ohio. *Pittsburgh Press* sports writer Carl Hughes strongly suspected that this climactic contest might be the Barons' last appearance in the AHL. It was not a case of fan apathy; in fact, it was quite the opposite: Cleveland, a minor-league hockey hotbed, was strongly rumored to be getting an NHL club for the 1951–52 season.

Fern Flaman's sore groin had improved enough so he could be listed as a maybe for Game Five. Earlier reports had declared the Leaf defensemen was undoubtedly through for the duration of the finals.

On the day of Game Five, the Canadian Press ran a very complimentary feature article about Ted (Teeder) Kennedy—the Toronto overtime hero from Game Three—and his unquestioned importance to the Maple Leafs. Frankly, however, it was absolutely unnecessary to point out the Toronto captain's immense value to his legions of fans across Canada.

"The Montreal Canadiens can have Rocket Richard and his goal-scoring wizardry," the story began. "Toronto hockey followers will settle for tenacious Ted Kennedy whose dogged center-ice play has brought the Maple Leafs to within one game of their fourth Stanley Cup championship in five years. Conn Smythe has called him the greatest playoff player in hockey. Around Toronto, and farther afield, many experts agree."

The lengthy story, which ran in the *Ottawa Citizen* without a byline, pointed out a very telling statistic from the first four games of the finals:

> Until [Harry] Watson and Howie Meeker got the range for a goal apiece at Montreal [in Game Four], the 25-year-old Kennedy's line had scored all Toronto's goals in the series. He was the main factor in standing off the challenge from the Boston Bruins in the semifinal series. Kennedy isn't the leading scorer [in the 1951 playoffs]—he has four goals and four assists in ten games—but he's been the number-one Leaf all the way.

The same article praised the very popular Teeder for his consistent excellence since he first joined the Leafs as a rookie seven years ago in 1944. Kennedy led the NHL playoffs in scoring in 1945 as Toronto barely held on to win the Stanley Cup against Detroit in the last year of the war, nearly squandering a huge three-game lead in the finals. When Kennedy was injured the following season, the Maple Leafs failed to even qualify for the playoffs in 1945–46. "[Kennedy] was a mainstay for the Leafs in their three consecutive Stanley Cups," insisted the author. "When he got hurt in semifinal play last year, the team bowed out to the Detroit Red Wings."[5]

Another Canadian Press writer focused on how overtime games had become the norm in the 1951 finals—and warned fans that an 11:45 p.m. Saturday curfew was in effect to comply with the Lord's Day Act in Toronto. "Considering the closeness of the previous games," penned Mel Sufrin, "there's good reason to expect that tonight's fifth game of the best-of-seven series might also go beyond regulation time."

Sufrin came up with a unique theory about why extra periods had been so prevalent in the championship round of the playoffs. He wrote,

> There may be an obscure psychological reason for these overtimes [in the finals]. It could be a reaction to the frustration during the regular season ... and the six teams of the NHL played a record number of ties.
>
> One thing is certain: Fans have not been at all disappointed to see Montreal and Toronto go into sudden-death overtime in every ... game to date. That probably goes double for Toronto supporters because their Leafs have won three of the four [games played to date].[6]

The Canadiens had arrived in Toronto a day before the Maple Leafs. Coach Dick Irvin, using a bit of reverse psychology, downplayed his team's chances. "There really wasn't much use making the trip here," he said. "We've given our best and the Leafs are ahead. I guess the semifinal with Detroit took too much out of us."[7]

Montreal general manager Frank Selke was considerably more optimistic in his comments to the press. "We've won games in Toronto before," he stated. "With a bit of luck, we can still go on to win the Cup."[8]

The Maple Leafs had not considered a Cup-clinching victory in Game Five to be a foregone conclusion—at least not publicly. "We have to go out and give everything we have—and a little bit more," stated Toronto coach Joe Primeau from the Leafs hideaway in St. Catharines. "It's a cinch those Canadiens are going to throw their best shot—and we don't want to return to Montreal."[9]

A United Press article reported that oddsmakers listed the Maple Leafs as a solid 8:5 betting favorite to finish off the Canadiens in Game Five and secure the Stanley Cup. "But all four previous games in the series have been settled in overtime," the article noted. "The Leaf players aren't breathing easily yet. Their chief worry, they admit, is still Maurice Richard."[10]

Joe Primeau acknowledged this sentiment to be true. He commented, "Richard is wonderful. Every time he gets the puck, I'm afraid he's going to score. I hope we take the Cup [on] Saturday night, but if The Rocket keeps up his pace, we'll have a tough time." Still, the Toronto coach had planned no specific tactics or personnel maneuvers to stifle the offensive prowess of Montreal's top gun. "We'll play him man-to-man without any special shadow," Primeau declared. "Whoever is opposite Richard will guard him."[11]

In his 1968 book, *The Lively World of Hockey*, historian Brian McFarlane deemed Game Five of the 1951 Stanley Cup finals to have broken "all records for sheer tension."[12] With the inevitable passage of time, living witnesses to that historic and thrilling contest are now a scarce commodity. As of August 2023, former NHL coach and *Hockey Night in Canada* commentator Harry Neale is one of the dwindling few people still with us who had been present at Maple Leaf Gardens that exciting Saturday night. He was a 14-year-old Torontonian on April 21, 1951. He attended the memorable game with his father. It was obviously a big event in his young life. Neale easily recalled many esoteric details from that special night in an interview he did about 50 years after the occasion.

> Dad worked for Imperial Oil. Once in a while he got tickets. [Authors' note: Imperial Oil was a longtime major sponsor of *HNIC*.] We sat in the south end blues, just off to the right. We were in the fifth or sixth row, good seats. You never had to stand up to watch the play sitting on the end … where Barilko scored. It was easy to see what exactly happened.[13]

Fern Flaman was back in the Toronto lineup, his groin injury apparently healed adequately enough for the rugged 24-year-old from Dysart, Saskatchewan, to participate in Game Five.

Tod Sloan might just be the most overlooked hero in the history of the Toronto Maple Leafs. In the decisive fifth game of the Stanley Cup finals, Sloan got both the home team's goals to enable the Leafs to go into overtime after 60 minutes of regulation play tied 2–2 with the visiting Habs. Moreover, Sloan's second marker came in highly dramatic fashion with just 28 seconds left in the third period. Without Sloan's pair of goals, there would be no Cup-clinching overtime goal by Bill Barilko. Yet how many Toronto hockey fans today know about Sloan's massive contribution to the Maple Leafs' 1951 Stanley Cup title?

The first 20 minutes of Game Five were played with neither Al Rollins nor Gerry McNeil surrendering a goal to the opposition. That was a rarity; it was the first scoreless opening period of the 1951 Cup finals where goals being scored early in games had been the norm. The first period, however, was not without incident. It began with a scary moment for Maple Leaf fans and specifically the team's popular captain, Ted Kennedy. He had to be carted off the ice on a stretcher in the first minute of play with what was later described as a wrenched back after slamming into the boards heavily. The worried crowd let out a discernible sigh of relief when Kennedy was back on the ice not long afterward seemingly having no lingering negative effects from the violent mishap.

Similarly, the second period began with a serious injury to a little-used Hab. In the first minute of the frame, Bob Dawes, a former Maple Leaf who had previously seen no ice time in either round of the Stanley Cup playoffs for Montreal, broke his right leg in several places when he mistimed a check on Ted Kennedy. The 26-year-old Dawes went crashing awkwardly into the boards. The Saskatoon resident would never play another game in the NHL.

It was Montreal's Maurice Richard who notched the game's first tally. It came 8:56 into the second period. A newsreel cameraman captured the goal: Richard shook loose from the Leafs' defensive alignment, faking Toronto defenseman Jimmy Thomson out of position. The Montreal superstar got a partial breakaway on Rollins, and put a deke on him. With an open net staring him in the face, Richard momentarily lost control of the puck, but recovered it just in time. He concluded the play by flipping the puck past the Toronto netminder with a backhand into the gaping cage. It entered the net a fraction of a second before a Maple Leaf defenseman was about to prevent Richard from shooting. The Canadiens took a 1-0 lead. The goal also meant that Richard had kept up his terrific scoring streak. He had found the net in all five games of the 1951 Stanley Cup finals. (Richard had also scored in four of the six semifinal games Montreal played versus Detroit—but, curiously, he never scored more than one goal per game.) He had further extended his playoff scoring record to 64 points.

The Maple Leafs were a resilient bunch, however. About three minutes after Richard's tally, Tod Sloan leveled the score for the hometown Maple Leafs. The goal delighted the overflow crowd of 14,577—described by one journalist as "hysterical and jampacked."[14] (Among that total were approximately 2,000 standees who were unable to get seats for the all-important game but were content to be in the building even if they could not sit down for its duration.) Sloan deftly accepted a sharp pass from teammate Ted Kennedy at the Montreal blue line and skated past both Doug Harvey and Bud McPherson. The latter seemed to be caught flat-footed on the play. Sloan moved in on McNeil. Like Richard had done, Sloan put a nifty deke of his own on the Montreal goaltender that sent him sprawling. With the whole upper half of the net to aim for, and McNeil lying on the ice hopelessly out of position, Sloan made no error. He flicked the puck into the top of the net to tie the score, 1-1. The tense rooters at Maple Leaf Gardens roared with joy. The time of Sloan's equalizer was precisely 12:00 of the second period. That marker ended the scoring for the middle stanza. Game Five was up for grabs despite the Leafs enjoying a wide advantage in territorial play.

10. Game Five

An unheralded Hab, Paul Meger, from the small town of Watrous in Saskatchewan, restored the visitors' one-goal edge early in the third period. Meger had played just 17 regular-season games for Montreal in 1950–51, scoring two goals and adding four assists in those appearances. He had become a postseason regular, though. This night was his eleventh playoff contest of the season. Meger's important goal was a casual and timely backhander; he simply redirected a pass that teammate Doug Harvey cleverly sent to him through the legs of Toronto's Joe Klukay at 4:47 of the period. It turned out to be the Habs' final goal of the 1950–51 NHL season.

The Maple Leafs had slightly more than 15 minutes remaining in the final period to find a gap in Gerry McNeil's armor for a game-tying goal. They almost used every allowable second to do so, but Toronto did eventually succeed in the task with the clock showing less than 60 seconds to play in the third period. The Leaf supporters were not going to allow their team to lose quietly. "The crowd stood and stamped in a frenzy," reported a United Press scribe in the *Boston Globe*.

Toronto coach Joe Primeau pulled netminder Al Rollins for an extra attacker with about a minute left on the Maple Leaf Gardens clock. After a stoppage, a key faceoff was held in the Montreal zone. Ted Kennedy, widely considered the best faceoff man in the NHL, looked across the ice to the spot where the puck would be dropped. He saw Billy Reay of the Canadiens waiting for him. Kennedy frowned. He knew that Reay was one of the few men in the league who routinely bested him on draws. Luckily for Kennedy and the Leafs as a whole, Montreal coach Dick Irvin did not realize that was the case. He opted instead for a wholesale line change, calling Reay to the bench and replacing him with veteran Elmer Lach. Kennedy breathed a sigh of relief as he knew Lach seldom won faceoffs against him. Primeau did not make a change; he left the same six Toronto skaters on the ice: Kennedy, Sloan, Mortson, Watson, Bentley, and Smith. Irvin would later defend the line change by insisting he was playing the probabilities. He simply wanted the best possible lineup on the ice to attempt to preserve the Habs' tenuous lead for the final minute of the third period. The thoroughly reliable Ted Kennedy won the hugely important draw for Toronto.

"I got it clean back to Bentley," Kennedy recalled 50 years after the fact. "Lach disentangled himself with me and rushed right out to Bentley. Max gave him the double-shuffle, walked in about three strides, and let it fly."[15]

Sid Smith recalled what happened after Kennedy won the faceoff and slid the puck to Max Bentley. "Max's shot either hit my leg or the referee's. [The puck] popped down beside me and I shot it. I could see it hit the post. Then, all of a sudden, the light went on. What happened? It deflected across to Sloan who was on the right side. He just batted it in. He saved our bacon right there."[16]

Sloan potted his second goal of the night—likely the most important tally he ever scored in his fine professional hockey career. More importantly, Toronto had leveled the score in Game Five at two goals apiece. There were just 28 seconds left on the clock. Nearly seven decades later, TheHockeyWriters.com would declare it the biggest moment of the entire 1951 Stanley Cup playoffs.

Maple Leaf Gardens was in an uproar. An anticipatory and optimistic chant of "We want the Cup!" echoed through the 20-year-old building. Sloan had scored 31 goals for Toronto during the 1950–51 regular season, but they were all insignificant compared to the one he had just knocked past McNeil late in Game Five of the Stanley Cup finals. The third period's dying moments ended without any further scoring. The fifth consecutive overtime stanza of this remarkable championship playoff series would be required to decide Game Five's victors—and perhaps the Cup champions.

When the overtime began, the Leafs continued to apply the same level of pressure they had during regulation time. However, it was the Canadiens who had the best early chance. Maurice Richard went in alone on Al Rollins. After a deke on the Toronto netminder, Richard appeared to have an unguarded net in which to deposit the puck. But, seemingly out of nowhere, came Maple Leaf defenseman Bill Barilko to slide in front of the Rocket's shot and deflect it out of harm's way. Not long afterward, another act of Barilko heroics got him on the scoresheet—and into hockey lore.

Toronto advanced the puck across the Montreal blue line. Harry Watson collected the disc and fired a pass to teammate Howie Meeker who was in front of the Habs' net. Meeker never really controlled the pass. The puck struck his stick, grazed the side of the goalpost, and rolled behind the cage. Meeker got to it first. Chasing him was Montreal defenseman Tom Johnson. Meeker attempted a wraparound with no success, but he retained control of the puck. He tried to feed it to Watson who was positioned in front of goaltender Gerry McNeil, but Watson was watched closely by defenseman Butch Bouchard. The puck went in the vicinity of Watson who took a swipe at it and missed. The puck hit a skate—likely it was Bouchard's—and bounced toward the faceoff circle.

Bill Barilko saw an opportunity and charged forward from his defensive position. He narrowly missed colliding with teammate Cal Gardner, which slightly put him off stride. McNeil, who had been down on the ice to prevent Meeker's wraparound attempt, was slowly regaining his feet. He was not quite aware of where the puck was nor of the imminent danger coming from the advancing Leaf defenseman. Barilko lunged at the puck with a backhanded swat. McNeil did not see it heading toward to the top of his net until it was too late to do anything about it. It was entirely pure luck, but Barilko's shot could not have been placed any better.

For years McNeil sincerely thought Barilko had scored the series-deciding tally with a slapshot. In a 1975 interview he said as much. Newsreel footage of the game clearly shows Barilko scoring his goal on a backhand shot. Be that as it may, it was wrongly described as a "blistering drive" in some newspaper accounts in the days that followed Game Five. In Brian McFarlane's 1968 book, *The Lively World of Hockey*, he too wrongly wrote that Barilko scored on a slapshot. Al Nickleson made the same incorrect assertion in his report on the game for the *Globe & Mail*. The shot Barilko launched toward the Montreal net certainly had some pace to it; it was more than just a flick. Its speed, however, was nowhere close to that of a slapshot.

"It was as clean as a hound's tooth," wrote Red Burnett in his game report for the *Toronto Star*. "McNeil never had a chance."[17] Both Meeker and Watson earned assists on Barilko's dramatic goal.

A United Press reporter described the climactic moment of Game Five: Bill Barilko's game-winning goal that occurred 2:53 into the fourth period. "The curly-haired defenseman clinched the contest on a 20-foot shot ... when he converted Howie Meeker's setup,"[18] wrote the unnamed scribe, whose synopsis of the game ran in the next day's Sunday *Boston Globe*. (He correctly called it a backhand.) Game Five featured the briefest overtime period of the 1951 Stanley Cup finals; it was two seconds shorter than Game Two—the only game in the series won by the Canadiens.

Proving that not every scribe saw the game-ending play the same way, the writer continued with his version of the sequences leading up to the goal. "Meeker started the big play by firing a shot that goalie Gerry McNeil kicked aside [sic]. Harry Watson spun the puck back to Meeker who placed it on the big Barilko's stick for the crusher."[19]

The famous and terrific image of Barilko scoring the Stanley Cup–winning goal was snapped by one of the Leafs' two official club photographers, Nat Turofsky. (The team's other photographer was his brother, Lou. The twosome owned a Toronto photo studio. They had been employed by the club since 1928.) It shows the off-balance Leaf falling forward, with the puck striking the mesh inside the net above the helpless McNeil's blocker. James Marsh, who attended the game as a seven-year-old with his grandmother, wrote years later, "Turofsky on his Graflex camera, [displayed] such exquisite timing that he caught the puck in the net before the goal light had flashed."[20] Perhaps only one fan in the photo realizes a goal has been scored. To this day, Turofsky's 1951 masterpiece remains the most requested photograph in the Hockey Hall of Fame's large archives. The fact that the Hockey Hall of Fame is located in Toronto might be part of the reason for its enduring popularity.

The Nat Turofsky photograph of Bill Barilko's goal merited the top half of a page in the April 23 edition of the *Toronto Star*. (The were no Sunday newspapers published in Toronto in 1951, so there was a lengthy wait before most people got to look at what the photographer had snapped in such a timely manner.) The bottom half of the page contained an ad for the very Canadian product of Beehive corn syrup, an omnipresent sponsor of the NHL and hockey in general. The advert also served as a congratulatory message to the Cup-champion Maple Leafs. The advertisement claimed every member of the Toronto hockey team swore by the benefits of this easy-to-digest, marvelous, sweet, and tasty "energy food."

Foster Hewitt's call of Bill Barilko's historic goal on the English-language CBC radio was heard by approximately three million Canadian radio listeners that Saturday night. (There were only about 14 million Canadians in 1951.) His broadcast has been preserved for posterity. Here is what the famous hockey voice said during the last 33 seconds of the season-ending game:

> … Watson comes back fast at center ice…. Skating down the left wing…. Into the corner…. Shoots and hits the side of the net. Here it's right in front to Meeker! Meeker went by the net. Centered out in front! McNeil fell. In front again. Watson shoots. He shoots, he scores! Barilko! Barilko has won the Stanley Cup for the Leafs! Barilko shoots it into the net while McNeil was left all by himself. The Toronto Maple Leafs are the world champions….[21]

Although he quickly corrected himself, Hewitt had initially misidentified the shooter as Harry Watson. Watson, in fact, *had taken a swipe* at Meeker's centering pass, but he missed the puck entirely. Hewitt likely erred because he had not figured Toronto's #5 to be anywhere near the Montreal net. In fact, Before the overtime began, coach Joe Primeau had cautioned Barilko against taking unnecessary or reckless chances during the overtime and not stray too far from his defensive position. Primeau probably would have been content if Barilko had stayed near the center red line to thwart any chance of a Montreal counterattack. Given what happened, both Primeau and Barilko, who was always a bit of a maverick, could both laugh at the fact that the latter had clearly ignored a direct order from the former—and was greatly rewarded for his disobedience. Primeau, like Barilko, was hoisted on the shoulders of the Leaf players in triumph and celebration.

Making Barilko's goal even more remarkable was that he had scored it while playing with a broken nose! The mishap had occurred after Barilko collided with Montreal's Bert Olmstead in the third period which sent the Leaf tumbling into the boards. Milt Dunnell lauded Barilko's courage in returning to the game, suggesting that many NHL players would have been through for the night—and perhaps longer—after sustaining such an injury. It would almost certainly be the case today.

At her home in Timmins, Anne Barilko was listening to the HNIC broadcast on the radio. She recalled becoming overjoyed when Toronto scored—and even more so when Foster Hewitt announced that her big brother was the goal scorer.

Harry Neale remembered Barilko's game-winning tally vividly. He told Barilko biographer Kevin Shea, "[It's as if] I went to the game yesterday. Every time I see that picture of Barilko scoring, I [recall] I was about 50 feet away."[22]

The Boston Globe's report on the game—which was relegated to the sixth page of its Sunday sports coverage as baseball dominated—accurately noted, "The tally climaxed one of the most grueling Stanley Cup finals in history, which saw the bitter rivals go into sudden-death overtime in every one of the five games. It was the fourth Stanley Cup championship

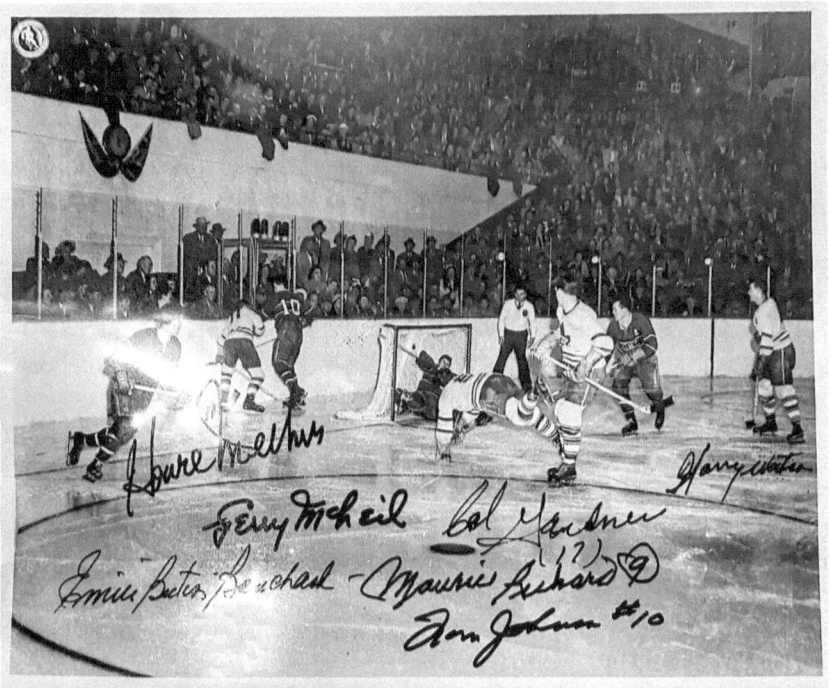

The famous image of Bill Barilko's goal has the autographs of seven of the nine individuals captured by the photograph. Only the signatures of Bill Barilko and referee Bill Chadwick are missing (courtesy Mark Fera).

in five years for the Toronto club, and its sixth in ten seasons."[23] In 1951, that represented a string of excellence unmatched in the modern era of the NHL.

Barilko's mother, Faye, was in Maple Leaf Gardens but she did not see her son's thrilling Cup-winning goal. When the overtime began, she nervously shut her eyes tightly and dared not open them until she heard the crowd's deafening roar. When she realized what had happened, Faye Barilko, began shouting repetitively in her broken English to no one in particular, "My Billy score! My Billy score!"[24] It was Barilko's only point in the entire series, although he had picked up three minor penalties in the Leafs' five games versus Montreal.

Maple Leafs fan Tom Gaston, who attended the team's first game in 1927, co-authored a book in 2001 titled *A Fan for All Seasons* about his experiences as a longtime Toronto season-ticket holder. Of course, he was present to witness hockey history that April night. In his book, Gaston described the bedlam that overtook the arena in the moments following Barilko's overtime goal. "The crowd went crazy!" he recalled. "It may well have been the loudest I ever heard Maple Leaf Gardens."[25]

Toronto captain Teeder Kennedy had an interesting perspective on the Cup triumph in the grand scheme of things. He was annoyed that the Leafs had faltered in the 1950 Stanley Cup playoffs! Had they not, the 1951 victory would have been the fifth in a row for Toronto, he pointed out to the press.

The overtime loss was a huge disappointment to the underdog visitors in red. They were thoroughly outplayed over the entire course of the tension-packed game, but they may have deserved to win based upon their display of sheer grittiness. It was certainly a heart-breaking setback for Habs coach Dick Irvin especially, seeing his team unable to secure the game after leading the contest twice and having an edge on the scoreboard with a minute to play in regulation time.

In the grand scheme of things, the Habs had nothing to hang their heads about. Picked by more than one hockey expert to finish last in 1950–51, the Canadiens had ridden a late-season spurt to rise to third place in the NHL standings, and then produced a monumental upset win over the record-breaking Detroit Red Wings in the Stanley Cup semifinals. Those thoughts of their achievements were not preeminent in the minds of the just-defeated Habs, however. Disconsolate Montreal goaltender Gerry McNeil reputedly broke into tears shortly after entering the visitors' dressing room and sitting down. (According to scribe Al Nickleson, Maurice Richard was crying too.) Similarly, Habs coach Dick Irvin only nodded and shook his head in answering reporters' queries, before he abruptly fled from his disconsolate players.

10. Game Five

Not long before he died at age 78 in 2004, McNeil told author Kevin Shea that he felt utterly lost on the ice when the game and the 1950–51 hockey season ended so suddenly. "On most goals you have a sense they are coming and you get ready," he lamented, "but this one just happened. I didn't know how the puck got in. It was just a shocker."[26] McNeil recalled that his teammates were seemingly scattered everywhere on the ice surface and he could not wait to find the exit. To their credit, however, the Canadiens sportingly stuck around long enough to congratulate the Cup winners. The now-familiar end-of-series handshake line was not yet an ingrained hockey ritual in 1951.

McNeil's play had been terrific throughout the entire contest. At one point the Montreal netminder received a long ovation from the partisan Toronto crowd after making a particularly impressive save. Early in the game he had stopped a long screen shot by … Bill Barilko. A Canadian Press reporter said "the cool rookie … had snatched a rifle-like slapshot through a crowd of players" after which even the Leaf fans "roared their applause."[27]

A quarter-century later, McNeil was philosophical and accepting about what had happened to his Habs in that year's Stanley Cup finals. He told an interviewer in 1975,

> I always look back at the 1951 series. Even though we lost, I got as much of a thrill out of that series as I got out of winning the Stanley Cup [in 1953]. We were only a third-place club, not the strong Canadien club of a few years later. In the semifinal, we beat Detroit who had won the Cup the year before. That was something: knocking out the Cup champions and then those five straight overtime games in the finals. We achieved something.

As for the remarkable string of overtime games versus Toronto in the finals, McNeil further stated,

> I don't think it's ever happened before or since. It had to play hell with the nerves, especially for the goalkeepers. There was no leeway at all in any of those games. It was either a tie game or you were ahead by a goal or behind by a goal. The other players can take out some of their tension by slamming some guy into the boards, but in net you just stand there and hope the next shot doesn't hit the post and bounce in.
>
> I didn't know it was Barilko who had scored. Half the time I never knew who scored [against me]. I didn't give a damn who it was; it was a goal.[28]

The Canadian Press amusingly reported that Bill Barilko's play on the night was typical of him. "Bashing Bill Barilko's swashbuckling hockey produces far more penalties than goals," began CP correspondent Gerry Lougheed who did not merit a byline over his story that appeared in the *Ottawa Citizen*. (He got one in the rival *Ottawa Journal*, though.) "It ran true to form Saturday night when the blond defenseman got the referee's thumb twice and scored once. But that one goal was the big one of the 1951 Stanley Cup finals...."[29]

As the Maple Leafs celebrated on the ice, their fans grew restless. They resumed their chant of "We want the Cup!" for a while. They soon got their wish. Shortly thereafter, NHL president Clarence Campbell obliged by presenting Lord Stanley's glorious old bowl to Leaf captain Ted Kennedy. (Harry Neale recalled the ceremony as being very much off-the-cuff, not nearly as choreographed as it is in the twenty-first-century NHL.) Kennedy gleefully accepted the famous trophy, spoke a few complimentary words to the happy throng, and then handed the microphone over to coach Joe Primeau. In his speech, Primeau modestly took no credit whatsoever for the Leafs' triumph. He credited the success to both the players and to Hap Day, the previous Toronto coach.

The better team had won. Although he credited Montreal with having a tremendous team, Al Nickleson wrote in the *Globe & Mail*, "Any doubt as to the proper disposition of the Cup must have been dispelled by the tremendous closing fight ... of the champions."[30] Four different men had scored the four overtime goals for Toronto, demonstrating how balanced the Maple Leafs were. None of those players had ever scored an extra-time marker in Stanley Cup play prior to 1951—and not one of them ever managed the feat again.

The Cup triumph provided something of a hockey grand slam for Joe Primeau. He had previously coached the 1949–50 Toronto Marlboros to the Allan Cup title (the national senior amateur championship of Canada) and the 1946–47 St. Michael's Majors to the Memorial Cup (the country's national junior championship). No man before or since has managed that impressive "triple crown" feat. Moreover, Primeau did it in the space of just five seasons. Milt Dunnell of the *Toronto Star* reported in his April 23 column that Primeau would step down as the Leafs coach—as had been rumored throughout the Stanley Cup finals. "Like Gene Tunney," Dunnell penned, "Primeau will retire undefeated."[31]

The crowd also demanded that Toronto's other goalie, Turk Broda, step forward and say a few words. Despite the urgings of the public and his teammates—almost to the point of them dragging Broda to the microphone that had been placed on the ice surface—the shy, veteran netminder declined to make a speech. Broda had not even dressed for the final three games of the finals. He was nattily attired in a suit and tie. Having a ready backup goalie on standby in uniform was still a decade away from being the norm for teams in the NHL.

The Maple Leafs organization suffered a minor setback that same night—make that a *minor league* setback—although few fans in the

Toronto area cared very much about it. The Pittsburgh Hornets, the Leafs' top farm team, lost the seventh game of the Calder Cup finals in Cleveland to the hometown Barons. The score was 3–1. The star of the series was Barons goaltender Johnny Bower, who would eventually become a beloved member of the Maple Leafs. Former Toronto coach Hap Day was at the game at the Cleveland Arena on April 21—not in Maple Leaf Gardens—and thus he did not witness a major moment in Toronto hockey history, nor did he hear the praiseful comments about him uttered by his successor, Joe Primeau, during the latter's postgame speech to the fans who were in no great hurry to leave the premises.

The victorious Maple Leafs happily headed to the home team's dressing room to celebrate their triumph privately, which included the traditional quaffing of champagne from the Stanley Cup. (Howie Meeker recalled decades later that his hockey stick had vanished during the postgame celebration, so he could not give it to the Toronto equipment manager as was the norm at the end of a game. He seriously wondered if he would get in trouble with team management.) A special round of cheers was given to Barilko, who was informed he had been named the game's first star by Foster Hewitt on the *HNIC* broadcast. Tod Sloan was tagged as its second star. Gerry McNeil was honored as the contest's third star. All things considered, many observers thought the order should have been reversed. The Habs had been badly outshot by a 41–19 margin in Game Five. McNeil's acrobatic goaltending had kept Montreal in the hunt in the fourth period of a contest they probably should have lost decisively in regulation time but were instead just seconds away from winning. Moreover, in the large scheme of things, Sloan's two goals in regulation time were more important in the home team's victory than Barilko's one spectacular tally in overtime.

Al Rollins got out of his heavy and sweaty goaltending gear slowly, complaining to reporters within earshot that he felt like an old man from the cumulative effects of the tension-packed playoffs. Rollins was far from aged; he was just 24½ years old. It had been a remarkable rookie year for him. He had played superbly in the Stanley Cup finals. In the three games Rollins played since he had replaced Turk Broda in the Toronto net, he had allowed just five goals in 192 minutes and 55 seconds of play. That works out to a praiseworthy goals-against average of 1.56.

The Leafs were wise enough to prepare a large room adjoined to their dressing room in case a bigger place was necessary to celebrate the Cup triumph. It proved to be very necessary. Nevertheless, the anterior room soon became overcrowded with well-wishers, both invited ones and otherwise. One welcome person who managed to squeeze into the tight confines for the merriment was Faye Barilko. She was photographed

Champagne was flowing in the anteroom within Maple Leaf Gardens where the victorious Toronto Maple Leafs celebrated their Stanley Cup win. The four men at the front of the photograph (from left) are team owner Conn Smythe, Bill Barilko, captain Ted Kennedy, and Howie Meeker (courtesy Mark Fera).

happily ladling champagne from the Stanley Cup into her son's mouth. Bill was already nattily clad in civilian clothes when the photo was taken. When he was able to talk away from the usual victory hubbub and clamor, Barilko quietly told Milt Dunnell of the *Toronto Star*, "It's been a long time coming. This is something I've dreamed about all my life."[32]

Barilko's teammates happily reminded him that his contract would soon be expiring—and he now possessed some excellent and unique leverage for a substantial raise when he got around to negotiating his new salary for the 1951–52 season. Surely, he could expect to improve on the $9,000 he had earned with the Maple Leafs in 1950–51. The fact that he had slumped badly during the early part of the regular season and had almost been demoted to the minor league Pittsburgh Hornets was forgotten. On April 21, 1951, Toronto's #5 was on top of the world.

Journalist Gerry Lougheed recalled a statement Toronto's general manager had made to him just before the 1950–51 NHL season was about to begin. Lougheed wrote, "Away back in October, Conn Smythe ... said the team's playoff chances depended on how many boys [on the Toronto

10. Game Five

roster] became men. A lot of boys became men on Saturday night. Their birthday present was the Stanley Cup."[33]

The Leafs' victory celebrations continued, but the partygoers moved the location of the festivities from Maple Leaf Gardens to a local restaurant. While there, the Toronto players were informed by Conn Smythe that all the beans had been counted and the arithmetic calculated. The figures said each player on the Stanley Cup champions would be receiving bonuses of $2,500 from the NHL. It broke down to $500 for finishing in second place during the regular season, and $1,000 for each of the two rounds of playoffs they had won to capture the Cup. (The runner-up Canadiens pulled in $1,850 apiece for their postseason and regular-season efforts.) Conn Smythe would later present each Leaf player with a special memento of the championship: a silver box with an image of the Stanley Cup engraved on it. Barilko did not stay long at the party. After a brief appearance at the eatery, he opted to join some friends for a low-key celebration at a private home.

The bonus money the Maple Leafs received was not inconsequential. It was, in fact, a small fortune for many professional hockey players in 1951—even those vying in the lofty atmosphere of the NHL. Take the case of Fern Flaman, for example. Not long after the Maple Leafs' victory celebrations had died down, Flaman, a Stanley Cup champion, reported to his summer employment at a Boston brewery. It was not a cushy position at all; it was a tough manual-labor job mainly consisting of lugging heavy beer kegs throughout a large warehouse. A photograph of Flaman hard at work was widely circulated in Canadian daily newspapers.

Despite being on the losing end of the Stanley Cup finals, Maurice Richard was lauded in an editorial that appeared in the *Ottawa Citizen* a few days later. Sports journalist Tommy Shields glowingly wrote of him,

> The word "great" can be applied, without reserve, to Montreal's Maurice Richard. The Rocket, always a blazing figure in the playoff picture, took over playoff scoring records from Toe Blake by his outstanding work, and his last-game goal showed that he still was the Habs' big gun and inspiration, even in defeat. Whether or not they liked him before this series started, partisan Toronto fans must admit that Richard is entitled to a place among the most brilliant payers in the long history of hockey.[34]

In the five games of 1951 Stanley Cup playoff finals, Montreal had scored exactly 10 goals. The fabulous Maurice Richard, who was likely at the apex of his playing ability that spring, accounted for fully half of them. He also assisted on two of the other five goals scored by the defeated Canadiens.

In 2019, TheHockeyWriters.com website featured a retrospective piece about the whole 1951 NHL playoffs. It said, in part, "The '51 Stanley

Cup finals between Toronto and Montreal was one of the most highly anticipated series in the 'Original Six era' and is often looked upon by the period's contemporary observers as some of the best hockey ever played."[35]

With all five games between the Canadiens and Maple Leafs being decided dramatically in sudden-death overtime, it is extremely difficult to refute that statement.

Game Five Scoring Summary
Montreal 2 at Toronto 3 (OT)
April 21, 1951

First Period
No scoring

Second Period
1. MTL Maurice Richard (Bud McPherson) 8:56
2. TOR Tod Sloan (Ted Kennedy) 12:00

Third Period
3. MTL Paul Meger (Doug Harvey) 4:47
4. TOR Tod Sloan (Max Bentley, Sid Smith) 19:28

Overtime
5. TOR Bill Barilko (Howie Meeker, Harry Watson) 2:53

11

Post-Series Miscellany

On Monday, The *Toronto Star* reported that an enterprising 24-year-old male strayed beyond the bounds of the local commercial laws with his entrepreneurial skills. He was arrested outside Maple Leaf Gardens on Saturday evening. His crime? He attempted to sell a $5 ticket to Game Five of the Stanley Cup finals for the inflated price of $15. His case was dealt with swiftly. On Monday, April 23, he appeared in the local magistrate's court and quickly pled guilty to a charge of selling a sports ticket for more than it was worth, a misdemeanor offense. The man had the choice of paying a $10 fine or spending five days in the city's hoosegow. He opted for the former. Somewhat ironically, the culprit's name was John Sellars.

Not only were the NHL and AHL championships for the 1950–51 season decided on April 21, so were the National Basketball Association's champs. The winners, in seven games, were the Rochester Royals. They beat the New York Knickerbockers, 79–75, before 4,206 paying customers at the Rochester Sports Arena. With their hard-fought victory, the Royals avoided a catastrophic collapse. The had won the first three games of the best-of-seven finals, but the Knicks took the next three contests to force a winner-take-all Game Seven.

The awarding of the Stanley Cup and Calder Cup did not mean it was the end of the hockey season in Canada. The two major amateur trophies were still up for grabs. The arduous rounds for both the Allan Cup and Memorial Cup playoffs were not even close to being decided. In fact, the finals had not begun for either of the prized baubles. Games would extend well into May, something unheard of in the NHL in 1951.

The Stanley Cup was the seventh won by Conn Smythe as an NHL general manager—all with the Toronto Maple Leafs, of course. That achievement tied him with much more mobile Tommy Gorman whose seven Cups came with four different teams, two of which were now defunct. Three Gorman triumphs came with the old Ottawa Senators, one with the Montreal Maroons, one with the Chicago Black Hawks, and two with the Montreal Canadiens.

Dink Carroll of the *Montreal Gazette* wrote in the April 24 edition, "The Canadiens had recovered sufficiently yesterday from their Stanley Cup defeat to assemble at the Forum and have a group picture taken."[1] There were two absentees, however. Bob Dawes was still recuperating in a Toronto hospital with a compound leg fracture. Ross Lowe resided near Toronto. With no further games to play, Lowe chose not to make the trip back to Montreal with the rest of the Habs. The players on the Canadiens had an unofficial team party at the restaurant owned by Butch Bouchard in the east end of Montreal on Sunday night. Carroll added there would be no official wrap-up party for the team since they did not win the Stanley Cup. The scribe did say that the Habs "came close enough to make prospects for next season look especially bright, if a couple of new players can be added to bolster weak spots."[2]

Bill Tobin, the president of the Chicago Black Hawks, shed some important light on an incident from Game Four. He told the press that Conn Smythe had *not* gotten into a physical altercation with NHL president Clarence Campbell at the Forum after a penalty call went against Toronto's Max Bentley, as had been widely reported in newspapers across Canada. Tobin said the truth was that Smythe had tried to attack *him*—and Campbell had gotten into the middle of it as a peacemaker. Tobin did not divulge what exactly was said by either party to cause the ruckus, but he commented that Smythe likely knew that Bentley's hooking penalty was deserved because it happened right in front of him. "He was just trying to give his team a lift,"[3] Tobin surmised.

Three days after Toronto had finished off the Habs at Maple Leaf Gardens, the sports department of the *Montreal Gazette* was still bemoaning the bad breaks the Habs had gotten in the five-game championship series. A huge drawing created by the paper's house cartoonist, John Collins, spelled things out with more than a little bit of creativity on his part. He emphasized his point using upper-case letters in strategic certain phrases from "Barilko's goal," "Rollins' goaling," and so forth to vertically spell out THE BREAKS.

How Close Were the 1951 Stanley Cup Finals?

So how close were the 1951 Stanley Cup finals? It seems like a silly question considering all five games went into overtime before a winner was decided. Four of the games ended in 3–2 scores, while one finished with a 2–1 count. Even those factual statements do not do justice to the tightness of this series. An examination of the numbers gives more perspective.

11. Post-Series Miscellany

Counting the minutes and seconds of the overtime periods as well as the 300 minutes of regulation time the Maple Leafs and the Canadiens played in those five games, the elapsed playing time for the entire series was 321 minutes and 41 seconds. In other words, the Habs and Leafs were on the ice for the equivalent of sixteen 20-minute periods plus an additional 101 seconds. In all that time, Toronto never led in any game by two goals! On the other side of the coin, Montreal held a two-goal edge only once. It was a brief spell: The Canadiens led Game Two by two goals for only six minutes and seven seconds! Simple arithmetic says that the games were either tied or one team had a tenuous one-goal lead for 315 and 34 seconds. That is approximately 98.1 percent of the time.

The amount of time the two teams were tied during each game was also enormous. Over the five compelling contests, Toronto and Montreal were tied for precisely 165 minutes and 47 seconds of playing time. This accounts for about 51.5 percent of the total game time in the whole series. Thus, better than half the time during the five-game series, the scoreboard at the Forum or at Maple Gardens would have shown the score of any given game to be level.

In Games Three and Five, both won by Toronto, the Maple Leafs did not hold a lead at any time during regulation play. They did not surge in front until winning those two contests in overtime. Toronto never held a lead at all in Game Two—the only game in the finals that the Leafs lost. Montreal never held a lead in either Game One or Four, but the Habs never trailed by more than a single tally. Montreal actually led games for a longer stretch of time (85:57) than Toronto did (69:57)—an advantage of exactly 16 minutes.

For what it is worth, the two teams were almost level in penalty minutes in the five-game finals. Montreal was whistled for 47 minutes' worth of infractions while Toronto had 45.

The numbers do not lie. Despite being huge underdogs, and despite losing four of five games to the champions from Toronto, the Montreal Canadiens were an extremely competitive team during the 1951 Stanley Cup finals. Perhaps Dick Irvin was fully justified in bemoaning that the elusive breaks in the series simply did not go the way of the Habs. It had been quite a series. Here are the precise figures:

Total time played in the series: 321:41
Total time in which games were tied: 165:47
Total time in which Toronto led by one goal: 69:57
Total time in which Toronto led by two goals: 0:00
Total time in which Montreal led by one goal: 79:50
Total time in which Montreal led by two goals: 6:07

Why Did Toronto Win the Series?

Had the Montreal Canadiens emerged victorious in 1950–51, the narrative likely would have been that Maurice "Rocket" Richard had carried the team on his back and goaltender Gerry McNeil had stymied the Toronto Maple Leafs. However, there was no singular scoring superman for the victors, nor was there an awe-inspiring individual guarding the goal line for the victors. Simply put, Toronto had the steadier, more balanced team for the five-game finals compared to their overmatched opponents. More than 70 years later, we can peel back that simplification of how they did it and offer a little more analysis.

Let's begin with goaltending: The Canadiens used Gerry McNeil as their netminder for every second of every contest of the five-game affair. McNeil's losing record of one win against four losses might imply that he was subpar at his position, but that is quite far from being the case. The Montreal goalie had managed to keep his team in every contest and played well enough that his team could have (and probably should have) won more games than they ultimately did. Every reporter covering the Stanley Cup finals acknowledged McNeil's excellent play and its importance to the Habs' chances of achieving an upset win in the series. The Maple Leafs countered with a goaltending tandem of Turk Broda and Al Rollins. The aging Broda, who began the series for the first two games filling in for the injured Rollins, played well enough that his record could just as easily have been a pair of victories instead of winning just the one game. When Rollins took over the netminding duties for the remaining three games, he was even more stellar than his older and more famous teammate, backstopping the Maple Leafs to three straight overtime victories. McNeil was great, but the duo of Broda and Rollins was even more so.

All five games of the Cup finals went into extra time, of course. Each of those games produced a different overtime hero. The difference here being that the hero for the Montreal Canadiens, as was so often the case in 1950–51, was the unparalleled Maurice Richard who netted five of the 10 goals for his squad in the finals and the only overtime winner for Les Habitants. Toronto managed to produce four different overtime scorers: Sid Smith, Ted Kennedy, Harry Watson and the immortal Bill Barilko. These four superstars of the series accounted for nine of the 13 goals scored by the Maple Leafs against the Canadiens. Doug Harvey provided the lone overtime assist for Montreal and finished tied with teammate Bill Reay for second on the squad in points to Richard's seven with three apiece. Toronto, once again saw four players picking up helpers in the extra frames. Harry Watson, Howie Meeker, Max Bentley and Ted Sloan. (Sloan was the only player on either team to pick up two.) The more balanced offensive

11. Post-Series Miscellany

A publicity photograph of the 1950–51 Stanley Cup Champion Toronto Maple Leafs. Bill Barilko is standing in the back row, third from the right (courtesy Mark Fera).

showing by the Toronto Maple Leafs over the Montreal Canadiens proved to be a huge difference in the series' outcome.

Toronto also took timely advantage of critical errors by the Habs at opportune times. The tying goal in Game Five could be attributed to the Habs choosing the wrong faceoff man to face Teeder Kennedy in the final minute of regulation time. Furthermore, at least two of Toronto's four overtime goals was the direct result of careless (and fatal) Montreal blunders. If the Maple Leafs got the majority of the series' breaks, as the Montreal sports journalists often claimed, Toronto's diligence and hockey smarts certainly helped create many of them. As the adage states, "Luck is the residue of hard work."

If we look at coaching, Dick Irvin of the Montreal Canadiens was in his 22nd season behind an NHL bench, having previously won Lord Stanley's silver chalice twice with his current team and once as the man guiding the successful Toronto Maple Leafs in just his third season in the league. In 1950–51, Joe Primeau was in just his first season as the Leafs coach, but he would not have a lengthy tenure there. He would be replaced after Toronto failed to qualify for the Stanley playoffs in 1952–53. Primeau never coached again afterward—which was probably a shame, given his outstanding résumé in so many tiers of Canada's beloved sport. The experience of Dick Irvin was likely a major factor in why each game was as close as it was. Primeau was blessed to have the more balanced squad, which was good enough to offset his lack of NHL experience compared to the more seasoned Irvin.

Whenever any series in any sport is as closely contested as the 1950–51 Stanley Cup finals were, there are numerous factors which ultimately could be the reason a particular team emerges victorious. A lucky bounce here, or a player temporarily out of position there, can often turn the tide of such tightly fought matches. The caliber of the Maple Leafs team overall was just a bit better than that of the Habs. The passage of time would see more victors from the 1950–51 Cup champions earn their way into the Hockey Hall of Fame than their opponents. That list included such luminaries as Harry Watson, Ted Kennedy and Turk Broda for Toronto and Maurice Richard and Doug Harvey for Montreal. (Richard is one of only 10 players to have the customary three-year waiting period for entrance into the HHOF waived after his retirement in the spring of 1960 following Montreal's historic fifth consecutive Stanley Cup triumph.) Both coaches, Dick Irvin and Joe Primeau, would be enshrined in the Hall of Fame as well.

Whatever the reason or reasons for Toronto's eventual Cup triumph, the championship showdown of the 1950–51 NHL season provided hockey fans with five highly entertaining games of edge-of-your seat, end-to-end action. More than seven decades have steadily elapsed since Bill Barilko's dramatic heroics ended the series in the fifth game, but the 1951 NHL finals remains the only time in the long history of Stanley Cup play in which every game of a best-of-seven series—in any round of the league's playoffs—required extra time to determine a winner. In this spectacular championship tussle, 60 minutes was never long enough.

12

Studs and Duds of the 1950–51 Stanley Cup Finals

"One man can be a crucial ingredient on a team, but one man cannot make a team."[1]—Kareem Abdul-Jabbar

Team sports offer a fascinating study of human dynamics. Watching a team's quest for superiority within its respective league can often teach even the most casual observer some valuable lessons. "Quitters never win and winners never quit" is a saying heard in practically every locker room at every level of organized sport. Drive and determination, of course, can go a long way to showcasing a team's success. Sometimes the team that hoists the championship trophy is one that has demonstrated undeniable teamwork, operating as a well-oiled machine, while other times lucky bounces can be the author of destiny. Usually, a team's superstars carry the weight of the club on their shoulders. However, sometimes relatively unknowns are given a chance to rise to the occasion, pick up the slack of their slumping teammates, and become heroes, at least for a short time. Here is a look at the "studs and duds" of the 1950–51 Stanley Cup finals.

Montreal Canadiens: Studs

Maurice Richard was the most dominant player in the series on either team. The Montreal Canadiens only managed 10 goals in the five-game series. Richard scored half of them, netting exactly one goal in every game of the series. Three of those goals gave his team either the lead or the win; the other two leveled the score. Richard also assisted on a pair of Montreal goals, ultimately factoring in on 70 percent of his team's tallies. He was undeniably the top stud for the Habs.

After a starring performance in the Habs' amazing semifinal upset of Detroit, **Gerry McNeil**'s performance tailed off slightly in the finals. McNeil allowed 12 goals in six games to the Red Wings while giving up 13 goals in five games to the eventual Stanley Cup–winning Toronto Maple Leafs. The Montreal netminder gave his team an opportunity to win every game despite the Canadiens entering the series as heavy underdogs. So, despite his 1–4 win-loss record, McNeil was a stud.

Doug Harvey was the best offensive defenseman for the Canadiens as he finished the 1950–51 NHL season fifth on his team with 29 points. During Montreal's semifinal series versus Detroit, Harvey only had a pair of helpers, but in the finals, he picked up an assist on Maurice Richard's Game Two overtime winner with an excellent pass that sent the Rocket alone on Turk Broda. Harvey finished the series with three assists.

Although **Paul Masnick** had just two points for the series, the pair of goals he scored were timely ones. Like Richard, Masnick's goals either tied a game or put the Habs in the lead. Considering Masnick did not put the puck in the net even once during the six-game semifinal with Detroit, and he only had four goals and one assist in 43 games during the regular season, his two-goal performance versus Toronto elevated him to stud status.

Billy Reay led Montreal in the Stanley Cup finals with three assists, factoring in on nearly a third of all the goals for the Habs. It was a typically solid performance for one of the most underrated Canadiens of that era.

Montreal Canadiens: Duds

Ken Mosdell had a reliable regular season, in which he picked up 13 goals and 18 assists for 31 points (fourth most on the team) in 66 games during the regular season for the Habs. Mosdell was quite close to maintaining that scoring pace in the Canadiens' surprising semifinal victory over Detroit with a goal and an assist in six games. However, in the five-game finals, Mosdell never once factored into any of Montreal's goals. With such a close series, any points from any source could have turned the tide. Thus, Mosdell's statistical bagels relegate him to one of Montreal's duds.

In 1950–51, **Floyd Curry** posted very similar numbers to teammate Ken Mosdell. Curry, like Mosdell, had 13 goals but four fewer assists (14) in three extra games during the regular season. Also following in his teammate's footsteps, Curry had two points in the semifinals versus Detroit, albeit just a pair of assists. Continuing to mirror his fellow Hab, Curry failed to find his name attached to any of Montreal's goals in the finals against Toronto. For this reason, Curry finds his name affixed to the list of duds.

12. Studs and Duds of the 1950–51 Stanley Cup Finals

Bernie Geoffrion had a goal and an assist versus Detroit in the semifinal round but failed to produce even a single point in the Stanley Cup finals. Despite being only 19 years old and playing in just 18 games during the regular season, Boom Boom put up eight goals and six assists averaging 0.77 points per game. The Canadiens did not need much more scoring to turn the series around and Geoffrion was one dud that could have made a huge difference.

Considering that **Elmer Lach** finished the 1950–51 season second on the team in points with 45, notching 21 goals and sharing the team lead in assists with 24, his dismal performance of just a single goal came as quite a disappointment. Lach averaged 0.2 points per game in the finals, a considerable decline from his 0.69 points per game in the regular season.

Bert Olmstead only played in 39 games during the 1950–51 season for the Canadiens, but he averaged nearly a point per game as he finished the season with 38 points. Olmstead had two goals and two assists in the semifinal series versus Detroit, placing him second on the team to Richard in points for the series. Thus, his subpar performance of just a pair of assists in the five-game Stanley Cup finals must earn him a spot on this list of duds.

Toronto Maple Leafs: Studs

Bill Barilko only had a single point in the Stanley finals versus Montreal, a goal. However, it immediately became "The Goal" and catapulted him into instant fame with Toronto fans, enshrining Barilko as a beloved player. Barilko's unexpected disappearance and death that summer and subsequently becoming the subject of a very popular song by The Tragically Hip have immortalized Barilko's moment of fame for eternity and, in totality, have crowned him "King Stud" for the series—if one happens to be a Toronto Maple Leafs supporter.

During the Stanley Cup final, **Tod Sloan** led the Maple Leafs in scoring with seven points, coming from three goals and four assists. Half of Sloan's assists came in overtime. Sloan's Game One marker put his team up 2–1 late in the first period. His other two goals came in Game Five, the second of which was scored in the final minute of play to force overtime. Overshadowed by Bill Barilko's famous tally, Sloan's game-tying goal may be the most underrated marker in the long history of the Toronto Maple Leafs.

After being injured in the semifinals against Boston, goaltender **Al Rollins** returned to the net in Game Three of the Stanley Cup finals versus Montreal and proceeded to win all three contests in which he was involved. His minuscule goals-against-average of 1.56 is certainly enough to elevate him to stud level.

Sid Smith scored five of the 13 goals for Toronto, accounting for roughly 38.5 percent of the Maple Leafs' tallies. One of those goals was the Game One overtime winner, the other four goals were each the opening goal scored by the Leafs in the first four games of the series. Two of Smith's goals came within the first minute of play in both Game One and Game Four. Smith had 12 power play goals in 70 games during the regular season, but he elevated his play with the man advantage in the finals, pocketing a pair of power play markers in just five games.

Max Bentley led the Maple Leafs in scoring during the 1950–51 regular season with 62 points. Although he failed to score a single goal in the finals, he was able to pick up four assists, with one of his helpers coming in overtime.

Ted Kennedy carried his consistent play from the regular season into the playoffs. One of Teeder's two goals in the championship series was the Game Three overtime winner, while the other leveled the score in Game Two and sent that game into overtime.

In what amounted to a terrific last hurrah for a beloved veteran, **Turk Broda** was suddenly pressed into postseason service for Toronto due to an injury suffered by goaltender Al Rollins in Game One of the semifinals versus Boston. Broda promptly picked up a pair of shutouts versus the Bruins. Broda continued his excellence in net in the finals against Montreal. He won Game One and despite losing Game Two, his fine play has earned him a spot on this list.

Howie Meeker averaged about two points every five games during the 1950–51 regular season for Toronto. In the finals, he maintained that pace picking up one goal and one assist. His lone assist, however, was on Bill Barilko's goal that sealed the famous Stanley Cup victory for the Maple Leafs.

Harry Watson picked up 37 points in the regular season in the 68 games he played for the Maple Leafs. In the finals, Watson had a goal and two assists. Two of his points came in overtimes including his Game Four winner putting Toronto up three games to one at the time. Watson was one of the players who assisted on Bill Barilko's Cup-clinching goal in Game Five.

Toronto Maple Leafs: Duds

Danny Lewicki was in his first season in the NHL in 1950–51. As a rookie, Lewicki posted a very respectable showing of 16 goals and 18 assists. However, he failed to record a single point in any of the nine games he found himself in during the post season. A disappointment that has him firmly placed on the duds list.

Fleming Mackell was coming off his best regular season to date with 25 points. (He topped that mark several times later in his career as a member of the Boston Bruins.) His 12 goals during the 1950–51 campaign were more than half the total he scored in his first five seasons in the NHL. During the semifinals against Boston, Mackell found the net twice and added three assists. Thus, his inability to record a point in the Stanley Cup finals gets him a spot on the Maple Leafs' roster of duds.

Jimmy Thomson had a career year for the Maple Leafs in 1950–51. He scored only three times but added 33 assists for 36 points. It was the only time in the defenseman's 12 years in the NHL where he would score more than 30 points in a regular season. In the postseason, however, Thomson picked up just a single assist in Toronto's semifinal series triumph versus Boston … and then nothing at all in the Cup finals against Montreal.

Cal Gardner finished the 1950–51 regular season with 23 goals and 28 assists for the Maple Leafs. The 51 points accrued was good enough to tie with Sid Smith for 4th most on the team. Gardner only managed a single goal and an assist in the semifinals with Boston but in the Cup finals, Gardner came up empty failing to register a single point.

Joe Klukay was never one of the top performers, scoring-wise during his stint with the Maple Leafs, having recorded a career-best 31 points during the 1949–50 regular season. In 1950–51, he was just one point shy of his top seasonal performance. (Klukay would eventually raise this mark in 1953–54 as a member of the Boston Bruins to 37.) He managed to excel in the semifinal series versus Boston, scoring four goals and adding a trio of helpers, thus the bagels he threw up on the scoreboards in the finals has him on the list of duds for Toronto.

13

The Short Life, Disappearance and Recovery of Bill Barilko

Before He Was Famous

On Saturday, April 21, 1951, Bill Barilko became a household name in Canada just by scoring a timely goal in the Stanley Cup playoffs. But who was he before he scored the biggest goal of his hockey career (and probably the most famous tally in the long history of the Toronto Maple Leafs)?

On March 25, 1927, William (Bill) Barilko was born in Timmins, Ontario, in what is considered northeastern Ontario. It is located on the Mattagami River. The city's economy is based on mining and lumber. Mining was absolutely the major industry at the time of Barilko's birth. Gold was discovered in the area in 1909. A visitor is just as likely to encounter a francophone in Timmins as an anglophone. According to the 2021 census, half the current population of about 44,000 is bilingual. Like numerous Canadian towns and cities, cold and long winters made hockey a popular pastime in Timmins. A local joke says a year in Timmins consists of 10 months of snow and two months of bad hockey weather. Still, between 1921 and 1931—the decade in which Bill Barilko was born—Timmins' population grew from 3,800 to 14,200, indicating it was, despite the elements, a prosperous community.

Barilko's parents, Steve and Feodosia, were immigrants of what would now be called Polish/Ukrainian descent. Steve Barilko arrived in Canada in 1910 when he was 17 or 18 years old; his exact date of birth is uncertain. Feodosia Karpinchuk arrived as a 25-year-old sometime in late 1924. She was fleeing a period of the Russian Revolution when Poles were in serious danger of being overrun. A cousin had sponsored Feodosia's immigration process, which fast-tracked her to Timmins. Within three weeks of her

13. The Short Life, Disappearance and Recovery of Bill Barilko 143

arrival there, Feodosia was married to Steve Barilko. The circumstances behind the speedy marriage were never openly discussed in the family, but the three Barilko children (Alex, Bill, and Anne, born in that order) always assumed their parents' nuptials had been arranged well before their mother ever set foot in Canada.

There were not many luxuries in the spartan Barilko household. Steve Barilko worked as a full-time cook in a mining camp and was often only home on weekends. He learned to speak English quickly through his interactions with the miners. Faye, however, never had any formal education during her life, never learned to read or write, and spoke in broken English until the day she died. Steve tried to teach his wife whatever he could about the language with only partial success. (Nevertheless, according to Maple Leafs superfan and Bill Barilko authority Mark Fera, English was the language most often spoken in the Barilko household.) When roads in the region became more plentiful and accessible all-year round, miners no longer needed to permanently reside in camps. Accordingly, cooks for the men were no longer required. Steve was now out of a permanent job and had to seek employment wherever he could find it. The Barilko family lived modestly, occasionally teetering on penury.

Sports were a foreign concept to both Steve and Faye Barilko, but not to their boys. Bill played outdoor hockey for recreation as did his brother, Alex, who was 13 months older. "Alex was the better hockey player, but Bill worked harder,"[1] opined Fera. The second son was a late bloomer when it came to Canada's favorite sport. The two Barilko boys did not have skates at the same early age that most other Canadian boys normally got them. Initially, Bill was such a poor skater that he played in goal during most of his formative hockey years. However, endless practice, going forward and backward, eventually made his skating passable. (It never really reached NHL caliber.) All the skating was done outdoors, quite often in frightfully cold weather. Timmins sometimes had as many as 17 public outdoor rinks when the Barilko children were growing up. The lone indoor arena in the community burned down in a 1947 fire. For years afterward, Timmins had no real hockey arena. Nevertheless, with every boy in town seemingly spending every spare moment on the ice, northern Ontario became a hockey hotbed. Scouts routinely enticed promising players to join prestigious amateur teams in southern Ontario towns and cities.

At school, Bill constantly struggled. He was a poor student. His spelling was especially atrocious. Not surprisingly, he had precious little interest in anything related to academics. Bill spent three years trying to get through the eighth grade. With his mother's blessing, he finally gave up on schooling altogether at age 15 and worked for a time as a truck driver.

Bill's winning personality made him a popular fellow with most everyone he encountered.

By the end of the Second World War, Bill Barilko was playing defense for the Holman Pluggers, a very talented juvenile team that won several regional and provincial titles. Two years earlier, he had been the team's stick boy and emergency backup goaltender. The Pluggers—named for and sponsored by local mining supply company—graduated several players into the National Hockey League. The most noteworthy was Allan Stanley, who was a year older than Barilko. (Stanley would eventually play 1,244 games in hockey's top professional circuit before retiring in 1969 at age 43.) Barilko's dedication to the sport kept paying off. By age 17 he was playing defense for Timmins' strong senior amateur team. That same year, as one of Ontario's most promising junior hockey players, Barilko was selected to play in the equivalent of a prospects game at Maple Leaf Gardens in Toronto.

Sadly, Steven Barilko, Bill's father, never lived to see his son reach the pinnacle of hockey. He died in his early fifties in 1946, the result of a tragic fall down a flight of stairs at his place of employment.

By the 1946–47 season, Barilko had signed a pro hockey contract. He was playing for the Hollywood Wolves of the Pacific Coast Hockey League—the lowest possible tier in the professional sport's ranks. The pay was lousy but there were some undeniable perquisites. The weather in exotic Hollywood was marvelous, certainly superior to what he was used to in Timmins. There was also the frequent hobnobbing with Hollywood starlets. Bill Barilko was a strikingly handsome, fair, curly-haired, blue-eyed young man and something of a local celebrity because he was an athlete. Hollywood press agents sometimes had Barilko pose for publicity pictures with upcoming starlets. It was a win-win-win situation. The movie studios and the hockey team both got publicity, and of course, it was highly doubtful that Bill had any gripes about the obvious benefits of his exploitation.

On February 5, 1947, in the middle of a Hollywood Wolves home game, Barilko was notified that he was urgently needed elsewhere up the pro hockey ladder. The 20-year-old Barilko was ordered to report immediately to the Pittsburgh Hornets, the Toronto Maple Leafs' affiliate in the American Hockey League. He never suited up for a single minute with that AHL club. The Leafs were suddenly battling a spate of injuries too—especially among their defensive corps—so Barilko was quickly rerouted to Toronto. It was an almost unheard-of promotion at the time. (The equivalent today would be a player suddenly ascending from the East Coast Hockey League to the NHL with no stops between the two.) Barilko had a special hockey talent, though, that would soon be on display in the NHL.

13. The Short Life, Disappearance and Recovery of Bill Barilko

He was a bruising defenseman who could deliver clean, punishing, and highly effective body checks to opponents. It earned him the alliterative nickname "Bashing Bill." Barilko played in the final 18 regular season games for Toronto—and in the Maple Leafs' 11 Stanley Cup playoff games that spring.

Newspapers in Toronto found out what their counterparts in Hollywood already knew: Images of Barilko on their pages were always popular with female readers. "Photographers loved snapping pictures of the young, dashing Barilko alongside any pretty girl they could find. He was quickly becoming one of Toronto's most eligible bachelors,"[2] wrote Jamie Hayes in a nostalgia article years later.

"[He] could hit like a ton," teammate Howie Meeker glowingly said of Barilko. "He made [our defense] big, he made it tough, and he made it mean."[3] Ted Kennedy remembered that Barilko was an impressive physical specimen. While not an excellent skater, the Leaf captain remembers Barilko being strong on his skates and having a love for the physical aspects of hockey. "When he got somebody along the boards, he'd rub him out. He had a back on him that was huge. [It] was about four feet wide."[4]

In his very first NHL game, on February 6, 1947, Barilko leveled two big-name Montreal Canadiens with his soon-to-be-feared lethal bodychecks. The victims were two of the Habs' biggest stars: Maurice Richard and Butch Bouchard. Not long afterward, Bashing Bill sent Milt Schmidt of the Boston Bruins airborne with a perfectly timed hit. A photo of the incident was widely published in newspapers across Canada.

In an early interview he did with a scribe from the Toronto *Globe & Mail*, Barilko stated he intended to make pro hockey his livelihood for as long as possible and he would strive to stay in the NHL with the Maple Leafs. He timed his ascension quite well. The Leafs won three straight Stanley Cups in 1947, 1948 and 1949—a first for any team in the modern era of professional hockey. In the 1947–48 season, Barilko led the NHL in penalty minutes with 147. He was obviously a tough customer. He was durable too. In 1948–49 he played in all 60 regular-season games for Toronto.

The team's streak of Cup championships ended in 1950 with a heartbreaking seventh-game loss in a playoff semifinal series to Detroit, but thanks to a much-talked-about goal scored by Bill Barilko, the bruising basher from Timmins, the Stanley Cup returned to Toronto in the spring of 1951. That season had been oddly difficult for Barilko. He seemed to shy away from his legendary bodychecking early in the season. He was rumored to be heading for demotion to Toronto's top farm team in Pittsburgh, but he suddenly turned his game around. *The Hockey News* edition of January 6, 1951, featured an article that noted, "Bill Barilko has been a big disappointment this season. His play has fallen way off and he's been riding the bench in a number of games of late. This has been one of Barilko's poorer seasons." However, the demotion of some of Barilko's teammates seemed to jolt him out of his funk. Things turned around rapidly. By the first week in March, Barilko had been named Player of the Week by that same hockey publication.

When the 1950–51 NHL season ended, the 24-year-old Barilko's overall stats showed he had played slightly more than four seasons with the Toronto Maple Leafs. Over that time, he had played in 252 NHL games, scored 26 goals, tallied 36 assists, and had accrued the sizable total of 456 penalty minutes. (He had even scored on a penalty shot versus Boston in a 1950 game!) In his 47 career NHL playoff games, Barilko had scored five goals, assisted on seven others, and amassed 104 minutes in penalties.

There was no doubt that Bill Barilko belonged in the NHL and had become a reliable fixture on the roster of the Toronto Maple Leafs.

His Disappearance

> "Bill Barilko—national hero, man of mystery."[5]—Was El-Halabi, *Bleacher Report*

The death of Bill Barilko has sometimes been called Canada's version of the Buddy Holly tragedy. Except for the fact that they were both very young men at the time of their deaths and they both perished as passengers in aviation mishaps, there really is no comparison, however. Holly's airplane crashed a few minutes after takeoff. Its wreckage was found within hours. The small aircraft carrying Bill Barilko flew off from a remote fueling station and went down somewhere in the thick forests of northern Ontario. His fate was a much-pondered mystery that lasted for nearly 11 years.

On the night of April 21, 1951, Toronto Maple Leaf defenseman Bill Barilko scored the Stanley Cup winning goal to defeat the Montreal Canadiens before a raucous, overflow crowd at Maple Leaf Gardens. Slightly more than four months later he was presumed to be dead. The small airplane in which Barilko was a passenger had disappeared somewhere over the thickly tree-covered and largely inaccessible regions of rugged northern Ontario.

As was his summer tradition, the 24-year-old Barilko returned to his hometown to visit and stay with his widowed mother in Timmins, Ontario. On Friday, August 24, 1951, the Toronto Maple Leaf defenseman accepted an invitation on short notice to join a local dentist, 49-year-old Dr. Henry Hudson, on a flight aboard Hudson's private aircraft. It was a standard Fairchild 24 floatplane, common to the region, which had been painted a distinctively bright shade of yellow. Their destination was the small community of Seal River, a remote village on the shore of James Bay in northern Quebec. The hard-to-get-to locale was a favorite relaxing spot of Dr. Hudson's, who, according to later newspaper stories, had been a licensed pilot for about five years. Whenever the fickle weather of northern Ontario allowed it, the dentist often flew to James Bay during the summer weekends to engage in his favorite hobby. Hudson wanted Barilko to accompany him for one of his fishing outings. (The offer was made to Barilko after another friend of Dr. Hudson, a local man named Archie Chenier, suddenly cancelled on the dentist because he was unexpectedly summoned to work by his employer.) Ironically Barilko never ate fish himself—he hated the taste of them—but like Dr. Hudson, Barilko too loved fishing as a relaxing summer pastime. He quicky and happily accepted the fateful invitation.

Barilko's 52-year-old mother, Feodosia, was nicknamed Faye or Fay; spellings vary depending upon the source. She later told the *Toronto Star* that she had had a premonition that something bad might happen to Dr. Hudson's airplane when it was flying over the dense bush in the middle of nowhere. (In a 2021 interview with TV Ontario, Barilko's nephew, Frank Klisanich, said that his grandmother was not specifically opposed to Bill going on the fishing trip; however, she was opposed to him departing on a Friday. Faye associated Fridays with bad luck because her husband had died suddenly on a Friday five years earlier. Bill Barilko, had been born on a Friday, however.) Accordingly, Faye urged her son to change his mind about accepting the dentist's kind offer. The handsome hockey player cavalierly laughed at her superstitious motherly concerns. Her son's dismissive reaction angered Faye so much that, in a fit of pique, she rashly refused to say goodbye to him when he left her house to meet Hudson for their flight.

Their pontoon plane departed from a lake located in South Porcupine, Ontario. The men told friends and family members they would likely return on Sunday—or Monday, at the very latest—if bad weather happened to set in. In northern Ontario, that scenario was always a distinct possibility at any time throughout the year. Certainly, Barilko wanted to return home on Sunday. He and three other NHL players from Timmins were going to be treated to a special farewell dinner on Sunday evening at the home of a hockey-loving private citizen before they headed off to their respective clubs' training camps. Hudson also had his usual schedule of dental patients to see on Monday. Thus, everyone who knew about the men's trip fully expected the two fishermen to return to Timmins sometime on Sunday.

Rupert House (also called Rupert's House or Ruppert's House in

1951)—now known by its traditional native name of Waskaganish—was a tiny stopover community in Quebec for the region's bush pilots. Dr. Hudson set his airplane down there to have it refueled. He and Barilko cheerfully conversed with a chatty 18-year-old named James Crawford who took care of filling the plane's gas tank. (Crawford was not a hockey fan at the time, so he had no idea he was talking to the man who had scored the famous Stanley Cup–winning goal for the Toronto Maple Leafs just four months earlier.) Barilko told Crawford that he and Dr. Hudson would be fishing for Arctic char and, as a gift, would bring him a sample when they returned to Rupert House on their way back home, likely on Sunday. Crawford loved fresh fish, so he was delighted by that promise. The two travelers said their goodbyes to the happy teenager and departed for their destination at Seal Lake.

When they arrived there, the twosome would have established a campsite near the water, erecting their tents. They presumably would have begun fishing immediately. Evidently it was a happy and hugely successful vacation for the two avid fishermen. The fish at that locale were more than plentiful—and they were eagerly biting. About 150 pounds of Arctic char were stored in the plane's pontoons when they departed for home! On their way back to Timmins, Barilko and Hudson made a special stop in tiny Fort George, Quebec (now known as Chicasibi). Concerned about the extra weight from the massive volume of fish now in their airplane, the men received permission from the Shepherds, a local missionary family, to leave their bulky camping supplies and fishing gear with them until they returned to the region sometime in 1952. Barilko, in high spirits, told the awestruck Shepherd children that he would get them Maple Leaf hockey tickets if they were ever in Toronto during the NHL season. The Shepherds cordially invited the men to their house for tea, but Dr. Hudson politely declined the pleasantry. He insisted they had to be home for supper in Timmins that night—and to put their heavy cargo of fresh fish on ice before it spoiled.

The twosome made one further stop at Rupert's House to refuel their yellow aircraft. A 23-year-old employee named Dan Wheeler completed the task this time. He later recalled that Dr. Hudson looked noticeably tired. That was understandable. Their flight had been a rough one against high winds and with darkening cloud cover overhead. Although he was not working at the time, James Crawford had seen the yellow aircraft descend to the landing strip. He hurriedly approached to reconnect with the two fishermen to see if he would be given his promised fish. Barilko faithfully kept his word and gave him a large sample of the Artic char. (Crawford recalled Hudson was annoyed by his friend's generosity. Eschewing tact, the dentist rudely told Barilko a smaller fish would have

13. The Short Life, Disappearance and Recovery of Bill Barilko

been more than an ample gift for the teen.) Crawford later estimated there were about 60 such fish stuffed into the airplane's pontoons—a storage method the young man had never seen before.

Dr. Hudson reaffirmed they needed to get home to Timmins before the fish went bad and their suppers got cold. He and Barilko reboarded the aircraft after just a short stay. It lifted off at about 4 p.m. on Sunday, August 26. The airplane, laden with its heavy load of Arctic char, struggled to gain altitude as it flew into a graying sky, but it eventually traveled beyond the sight of the two people they had spoken to at Rupert's House. The estimated distance of the return flight was 236 miles, ordinarily a trip of about three hours.

The hockey players' special Sunday night dinner was delayed while everyone waited for the tardy Bill Barilko to arrive. When he did not show up at a reasonable time, they began the meal without him. No one was especially alarmed by Barilko's absence that evening. The prevailing feeling was that he and Dr. Hudson had simply stayed an extra day at Seal Lake to get in some additional fishing. Also, there was no immediate concern because the twosome had said they might extend their trip into Monday if they faced inclement weather for the trip back to Timmins.

However, when Dr. Hudson was not home by late Monday to see any of his scheduled dental patients—one was Allan Stanley of the New York Rangers—something was seriously wrong. His receptionist eventually reported him missing to the local police. Fear gripped the Barilko household when Bill failed to return to Timmins. "Why my Billy no come home?" Barilko's mother hysterically repeated to her other children. When the men's unexplained absence extended into the next day, the Tuesday, August 28 edition of the *Toronto Star* broke the story under the ominous headline, "Barilko Vanishes in North." Shortly thereafter, most dailies across Canada were running stories about the two missing fishermen—with the focus, of course, primarily on the famous Toronto Maple Leaf hockey player—and their elusive private yellow pontoon aircraft. (Many newspaper stories referred to Barilko as being 25 years old. That was incorrect; he had celebrated his 24th birthday on March 25.) By the following day, with still no word from the missing duo, the story became front-page news nationwide. Predictably, the closer one lived to Toronto, the more intensive coverage the twosome's disappearance received in the daily newspapers.

Somewhere along the pair's journey home, something had gone terribly awry. The single-engine plane and its two occupants simply disappeared. There had been sightings of a yellow airplane by observers on the ground who saw it struggling through the air. On Tuesday, when the men had still not yet returned home, a massive search initially employing six

Bashing Bill Barilko, Hockey Hero Missing On Northern Air Trip

Bill Barilko Hero of Leaf Cup Win
That was the headline on the sports pages less than four months ago. Today front-page headlines read:
Barilko Missing on James Bay Flight
Yesterday a full-scale search was under way in the hope of locating Bill Barilko, hero of last spring's Stanley Cup victory of the Toronto Maple Leafs, and his companion, Pilot Dr. Henry Hudson, a Timmins dentist, who were reported to be 50 hours overdue on a plane flight from James Bay to Timmins. The brawny blond defense bucko and Dr. Hudson left Rupert House on James Bay Monday at 7 p.m. after a fishing trip and haven't been heard from since.

One of the early newspaper reports about Bill Barilko's disappearance erroneously states the hockey player was last seen at Rupert's House on Monday (August 27) rather than Sunday.

low-flying aircraft from the Canadian government and military began. It began as a small operation on Tuesday, but that was curtailed after just a few hours due to an electrical storm in the region. The operation resumed and expanded exponentially over the next few days. In what one Canadian Press story ridiculously called "a tree-by-tree search," it turned up absolutely nothing despite 17 planes eventually being involved in the unsuccessful operation. A total of 1,345 flying hours were logged by hopeful aviators trying to find Dr. Hudson's missing airplane by flying over what was accurately described as some of the most desolate terrain in North America.

In the Canadian Press coverage, Faye Barilko was reported as being "near hysteria" over the fate of her missing son. After four days with little to no sleep, the 52-year-old widow was flown in a special airplane to Kapuskasing, about 75 northwest of Timmins. That was where the Royal Canadian Air Force had set up an "advance search base." The aircraft had been hired by the *Toronto Star*. She had readied herself to personally descend into the thick bush at the first sure sign of a sighting. She had always brought Bill luck when she traveled to Maple Leaf Gardens to watch him play, Faye said to the media. Perhaps her mere presence over the

13. The Short Life, Disappearance and Recovery of Bill Barilko

search area might be able to summon some more important magic than the result of a hockey game. Alas, that was not to be the case.

Confusion and conflicting reports initially trickled out of Timmins. Dr. Lou Hudson, the dentist's brother, first claimed he had seen his sibling's airplane "buzz" his house several times on Monday afternoon! This story was quickly debunked by local aviation records. As late as Wednesday, August 29, Phyllis Hudson, the dentist's wife, stoically refused to even consider the worst-case but highly probable scenario. "As far as I am concerned, they are not missing," she firmly told a Canadian Press reporter. "They are out of gas and down on some lake. My husband is a very careful pilot. Bad luck or lack of gas may have forced him down."[6] Harry Watson, who assisted on Barilko's famous goal, was more realistic. He said in a 2002 interview with Barilko's biographer Kevin Shea, "At first there were hopes they would be found alive, but as time went on, you just knew they wouldn't."[7] An optimistic story in Tuesday's *Toronto Star* about a bush fire that could perhaps have been set as a signal by the missing men turned out to have no merit whatsoever.

The extensive 1951 search found nothing. The only news that occasionally came from the operation was when ground searchers themselves went missing in the labyrinth of thick forest. That happened at least twice. Each time the wayward volunteers were safely found.

The estimated price tag for the unsuccessful search reached a whopping $385,000—a fantastic sum in 1951. About 100,000 square miles were eventually flown over by all those aircraft. It was the classic needle-in-a-haystack situation for everyone involved with the search party. The breadth of this operation has never been surpassed in Canadian history.

"There was no hope of finding Bill [alive]," Allan Stanley ruefully said years later. "You can't even believe the trees up in that country. The tops of the trees are packed so closely together that it looks like a can of asparagus. There was no way to find him unless it was by accident."[8]

The Maple Leafs' 1951 training camp opened on September 21, minus Barilko, of course. His home jersey and other paraphernalia were optimistically ready for him in his cubicle at Maple Leaf Gardens. (Tim Horton, another northern Ontarian, replaced Barilko on Toronto's defensive corps.) Saturday, October 13, opening night of the 1951–52 season, had the Leafs hosting Chicago. The visitors won, 3–1. Maple Leaf Gardens was a subdued place as Barilko's absence was palpable. Barilko's #5 sweater, it was reported on the front page of the *Ottawa Citizen*, would presumably remain ready for him to don "until its owner is found."

On October 30, with the season well underway, the club's management announced the team was offering a hefty $10,000 reward to anyone who might know the whereabouts of the missing aircraft and its occupants—as if a large sum of cash could suddenly make the wilds of northern Ontario more easily accessible. The money failed to generate any new clues to solve the ongoing mystery of what was now Canada's most famous active missing-persons case.

Before 1951 had ended, the Maple Leafs announced that they were withdrawing Barilko's #5 jersey from circulation. (It was not officially retired by the club until 1962.) Interestingly, Barilko had only worn #5 during the 1950-51 season. He had previously worn both #21 and #19 in his previous seasons as a Toronto Maple Leaf.

Years went by with no further news emerging about the two missing fishermen. Barilko and Hudson were eventually declared legally dead early in 1952—a fairly fast decision by missing-persons standards. Given the circumstances, however, it was a very reasonable one for the authorities to make. Phyllis Hudson, now a widow by decree, eventually remarried. She became Phyllis Duffy for the rest of her life, dying in May 1996 at the age of 90. Meanwhile, Faye Barilko kept clinging to the hope, against all odds and reason, that somehow her beloved Billy was alive and well somewhere. A year after Barilko and Hudson disappeared, several newspapers ran anniversary articles wondering about the missing twosome's fate. "What happened to Bill Barilko and Dr. Hudson?" the *Toronto Telegram* asked in an August 1952 story. "Almost any guess will do." This semi-regular act of commemoration and remembrance continued for a while, but even it stopped after a few years. The mysterious fate of the two missing Timmins fishermen slowly became history instead of news.

Frank Klisanich, Anne's eldest son, was born in 1951, the same year his uncle vanished. He said in a 2013 interview with the *National Post* shortly after his mother died, that the 1950s were especially hard on the extended Barilko family. They seldom talked about their absent Uncle Billy. The few times they did, his grandmother would pitifully insist that Bill must be out there, somewhere in the wilderness, lost and suffering from amnesia or something similar. She steadfastly clung to the faint and irrational hope that any day now her Billy would once again casually walk through the front door of the family house in Timmins.

Then, one drizzly spring day in 1962, a civilian helicopter pilot was hired to transport a passenger on a routine flight across a stretch of northern Ontario that was densely covered with forest ... and Bill Barilko's name would soon be front-page news across Canada again.

Finally Found: The Discovery and Recovery

> "It was kind of a funny parallel. The beginning of his Leaf career: right place, right time. The ending of his career:

13. The Short Life, Disappearance and Recovery of Bill Barilko 153

wrong place, wrong time."⁹—biographer Kevin Shea in a YouTube interview on the 70th anniversary of Bill Barilko's famous goal

On Thursday, May 31, 1962, nearly eleven years after Dr. Henry Hudson's private Fairchild 24 floatplane vanished somewhere over the densely tree-covered regions of northern Ontario, an alert helicopter pilot named Gary Fields keenly spotted something odd during a flight through light rain. It appeared to be the wreckage of a small aircraft in a forested area about 45 miles north of Cochrane, Ontario.

Fields was a civilian pilot who worked for Dominion Helicopter Services, a private Toronto-based transportation company. That fateful day he was flying an employee of Ontario's Department of Lands and Forests named Ray Paterick from Cochrane to Newpost Creek, a remote area that was under consideration for a hydroelectric-power project. During their 60-mile flight, Fields spotted what he later called "a glint of yellow" among the thick forest. Curious, he circled back and flew at a lower level. Both men clearly saw what they believed to be a pontoon and a strip of metal—almost certainly the wreckage of a small airplane. (Shortly after Barilko's disappearance, a railroad employee had told authorities that he had seen a plane apparently descending rapidly into a heavily forested area *south* of Cochrane. A large search had been undertaken there. Of course, it came up empty.) There was no place for Fields to land his helicopter anywhere near the crash site.

Unfortunately, there were no nearby landmarks to use as reference points. Nor were there reliable ways in 1962 of pinpointing where the helicopter had just flown—only a rough estimation could be made. Nevertheless, Fields—whose first name was misspelled as "Cary" rather than Gary in many subsequent newspaper stories—filed an official report about what he and Paterick had both definitely seen. This immediately prompted another Bill Barilko air search to be organized more than a decade after the first one. This time it would be much more condensed based on reputable evidence provided by two witnesses rather than the mere hopefulness that characterized the 1951 operation. It would include Fields and his helicopter. As with the initial search, two days of inclement, overcast weather maddeningly delayed its start.

Despite the government trying to suppress information about the renewed investigation in case it turned out to have no validity, stories that the ongoing Bill Barilko mystery might be solved began appearing in some pages of Canadian newspapers. The 1962 search began anew on June 3. It took until June 5 for Fields himself, by chance, to again fly his helicopter over the location where he had seen the glint of yellow on May 31.

(According to another version of the discovery story, the second sighting of the wreckage was made by another helicopter pilot, Ron Boyd, and his engineer Phil Weston and was duly recorded in Boyd's logbook.) The location was narrowed down this time as Lot 24, Concession III of northern Ontario's McAlpine Township. Fields easily understood why the wreckage had not been found during the vast 1951 search. Years later he told the *Toronto Sun*, "I saw that you had to be directly over the plane to see anything."[10] He noted, there were no scars on any of the trees. Thus, he surmised that Dr. Hudson's plane must have suddenly stalled and dropped straight downward into the soft, mushy swampland that was omnipresent in the area.

Fields' discovery was confirmed. Government spokesman J.W. Spooner was confident enough to contact the next of kin of both the Barilko and Hudson families by telephone before the media was officially informed of the newsworthy find. He told the men's loved ones the airplane's five identification letters—CF-FXT—were plainly visible from the air. This left no reasonable doubt that the downed plane was the aircraft that belonged to Dr. Hudson. Strangely, Dr. Hudson's widow, Phyllis, disputed the accuracy of those letters. She strongly insisted they should have also included DGZ among them. Ted Hall, a government official who was one of the key investigators, did not know where Phyllis Hudson had gotten that notion. Rather than disputing a grieving woman, he politely wrote in his investigation log, "We didn't argue."

When the grim news came to them, Barilko's sister and brother both accepted it calmly and with a measure of relief that their sibling's 1951 disappearance had at last been solved almost 4,000 days since the airplane had departed from the airstrip in South Porcupine. However, Barilko's 63-year-old mother was reported as being devastated by the news. Barilko's brother, Max, learned the news at his home in Montreal. "My sister and I can take it, but Mother is different," he told the *Toronto Telegram*. "This has been a great shock to her." Indeed, Faye Barilko required sedation upon learning the irrefutable truth that most everyone else had long suspected and perceived as inevitable. A sidebar story in the *Telegram* about the grieving mother featured the sad headline, "Hope of a Miracle Dies After 11 Years."[11] She had been visiting the home of her daughter and son-in-law in London, Ontario when the confirmation of the aircraft's discovery was deemed official. The rival *Toronto Star*'s headline was similar but less personal: "The Long Search Ends—Find Barilko's Plane."

The hard-to-get-to crash site was reached by a ground-search team the following day. A helicopter was able to land them in a clearing a mere quarter-mile from the wreckage. A second helicopter carrying journalists landed about three miles away on a knoll. The scribes reported on every aspect of what they saw. Some of it was grisly. The aircraft, as it crashed, had scraped out a hole eight feet long and three feet deep in the soft, muddy earth. Its wings had been sheared off in its descent through the thick forest. Young trees and new foliage had begun to grow through parts of the shattered airplane.

In the aircraft's fuselage, portions of two partial skeletons were found strapped into their seats. (Peter Worthington of the *Toronto Telegram* accompanied the land-search group. He described the men's bones as "moss-covered and weather-worn."[12]) Worthington also agreed with Fields. In his newspaper report, Worthington stated, "The lack of burned material suggested the gasoline tanks were empty at the time of the crash and exploded because of fumes. Every flier I've spoken to here thinks signs point to the plane running out of gasoline."[13] Worthington speculated that Hudson knew his plane was out of gas and probably spent his final moments frantically searching for water on which to land his pontoon-equipped aircraft. The unlucky pilot fell short of a small, shallow lake by only about 30 or 40 feet.

Worthington experienced an uncomfortable feeling wandering around at the crash site. He wrote, "Poking around the wreckage somehow seemed like tampering with a grave. I saw several splintered rib bones embedded in seeping bog by the pilot's seat. I stopped looking [after I saw that]."[14]

Barilko's identity was confirmed by a distinct belt buckle he had been wearing. Similarly, an expensive watch belonging to Dr. Hudson that he had bought while on vacation in Switzerland verified that he was the airplane's other occupant. Investigators deemed the cause of the crash to have been a combination of pilot inexperience, poor weather, and overloaded cargo. Because Barilko and Hudson had died in an unnatural way, autopsies of the two men were mandatory under Ontario law. Those procedures were done in Toronto at the lab of the Ontario Attorney-General. Not surprisingly, the reports concluded that both Barilko and Hudson had likely died instantaneously upon the airplane's violent impact with the ground. That was comforting news for the two families. At least they knew their fishermen had not suffered slow, agonizing deaths.

Barilko's disappearance had become part of Canadian lore since 1951. Thus, despite the lengthy passage of time, the discovery of the airplane and its two long-dead occupants was prominent news across Canada. "One Body Barilko's" declared the page-one headline in the *Montreal Gazette*. It was also the lead story on the CBC's national TV newscast on Thursday, June 7. That same day, the Canadian Press duly reported, "The bodies of Bill Barilko and Dr. Henry Hudson were found today amidst the smashed wreckage of their airplane in the northern Ontario bushland, ending one of Canada's longest-standing aviation mysteries."[15]

Hockey writers and historians were quick to realize that less than two months earlier, the Maple Leafs had won the 1962 Stanley Cup championship—the club's first Cup since Barilko's ill-fated fishing trip nearly 11 years earlier. The news of his plane finally being found coincided with the day the 1962 NHL's intra-league draft began in Montreal. The Barilko story got considerably more news coverage across Canada than the goings-on of NHL magnates in a hotel conference room in the heart of Quebec (and the World Cup soccer tournament taking place in Chile). One of the veteran players drafted that day was Bert Olmstead—who had played for Montreal in the 1951 Stanley Cup finals against Bill Barilko's Toronto Maple Leafs. Another participant in that championship series was also making news that same day: Doug Harvey, it was reported, was pondering retirement.

Helicopter pilot Gary Fields knew nothing whatsoever about the missing hockey player before he spotted the downed plane. He was informed by friends about the reward money offered by the Toronto Maple Leafs back in October 1951 for any information that would help find Bill Barilko alive or dead. Fields was urged to apply for it—and he did. He told a reporter, "I was lucky enough to spot the wreckage twice. I don't imagine I'll be lucky enough to get $10,000."[16] He was correct. Stafford Smythe, the president of Maple Leaf Gardens, said the reward deadline had expired on January 1, 1952. Smythe had not made up that restriction simply to avoid paying Fields; that important tidbit of information did appear in news stories about the reward when the it was offered by the Toronto hockey club in the autumn of 1951.

The wreckage of Dr. Hudson's aircraft was not fully removed from the crash site until October 2011—more than 60 years after the aviation accident occurred. One member of the group who went on the journey to retrieve the airplane wreckage for preservation was Sandra Cattarello, an elderly female cousin of Barilko's. Another was an aging Archie Chenier—the fellow who had backed out of the August 1951 fishing trip, thus allowing Bill Barilko to take his place. Hockey enthusiast Dave McGirr, a onetime Timmins resident, was another of the 16 people who trekked to the crash site. McGirr said,

> It was a very proud and emotional experience to be involved in the recovery of Bill Barilko and Dr. Henry Hudson's plane. A major reason for this mission was to highlight the legacy of a great Canadian legend and to underline that Bill Barilko was from northern Ontario. He should be in the Hockey Hall of Fame.[17]

An 11-minute documentary about the airplane's recovery, titled *The Mission*, aired in 2016 on The Sports Network in Canada. It received very positive feedback.

Barilko's grave had been a marked cenotaph for a decade. With his remains found, this sad aspect of his tragically short life could now change. His headstone in the Timmins Memorial Cemetery where he was laid to rest is engraved with two hockey sticks with pucks, and the four years in which his Toronto Maple Leafs won the Stanley Cup. It also contains the notation, "Died Accidentally Aug. 26, 1951—Buried June 15, 1962." Faye Barilko was a woman of modest means, so the NHL kindly sent her a bank draft for $845 to cover some of her son's funeral costs. The money came attached to a letter of condolence from league president Clarence Campbell. Ted Kennedy, the captain of the 1950–51 Leafs, was supposed to represent his team at the funeral. He made the long drive to Timmins only to learn from the locals that because of the required autopsy on Barilko's skeleton, he had arrived a week too early for the services. Kennedy promptly turned his car around, drove back home, and chose not to return. When the funeral was finally held, teammate Harry Watson was one of the pallbearers who carried Bariko's casket from the hearse to his grave. Another pallbearer was Barilko's childhood friend, Gaston Garant. He recalled years later, "It was light as a feather. Nothing but a few bones."[18]

Another pallbearer was Allan Stanley—now a Leaf and a member of the 1962 Stanley Cup champions. "It was very sad," he recalled. "But ... it was a great relief to have closure. [It ended all the speculation.] People claimed they saw Barilko in Russia. There were crazy rumors."[19] Uniquely, Stanley would also be a pallbearer at the 1974 funeral of Tim Horton, the defenseman from Cochrane who had replaced Barilko in the Toronto lineup. Like Barilko, Horton had died while still an active player. (His death was the result of a single-vehicle car mishap.) Unlike Barilko, Horton was competing in the NHL at the very advanced age of 43.

In 2021, an enormous commemorative billboard was erected on the outskirts of Timmins in Barilko's memory. It shows a very enlarged, familiar photo of the smiling young hockey player raising his right fist in triumph not long after scoring the Stanley Cup–winning goal on April 21, 1951. Local journalist, historian and filmmaker Kevin Vincent noted, "The public's reaction to the billboard has been very heart-warming. People [in Timmins] obviously share this sense of pride about Bill Barilko."[20]

There have been conspiracy theories connected with the ill-fated airplane trip in the many decades since it occurred. The fact that the crash site near Cochrane was noticeably off the typical course that Henry Hudson should have been flying to get to Porcupine Lake—by some 36 miles—is a major reason why the battered aircraft was not found in the initial 1951 efforts. It also fosters speculation.

The most enduring—but totally unproven—claim is that Dr. Hudson was perhaps involved in an illegal but profitable practice known colloquially as "high-grading." It is the smuggling of gold out of Canada to secret American buyers. The Canadian government controls its gold supplies strictly, but dentists in 1951 had access to virtually unlimited qualities of the precious metal to use for patients' fillings. Timmins is famous as a gold-mining area. Dr. Hudson had access to a private airplane. Fishing trips could be used as a ruse to transport large quantities to remote places in northern Ontario and Quebec to meet up with American criminals posing as fishermen. Louise Hastings, Barilko's steady girlfriend—who apparently was about to become Barilko's fiancée—recalled decades later,

> I remember fighting with people when Bill disappeared. So many people around [Timmins] thought it was a hoax. They didn't think he and Dr. Hudson had gone fishing. They thought they'd flown somewhere and picked up gold. Bill would never have been involved in anything like that.[21]

Kevin Vincent strongly thinks otherwise. Seventy years later Vincent claimed there was a "one thousand percent chance" that the airplane trip that Barilko and Dr. Hudson made on the last weekend of August 1951 was not solely for the purposes of an innocent weekend of sport fishing. He said,

> Virtually every dentist in Timmins in that era was involved, in one way or another, in the gold-smuggling industry. It's endemic to this particular community. They needed to find innovative ways to get the gold out of Timmins. Dentists were, of course, allowed to possess gold. The theory that they might have been smuggling gold or that there was some sort of connection to it is very, very plausible. It's part of the story that we need to share with the world.[22]

Moreover, Dr. Lou Hudson, the dentist's brother, had once been shot in broad daylight by an unknown assailant while he was attending a curling bonspiel in Toronto! The wound was not a fatal one, but the man who pulled the trigger was never found and no suspect was ever named nor was a motive ever suggested. Gun violence of that kind rarely occurred in Canada in those days. Perhaps it was a dissatisfied gold customer who was out for revenge. Others suggested the motivation was more traditional: a romantic entanglement that suddenly turned violent one day due to jealousy. (As a totally unrelated aside, Lou Hudson was a hockey player of some repute himself—an Olympic gold medalist, having played on Canada's championship 1928 team at St. Moritz, Switzerland.)

According to Kevin Shea, a hockey historian who authored a terrific book in 2004 about Barilko's life, local scuttlebutt about Henry Hudson having a shady side of his personality was apparently quite commonplace throughout Timmins in the years between 1951 and 1962 when he and Barilko were famously missing. This inevitably led to some members of the community speculating if there was more to the dentist's disappearance than a tragic airplane misadventure. Peter Worthington, one of several journalists who examined the crash site in June 1962 just after the government officials had been there, noticed that the aircraft's pontoons had been split open by some very new ax blows. He figured the government's crash investigators had been issued orders to open them up for any evidence of gold smuggling ... and to do so before the press could arrive to witness the action and see the results. If the authorities did find anything incriminating in the pontoons, they certainly did not mention it publicly.

Does the fair-haired hockey hero fit into any of this smuggling speculation? Perhaps, say the imaginative theorists. Young Bill Barilko was a handsome sports celebrity with some connections to Hollywood (albeit thin ones by 1951), a lofty status which theoretically could have given him great access to many people with money and influence. Connections to prominent folks can always benefit someone who is up to no good. Could Bill Barilko really have been involved in a complex gold-smuggling racket with his hometown's dentist? No one has ever put forth even a scintilla of solid evidence that Barilko was anything more than an unfortunate passenger who was aboard an overloaded, doomed private aircraft on that tragic late August day in 1951—the summer when he never returned home from an impromptu weekend fishing trip with a family friend.

Had Dr. Henry Hudson, the middle-aged, fishing-loving dentist led a dangerous double life as an international gold smuggler? Since it is now more than 70 years after his pontooned airplane plummeted to the forested earth of northern Ontario, that is one mystery that will likely remain forever unsolved.

Honored Fifty Years After His Goal

A special ceremony was held at the Air Canada Centre on Tuesday, May 1, 2001, before that night's Stanley Cup playoff game between the New Jersey Devils and the Toronto Maple Leafs. Giving way to the unstoppable march of time, Maple Leaf Gardens was no longer the home building of Toronto's NHL club; the newer, fancier ACC was—and had been the Leafs' center of operations since February 1999.

The pregame gathering was organized to recognize the fiftieth anniversary of the Maple Leafs winning the 1951 Stanley Cup. Eight aging members of those 1950–51 Maple Leafs were present at the ACC to receive another cheer from the sellout crowd of more than 19,000 Toronto hockey supporters. They were Gus Mortson, Harry Watson, Danny Lewicki, Johnny McCormack, Bob Hassard, Fleming Mackell, Sid Smith, and Cal Gardner. However, the focus of the elaborate ceremony was on their long-dead teammate, Bill Barilko. His banner with the retired #5 was highlighted in the building's rafters. Newsreel footage of the 1951 Cup finals and still photos of the handsome 24-year-old defenseman appeared on the arena's large video board located above center ice.

Also present as a special guest was Bill Barilko's only surviving sibling, his sister Anne who was born in 1930, three years after he was. The 70-year-old was accompanied by what some people might have thought was an odd group of friends for a septuagenarian to have. They were The Tragically Hip, a hugely popular Canadian rock band. They and Anne Klisanich (née Barilko) had formed an unlikely acquaintanceship several years before. It was one that she instigated.

The members of the rock group were huge hockey fans, which is not an especially surprising interest for Canadian musicians to have. In 1992 they had released a song titled "Fifty Mission Cap" in which Barilko's 1951 disappearance and discovery 11 years later were the focal point of the lyrics. Lead singer Gord Downie had first learned about the tragic Bill Barilko story as a child from reading a factoid printed on the back of a hockey card. Journalist Bill Steer wrote in a 2021 article, "The song has been credited as singlehandedly reviving the Barilko legend that included an array of theories and speculation related to his sudden and no-trace disappearance."[23]

Predictably, Anne (Barilko) Klisanich, who was 62 years old at the time, had never heard of The Tragically Hip nor the song about her late brother until family and friends began casually mentioning the tune to her. Nevertheless, she was both impressed and grateful that hockey fans born well after Bill had died still knew something about him, his famous goal, and his unfortunate and sudden demise in the prime of his life.

In 1999, The Tragically Hip had a gig at the Hershey Centre in Mississauga (a Toronto suburb). That was the municipality where the 69-year-old Anne now resided with her husband. Upon learning about the concert, she took it upon herself to go the arena several hours before showtime to introduce herself to them. Of course, when she tried to enter the arena to pay the musicians an unscheduled visit, she was stopped by a dutiful security guard. She explained to him she was Bill Barilko's only sister; it was a tale he did not readily believe. Anne had come well prepared for such a challenge, though. She promptly produced her birth certificate, which had her maiden surname, and gave it to the man to show to the musicians. This document was apparently proof enough to convince him that her story sounded legitimate. He instructed her to stay put, then he walked down a corridor of the arena. A few minutes later the guard returned to Anne with a smile on his face. He returned the birth certificate to her. She was told

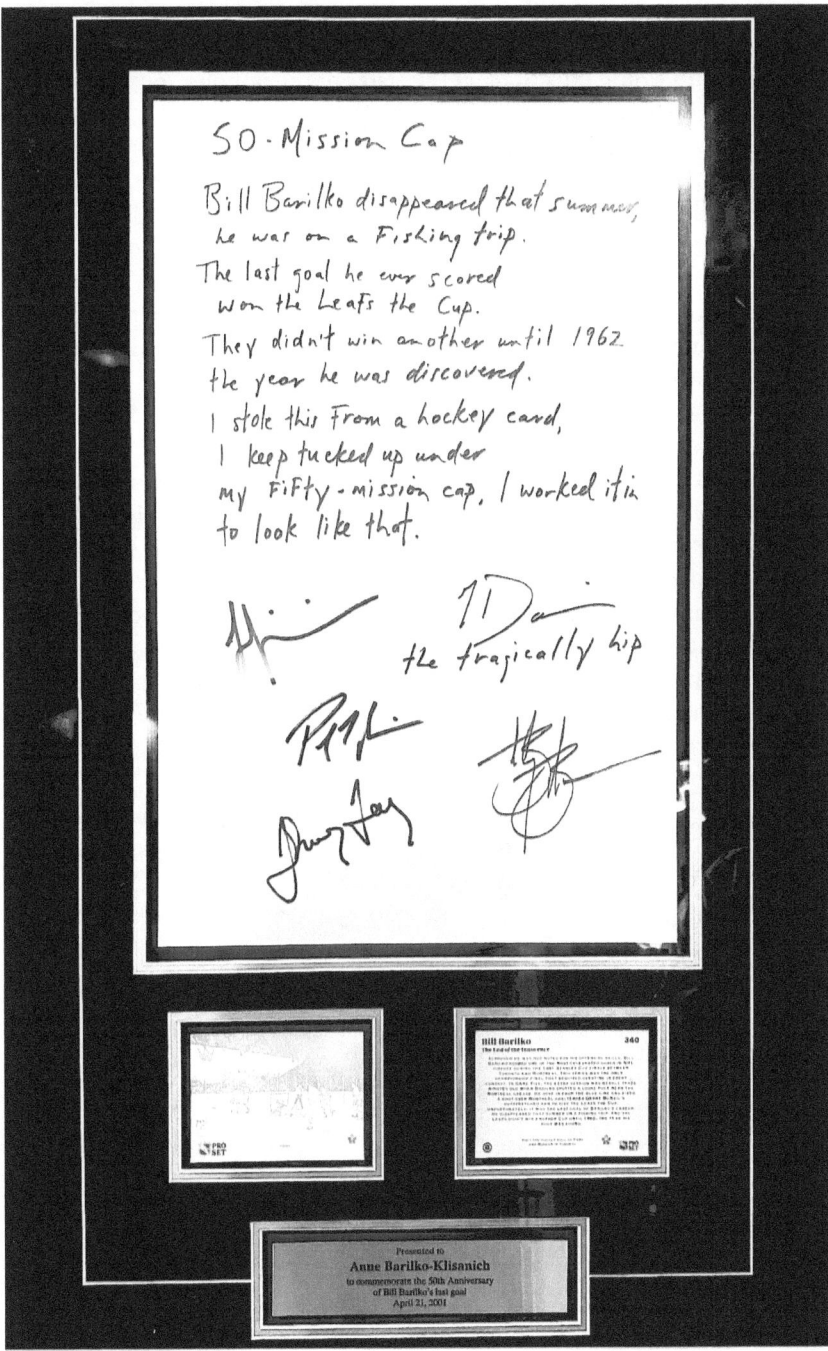

The lyrics to "Fifty Mission Cap." They were hand-written by Gord Downie and presented to Bill Barilko's sister, Anne, in a ceremony before a Toronto playoff game in 2001 (photo by Carl T. Madden, Courtesy Mark Fera).

that the group would love to meet the sister of the famous Toronto hockey player from yesteryear.

Anne was quickly escorted to a meeting with all the band's members who had just completed a soundcheck for that night's concert. They were thrilled to shake hands and pose for pictures with a genuine Barilko sibling. They politely asked her if she would like to stay for the show that evening as their special guest. She declined the unexpected offer, explaining she could not stay very long. She had to get home soon to prepare dinner for herself and her husband—a comment the musicians found very humbling but also endearing.

At the 2001 pregame ceremony, a plaque bearing the lyrics to "Fifty Mission Cap" was formally presented to 71-year-old Anne. (It is now in the collection of Mark Fera. The next chapter will explain who he is.) She also received the hockey card that had inspired Gord Downie—a Boston Bruins fan—to pen the song nearly a decade earlier. A portion of the tune was played over the ACC's loud speaker. Each member of The Tragically Hip then gave Anne a hug upon joining her on the blue-carpeted ice as part of the presentation.

That night the Maple Leafs fittingly played an overtime game against the New Jersey Devils. They lost, 3-2. It was the same score by which they had defeated the Montreal Canadiens on Bill Barilko's dramatic goal on Saturday, April 21, 1951.

Biographer Kevin Shea said in a 2021 interview that while the names of many of Barilko's 1950–51 teammates—such as Al Rollins and Fern Flaman—are becoming less and less well known to casual followers of the sport as time goes by, "It just seems as if you are a passionate or passive hockey fan, the name Bill Barilko, 70 years later, still falls off the tip of the tongue because of his extraordinary story … a gentleman who passed away at age 24 in 1951."[24]

14

The Curious Case of the Two Barilko Pucks

Sports memorabilia collectors are always on the lookout for iconic historical items. In NHL history, there are very few moments more iconic than Bill Barilko's Stanley Cup–winning goal in 1951. So ... what happened to the puck that was used to score the famous goal? The question is more complicated to answer than one might expect.

For more than five decades there was no disputing where it was: It was in the possession of the Hockey Hall of Fame in Toronto. Apparently, this was news to a man named Harry Donohue who claimed to have possessed the historic black disc within a short time of the Game Five's conclusion. In 2014, his descendants were going to donate it to the Hall of Fame—until they were informed that the keepers of the Hall already had the "Barilko puck" on display! That news was certainly unsettling to the Donohue family. Regardless of which puck was legitimate, obviously one thing was indisputable: At least one of the black discs had to be a phony.

Harry Donahue was a 16-year-old hockey fan who was in attendance at Maple Leaf Gardens on Saturday, April 21, 1951, to see the Toronto Maple Leafs win the Stanley Cup. Dressed in his best suit, Harry was accompanying his father, Jeremiah, a pub owner from Hamilton, Ontario. Harry held four season tickets for the Leafs in 1950–51. Seconds after the famous Barilko goal was scored, Donahue asked his father if he could go onto the ice surface and retrieve the puck from the Montreal net. His father said yes—provided he got permission from a Gardens usher! Harry dutifully approached a nearby uniformed attendant—and remarkably got the okay to do so. Times were much different in 1951.

Accordingly, Harry rose from his Red Section seat near the Montreal blue line, 10 rows from the ice. He vaulted over the low glass and boards there, rushed madly onto the ice, and plucked the puck from inside the Montreal net while the Leafs were celebrating their win and the Canadiens were skating toward the visitors' bench with glum expressions on their faces. Then he scrambled back to his waiting father with the puck securely in his grasp. As he clambered back over the boards and into the seating area, another spectator promptly offered him $20 for the historic disc—certainly a substantial sum for a teenager in 1951. Harry did not consider the money for very long. He declined the cash. It was the historic puck that was important to him. Within a few days, Jeremiah proudly had a wooden pedestal and an accompanying plaque made for the puck, identifying it and its historic importance. Over the following decades, family members occasionally brought the puck to social gatherings to proudly show it off as a cherished artefact of Stanley Cup history. (On one occasion, it was nearly dropped down a drainpipe.) Of course, the puck's historic value took on even greater significance following Barilko's August 1951 disappearance somewhere in the vast northern Ontario wilderness.

Harry Donohue died in 2013 at age 78. Later that year, Harry's descendants—especially his son Dan—thought it would be a terrific gesture to loan the puck to the Hockey Hall of Fame as a tribute to their late father. That was when they received the shocking news that another "Barilko puck" was already on display there—and had been since the Hall first opened its doors to the public on the grounds of the Canadian National Exhibition in Toronto in August 1961.

Donohue's version of events runs contrary to what was once popular lore, however. The scuttlebutt for decades was that the "Barilko puck," through one means or another, ended up in the possession of Jimmy Main, a wheelchair-bound youth. Often referred to in the print media as "a cripple" in the common vernacular of the era, Main was stationed in the front-row seating area of Maple Leaf Gardens alongside the goal judge at the end of the rink where Barilko scored his historic overtime goal. One version of the story has the puck bouncing out of the Montreal net and settling near the feet of an angry but unnamed Montreal Canadien. This unidentified Hab is said to have whacked the disc in frustration, sending it into the first row of seats behind the protective glass—and very near the vicinity of Jimmy Main. Another version has referee Bill Chadwick picking up the puck lying near him, skating over to Main, and kindly handing it to him as the ultimate souvenir of the game. Shortly before Main died, he gave the puck to a friend named George Fletcher. Fletcher eventually donated the puck to the Hall of Fame, although there is no paperwork in the Hall's archives to absolutely verify this gift. Be that as it may, there are several problems with both of those acquisition stories featuring Main.

If Main had been watching the Game Five from the front row, it would be almost impossible for a puck to be fired over the high glass and then land in the row immediately behind the glass. Presumably it would have fallen well behind the first row of seats—likely dozens of rows to the rear

14. The Curious Case of the Two Barilko Pucks

of where Main was located. Similarly, the presence of the high glass would make it very difficult for referee Chadwick to relay the puck to someone sitting there. Furthermore, Chadwick never claimed to have handed the puck to anyone or to have even picked it up after the game. In newsreel footage of the Barilko goal and its aftermath, Chadwick is clearly shown skating away from the net, ignoring the puck altogether, presumably to report the goal to the official scorekeeper. It was noted in some reporters' stories about the game that Chadwick and his two linesmen promptly hustled off the ice once the goal was scored to let the players celebrate or commiserate by themselves, depending on which uniforms they were wearing. That is still standard procedure among today's hockey officials in such series-ending circumstances.

Photographs and video evidence of the moments after the goal (found in the collection of the City of Toronto's municipal archives) show the puck is still sitting inside the Montreal net; it had not bounced out, as an important aspect of the Main story claims. The puck is lying near what would have been the left goalpost for the Toronto shooters or the right goalpost from the perspective of Montreal goaltender Gerry McNeil. That is exactly where Donohue claimed he had picked it up.

However, the most damning evidence against Main's claim being true is the puck itself. Main's disc, manufactured by Spalding, is embossed with an NHL crest that was used on league pucks from 1920 to 1943. There is no way an NHL game played during the 1951 Stanley Cup playoffs would have a puck bearing a crest that was out-of-date by nearly a decade at least. On the other hand, the Donohue puck features reddish-orange octagonal crests that were attached to both

The puck with which Bill Barilko scored the goal to end the 1951 Stanley Cup finals. The orange octagons on each side helped to verify its authenticity (photo by Carl T. Madden).

sides of all pucks used in NHL games between 1950 and 1958. That jibes perfectly with Barilko's 1951 overtime goal. It is quite astonishing that, over the years, no Hall of Fame curator nor scholarly fan bothered to question or even seem to notice the anachronistic nature of Main's puck.

Then there is the newsreel footage from Game Five. It captured something quite remarkable. "[It] is as clear as day if you are looking for it,"[1] wrote Brian Costello of *The Hockey News* in an online 2016 article about the Barilko puck controversy. Seconds after Barilko scored, an object was tossed onto the ice surface. It was almost certainly a puck. "What we see is a puck being thrown onto the ice—probably from the upper level of Maple Leaf Gardens judging by the path of its movement—and coming to rest in the high slot near the faceoff circle,"[2] Costello asserted. It bounced about 10 feet in front of the net, skittered along the ice, and gently collided with a Montreal player's skate by the far circle, the one that would have been to the right of McNeil. The Hab it softly struck was #15, Bert Olmstead.

Perhaps that weirdly discarded puck is what ended up afterward in Main's possession in some roundabout way rather than the true game-winning puck that was brazenly filched from the net (with an usher's permission) by Harry Donohue. That is likely why Main believed he had received the legitimate article. One important question remains: Why would anyone choose to throw an old puck onto the ice at that particular and noteworthy moment in hockey history? Unless someone confesses to being the puck-thrower all these decades later, the reason for the bizarre action must be left entirely to speculation. Nevertheless, the fact that a second puck was hurled onto the ice by an unknown person, motivated by who-knows-what, is probably the most likely reason why the confusion about the two Barilko pucks exists today.

"I'd love to see that Barilko puck on display [in the Hall of Fame] in my dad's name," Dan Donohue said in a 2015 interview. "A few years before he died, he said to me 'Dan, whatever anybody ever says to you about the puck, just know this: it's the real thing.'"[3]

With so much evidence against its legitimacy, the Hockey Hall of Fame no longer displays the Jimmy Main disc as the Barilko puck. Since March 2020, the Donohue puck has been in the possession of Mark Fera, a middle-age hockey fanatic who has a massive and thoroughly impressive collection of Toronto Maple Leafs memorabilia—with special emphasis on Bill Barilko-related artefacts. The puck is in good hands. It is not exactly Fera's property. With the permission of the Donohue family, Fera says he has it on permanent loan, or at least something akin to it without elaborating on the specifics of the arrangement. The 50-year-old keeps the historically significant disc on the original wooden stand crafted by Jeremiah Donohue in 1951, but he often stores it securely in a safe. On June 29, 2023,

14. The Curious Case of the Two Barilko Pucks

The historic "Barilko puck" on its wooden pedestal. It was built specially by Jeremiah Donohue to showcase the historic disc his son Harry retrieved from the Montreal net shortly after Game Five ended (photo by Carl T. Madden).

he thoughtfully had the puck at the ready for a pair of eager visitors to his home to see it, examine it, and handle it.

On that Thursday, Fera granted the two authors of this book the wonderful and tremendous opportunity to see his collection of Toronto Maple Leaf paraphernalia. Fera says he holds the world's largest collection of game-worn Leaf jerseys. We do not doubt this assertion for a moment. He estimates the total to be somewhere close to 300. Fera recalled that his fiancée (now his wife) humorously claimed he had "a strange fixation with men's used clothing."[4] All levity aside, it is a breathtaking display of memorabilia spanning the days of the Toronto Arenas more than a century ago through to the present-day Maple Leafs. The collection began with Fera's acquisition of a game-used Greg Terrion hockey stick in 1982 when he was just nine years old. It has steadily grown over the following four decades well beyond his ability to showcase every item in his vast collection. A sizable percentage is always locked away in storage.

As for the elusive Barilko black rubber disc, Fera confidently told us with a smile, "The controversy has ended; I have the puck."[5] Fera also has a Bill Barilko hockey stick with the #21 engraved on it, meaning it came from one of his first two seasons with the Leafs; a rare team photograph featuring the youthful defenseman as a member of the minor-league Hollywood Wolves; souvenirs from the appliance business on Toronto's Danforth Avenue co-owned by the two Barilko brothers; the only known ticket stub from Game Five of the 1951 Stanley Cup finals; one of Barilko's seasonal contracts with the Maple Leafs; autographed programs and photos galore, and dozens of other pieces of hockey history specifically connected to Toronto's tragic #5. Fera impressively seems to have an encyclopedic knowledge about every single memento he has steadily accrued over the years.

Fera also possesses something truly unique: the wreckage of the Fairchild 24 airplane in which the young hockey player and his dentist friend perished in August of 1951! Fera was one of the 16 volunteers who salvaged what was left of it on an unpleasant October day in 2011—one that showcased just about every possible weather option in northern Ontario. In fact, Fera personally hauled a huge chunk of the fuselage on his back to his truck to begin its long overdue voyage out of the wilderness. Fera has no qualms about having what many people might consider to be a morbid souvenir. "The Hockey Hall of Fame doesn't want anything to do with someone's death," he explained to us. "But I see no problem in having it among my collection."[6] (He points out to critics that it was recovered with the full blessings of both the Barilko and Hudson families.) Fera says that people have occasionally made him offers to purchase pieces of the doomed airplane. He refuses to consider such entreaties on the grounds that it would be a form of desecration. "I treat [the wreckage] with respect. It should be displayed. It completes the Bill Barilko story."[7]

What does Fera think happened to the Fairchild 24 on its fateful flight back to Timmins? He mainly suspects the stormy weather that afternoon caused the fatal crash. However, his research into the case has also

14. The Curious Case of the Two Barilko Pucks

A portion of Dr. Henry Hudson's Fairchild 24 seaplane in which Bill Barilko lost his life in August 1951. It is part of Mark Fera's collection of Toronto Maple Leaf memorabilia. Fera helped recover the wreckage in 2011 (photo by Carl T. Madden).

determined that Henry Hudson was not the extremely safe pilot his wife told reporters he was back in the summer of 1951. Instead, Fera says that Hudson was known in Timmins to be a maverick pilot—a "crazy cowboy"[8]—who often took needless risks in the sky. (For example, Hudson occasionally flew his aircraft under bridges just for the heck of it!) Hudson was also known to fly with low fuel levels. Prior to that tragic August afternoon in 1951, he had always escaped bad luck. Fera figures it was simply a case of the odds finally catching up with the fearless flying dentist and, unfortunately, his famous hockey-playing passenger.

15

Oops! The Stanley Cup Engraver Had a Bad Day

"Once [your name] is engraved, it can never be forgotten."
—NHL promotional ad from the 2015 Stanley Cup playoffs

The Stanley Cup is unique among the major team trophies in North America for featuring individuals' names on it. The first championship club to take the liberty of having its members' names engraved on Lord Stanley's famous trophy was the Montreal Wanderers back in 1907. This did not become the norm, however, for many years. For the next decade and a half, some teams did it while others did not. Starting with the victorious 1924 Montreal Canadiens, it has been done each season without exception. Since to err is human, there have been numerous mistakes by engravers over the years. Following the 1951 Stanley Cup playoffs, the champion Toronto Maple Leafs were subjected to more than their fair share of careless engraving boo-boos. There were five mistakes—yes, five—in listing the winners' names on hockey's grandest prize. Here they are:

Gus Mortson's last name was misspelled WORTSON with a "W" instead of an "M."
Danny Lewicki's last name was badly misspelled as LEWESKI, with the fourth letter being an E instead of an "I" and an "S" replacing the "C" as the fifth letter.
Ted Kennedy's name was misspelled as KENNEDYY with an extra "Y." Also, his position as the Maple Leafs captain, which should have been noted, was wrongly omitted.
The last name of Toronto team chairman William A.H. MacBrien was misspelled as McBrien, with the "A" in his surname omitted.
Elwin "Al" Rollins' first name was misspelled as ELVIN with a "V" instead of a "W."

A replica of the Stanley Cup was created by the NHL in 1992. This offered a terrific opportunity to make amends. Accordingly, four of the above engraving errors were fixed on the new version of the trophy. However, the Rollins mistake remarkably escaped detection again and was not corrected. This blunder is all the more unfortunate as the 1950–51 Toronto Maple Leafs were the only Cup winners that Rollins ever played for in an NHL career that lasted from 1949 to 1960. As of August 2023, the engraving error remains uncorrected.

16

Postscripts

"To win the Stanley Cup ... the feeling you get is hard to describe. It's great, but it's mixed with a feeling that you're so doggone glad it's over. You have spent so much of yourself, you're glad you don't have to spend any more. You have been driving for so long you have this feeling of relief—like a load off your shoulders—that now you are going to be able to get some rest."[1]—Joe Primeau, coach of the 1950–51 Toronto Maple Leafs

What became of the principal characters of the 1951 Stanley Cup playoffs, particularly those significant Leafs and Canadiens who faced off in the finals? Here are some postscripts to their careers and lives and those of peripheral figures of the 1950–51 NHL season.

Anne Barilko (Klisanich), Bill's sister and the youngest of the three Barilko siblings, died in January 2013 at the age of 82. All her life she never tired of talking about hockey, showing her five scrapbooks full of newspaper clippings about her late brother Bill, and discussing his famous goal to win the Stanley Cup for the Toronto Maple Leafs on April 21, 1951.

Feodosia (Faye) Barilko, Bill's mother, passed away in 1982. Her remains were interred beside her late husband (who had died in 1946) and her beloved Billy in Timmins Memorial Cemetery. The gravesite is often visited by die-hard Toronto Maple Leaf fans in something akin to a pilgrimage. She never truly got over the loss of her middle child. In an interview late in her life, Faye Barilko said that hardly a day went by when she did not cry about the tragic fate of her son, the famous hockey hero.

Sixteen-year-old **Max Bentley** was given a tryout by the Boston Bruins in 1936. The team took one look at him, figured he was undersized for the NHL, and sent him packing. Not long afterward, the Montreal Canadiens gave the teenager a more serious look and thought he had potential. But when the Habs' team doctor examined him, Bentley was told he had a bad heart and could potentially die within a year. It was an inauspicious and scary beginning to an eventual Hall of Fame career. Health problems constantly dogged Bentley—he always looked pale at the best of times—but he played through them admirably. Bentley was something akin to a walking pharmacy as he took pills and medicines for diabetes, ulcers, kidney trouble and numerous other ailments. It is a wonder he could play at all—but he did amazingly well. Although Max Bentley is best remembered as a Maple Leaf, he played parts of six seasons in Chicago, winning two NHL scoring titles there, before being acquired by Toronto six games into the 1947–48 campaign. He quickly became a hugely popular part of the Leafs' strong offense, scoring 110 goals for Toronto in five years. Bentley, one of three brothers to play in the NHL, was notable for his fancy stick-handling and other deft maneuvers to avoid opponents' checks. (Scholarly fans often compared Wayne Gretzky's skill in those departments of the game to Bentley's.) With some of that clever puck-handling, Bentley led the rush that culminated in Bill Barilko's famous 1951 overtime goal. A serious back injury sidelined Bentley 36 games into the 1952–53 season. He was traded to the New York Rangers the following year where he got to play with his brother, Doug. It turned out to be the swansong to his NHL days. Bentley died in his Saskatoon apartment on January 19, 1984. He was only 63 years old.

The **Boston Bruins** produced mostly mediocre squads for the rest of the 1950s, although they did manage to get into the Stanley Cup finals in 1953, 1957 and 1958—losing to far stronger Montreal teams on all three occasions. That era would soon seem like "the good old days" for the club. Following the 1958–59 season, in which they dropped a hard-fought, seven-game semifinal to Toronto, the Bruins would set an embarrassing NHL record by failing to qualify for the playoffs eight straight times. Hope was on the horizon, however. Bobby Orr, Phil Esposito and a talented supporting cast would dramatically change the Bruins' fortunes coinciding with the beginning of the league's expansion era in 1967–68.

Émile (Butch) Bouchard was a superb defenseman for the Montreal Canadiens who possessed both a keen intellect and a sharp financial mind. He was a late bloomer in hockey, though, as he did not learn how to skate until he was 16. Bouchard caught on quickly, however. He accepted $75 per week to play senior "amateur" hockey because the figure was more than 10 times the amount he was getting working at a bank. As a teenager, Bouchard cagily bought a beekeeping operation from an estate and made the apiary so profitable that he was able to buy his parents a house. Somewhere along the line, Bouchard acquired the nickname "Butch" from an anglophone teammate who thought his surname closely resembled the English word "butcher." Bouchard, at 6'3", was a physically imposing player—especially for his era—but he rarely got into fights because opponents dared

16. Postscripts

not tangle with him. ("He appeared to be chiseled out of stone,"[2] teammate Dickie Moore once commented.) This fear did not apply to fans, however. (Bouchard once got into a scuffle with a woman at Boston Garden who had stabbed him with a hairpin!) Bouchard would team with Doug Harvey on Montreal's defense in an excellent pairing. Harvey would often go on offensive charges with the puck, content with the knowledge that Bouchard would remain in a defensive possession in case of a turnover. Bouchard played his entire 15-season, NHL career with the Habs, winning four Stanley Cups along the way. Bouchard was held in great esteem by both teammates and opponents. On February 28, 1953, the Canadiens held a special night for him at the Forum in which Bouchard was honored in a ceremony during the second intermission in a game against the Detroit Red Wings. Among the gifts Bouchard received was a new Buick automobile which was driven onto the ice. Bouchard himself was supposed to drive the vehicle off the ice when the ceremony concluded. However, Bouchard discovered the keys had gone missing. To the crowd's amusement, Ted Lindsay, Detroit's captain, skated forward, returned the keys he had somehow deftly stolen, and congratulated Bouchard on behalf of the Red Wings. Bouchard was an early advocate of NHL teams having specialized coaching for defensive units, power plays, penalty killers, and goaltenders—measures that eventually became the norm. Bouchard's son, Pierre, won five Stanley Cups with the Habs in the 1970s. Butch Bouchard died at age 92 on April 14, 2012. His #3 jersey had been retired by the Habs as part of the team's centennial celebrations in 2009. That same year he was made a member of the Order of Canada.

Long before **Frank Boucher** became general manager of the New York Rangers, he made a bit of history as a player in the 1924 Stanley Cup final between his Vancouver Maroons and the Montreal Canadiens. In the Maroons' 2–1 loss in Game Two, Boucher scored the lone Vancouver goal—while his brother Billy scored both goals for the victorious Habs! Such a scoring monopoly by siblings on opposite sides in a Stanley Cup game has not happened in the century of play since then. When the Pacific Coast Hockey League collapsed, Boucher joined the NHL as an original New York Ranger. The skillful Boucher was so infrequently penalized that he inspired Lady Byng, the wife of Canada's governor-general, to donate a trophy to be given to the NHL player who best combined talent with gentlemanly behavior. Boucher won it seven of the first eight years it existed and was finally allowed to permanently keep the original Lady Byng Trophy. As an NHL coach, Boucher was innovative. He believed in having more than one goaltender on his roster, even to the point of changing them frequently during games as he would any other player. That extreme idea did not pan out successfully, but the concept of employing two goaltenders became the norm in the NHL by the early 1960s. Boucher coached the Rangers to the 1940 Stanley Cup. (The team would not win another until 1994.) He was encouraged to resign by the Rangers in 1954 when he was told the owners of the team had lost faith in his abilities to create a winning team. He complied. It ended nearly three decades of Boucher being with the club in some capacity. During the 1960s, Boucher served as commissioner of the Saskatchewan Junior Hockey League. Ranked as one of the Top Ten New York Rangers of all-time, Boucher died on December 12, 1977, at the age of 76.

The 1950–51 season was pretty much the end of the line for one of the NHL's iconic netminders, **Turk Broda**. He did not fully retire after Toronto's Cup triumph in April 1951, but he probably should have. Following his club's dramatic victory, the veteran Toronto goaltender played a grand total of one more regular-season NHL game in 1951–52 and two more in Toronto's playoff semifinal versus Detroit. He lost all three of those games and retired as an active player. He had won 303 regular-season games and another 60 in the playoffs—all for Toronto. Shortly thereafter, Broda became a successful junior hockey coach, leading the Toronto Marlboroughs to two Memorial Cups in the mid-1950s. He was also frequently seen at horse racing venues. In 1972, while visiting his daughter, Broda experienced severe chest pains. Taken to a Toronto hospital, Broda was fitted with a pacemaker. He nevertheless died of heart attack while still hospitalized, at the young age of 58 on October 17. Broda's obituary in the *New York Times* called him "one of hockey's greatest 'pressure' players of all time." (Just two weeks later, Bill Durnan, Broda's great goaltending rival with the Canadiens, died of kidney failure at the even younger age of 56.) Despite his famous moniker, Broda was not Turkish at all. His ancestry was Polish. Broda acquired the nickname as a child because, when angered, his neck tended to turn red like a turkey's. Among the many honors Broda won in his short life—and beyond—was induction into the National Polish-American Sports Hall of Fame. That tribute occurred in June 2005, nearly 33 years after his death.

Despite his comments to the contrary during the Detroit-Montreal semifinal, NHL president **Clarence Campbell** did not make any substantial move toward placing a time limit on playoff overtime games, nor did he reinstate regular-season overtime that had been discontinued during the Second World War. (This was done in order to ensure teams could catch their scheduled trains on time in an era when passenger rail service was greatly reduced in North America.) The autocratic Campbell stepped down as NHL's prexy in the spring of 1977 after 31 years of tireless devotion to the league in which he saw it triple in size to 18 teams. Hugely respected and often feared, Campbell died of a respiratory ailment at age 78 on June 24, 1984.

16. Postscripts

Bill Chadwick, the esteemed referee who worked Games One, Three and Five of the 1951 Stanley Cup finals, lived to be 94 years old. In his obituary it was reported that his final years were marked by declining health. He died under hospice care on October 24, 2009. A Hall of Famer for his 16 years as the first American-born NHL official, Chadwick's success was all the more remarkable because of a handicap: He was legally blind in his right eye as a result of an injury he suffered while playing in an amateur all-star game at Madison Square Garden in 1935. He did not acknowledge his vision problem during his officiating career, but he did not deny it, either. Whenever fans or players complained that he was blind, he was known tell them that they were "only 50 percent right."[3] Chadwick, a New Yorker, gained huge local fame after his refereeing days had ended for being a broadcaster for the New York Rangers, on both radio and television, for 14 seasons beginning in 1967–68. His first five seasons were on the radio only; then Chadwick switched to television on WWOR-TV prior to the start of the 1972–73 season. In Chadwick's obituary for NHL.com, it was written, "If there were two voices that defined Rangers hockey of the 1970s, they were Chadwick and play-by-play man Jim Gordon. Working in tandem, they called more than 650 regular-season and playoff games, and were right there when the Blueshirts went all the way to the 1979 Stanley Cup finals."[4] During these broadcasts, Chadwick often mangled players' names—Jean Béliveau's name sometimes came out of Chadwick's mouth as "Gene Bellyvoo"—but his unique descriptions and phrases endeared him to New York hockey fans. "He handles the puck like a cow handles a gun," was one such Chadwick-ism. When Ranger games began airing on cable television via the Madison Square Garden Network, Chadwick and Gordon gained a national following. A Bill Chadwick Fan Club was even established in distant Hawaii.

Neil Colville, the rookie coach of the New York Rangers in 1950–51, only lasted 23 games into the 1951–52 NHL season before resigning due to health issues. Before his brief coaching stint, Colville had been an outstanding player with the Broadway Blueshirts from 1936 to 1949, excluding the war years when he was a member of the Canadian Army. Neil, his brother Mac and Alex Shibicky comprised an offensive unit for New York dubbed the Bread Line. Colville was voted to postseason NHL all-star teams as both a forward and a defenseman—something only Boston's Dit Clapper had ever done. Still a relatively young man—he was only 36 when he got the Rangers' coaching gig—Colville embarked on a completely different career after leaving hockey. He moved to Whitehorse in Canada's distant Yukon Territory to run the region's first television system. It was comprised of four channels and was pretty much a solo operation. According to an amusing 2002 magazine article about early Canadian television,

Colville did just about everything there. He slept in a bunk in the studio and learned to do all the necessary tasks to keep the four channels on the air, from repairing technical equipment to hosting live newscasts. Filling air time with literally any sort of programming was often a challenging endeavor. In order to occupy its hours, sometimes Colville's TV stations would provide soporific shots of Whitehorse's less-than-bustling Main Street or do live broadcasts of a bowl of swimming goldfish—the equivalent of a test pattern. Colville was elected to the Hockey Hall of Fame in 1967. He died 20 years later of bone cancer, on December 26, 1987, at age 73.

Floyd (Busher) Curry played right wing for the Montreal Canadiens for another seven years, retiring after the Habs' third successive Cup win in the spring of 1958, a six-game triumph over the Boston Bruins. Before turning professional, Curry had been on the Memorial Cup champion Oshawa Generals in 1944 and the Allan Cup champion Montreal Royals in 1947. In total, Curry played in 601 regular-season games for the Canadiens and notched 105 goals. Despite being a forward, Curry was never a huge offensive threat. His only 20-goal season came in 1951–52 when he scored precisely 20 goals. Curry managed just one hattrick in his 11-year NHL career, but he chose an auspicious date to achieve the feat. It came on October 29, 1951, versus the New York Rangers, when Princess Elizabeth—who would become Queen Elizabeth II exactly 100 days later—was at the Montreal Forum to witness it. Curry was on four Stanley Cup winners with Montreal. He stayed affiliated with the Habs in numerous capacities for the rest of his life, first working in sales and then as the team's traveling secretary. Later Curry coached the Habs' minor league affiliate, the Montreal (and Nova Scotia) Voyageurs. He eventually moved up to assistant general manager of the Canadiens and then became the club's director of scouting. He died at age 81 on September 16, 2006.

The **Detroit Red Wings** learned their harsh lesson from the disappointing spring of 1951 not to rest on their regular-season laurels and simply expect similar success to occur automatically in the postseason. In 1951–52, the Red Wings had another tremendous regular-season campaign, ending their 70-game schedule with a terrific 44–14–12 mark—another 100-point output. This time they saved their best for when it counted most. They romped over the Toronto Maple Leafs in four straight games in one Stanley Cup semifinal and followed up that dominant series with another four-game blowout of the Montreal Canadiens in the finals. (The Canadiens had finished in second spot in the league standings in 1951–52, 22 points behind the front-runners from Detroit.) In eight playoff games in the spring of 1952, Terry Sawchuk cemented his status as an all-time great netminder—even though he was still just 22 years old. Sawchuk allowed just five goals in those pair of series sweeps for a microscopic

0.62 goals-against average. He did not surrender a single goal in the Wings' four games at the Olympia—a fantastic achievement. The Red Wings' perfect 8–0 record during the 1952 Stanley Cup playoffs was equaled by only one other squad during the romantic six-team era of the NHL: the 1959–60 Montreal Canadiens. Detroit would win back-to-back Cups in 1954 and 1955 (upending the Habs both times in the finals), lose to Montreal in the 1956 championship series—and then fall into mediocrity or worse. The Red Wings did not win another Stanley Cup until 1997.

Fern (Ferny) Flaman, frequently Bill Barilko's defensive partner, spent the first six years of his NHL career as a Boston Bruin. Fourteen games into his seventh campaign with the Bruins, during the 1950–51 season, Flaman was traded to Toronto. The timing of the deal allowed the resident of Dysart, Saskatchewan to be on the Maple Leafs' Cup-winning team that spring. It was the only time he played on a Stanley Cup championship team. Never much of an offensive threat—that was not his job—Flaman compiled just 30 goals in 911 NHL games. It was Flaman's rugged and excellent defensive prowess, however, that enabled him to remain in hockey's top league as long as he did. Flaman accrued 1,372 penalty minutes over his 14-year career. He was dealt back to the Bruins at the end of the 1953–54 season where he eventually became the team's captain. (Quite popular among Bruin fans, in 1961 Flaman was given a five-foot-tall portrait of himself as his playing career was nearing its end. It had been paid for entirely by donations from his admirers. Flaman cherished the memento and displayed it prominently in his home for the rest of his life.) Five times in his career, Flaman finished among the top five vote-getters for the Norris Trophy, although he never won it. Flaman would go on to a highly successful coaching career, briefly with the Rhode Island Reds of the American Hockey League, followed by 19 seasons with the Northeastern Huskies in the NCAA ranks. When Boston Garden hosted its last game in September 1995, during the postgame alumni skate, the 68-year-old Flaman and Terry O'Reilly both made impromptu detours to the Bruins' penalty box. There they sat, grinning for the benefit of photographers. Flaman died of cancer on June 22, 2012, at age 85. Upon learning of Flaman's death, Milt Schmidt told the *Boston Globe*, "I played with him and I played against him, and there was no one tougher in the National Hockey League. He was a real stay-at-home defenseman who rarely got caught up-ice. He was a quiet leader who never backed down from anybody."[5]

Center **Cal Gardner** spent one more season in Toronto before being dealt to the Chicago Black Hawks in September 1952 in a much-discussed transaction. He was one of four Maple Leafs traded to the Hawks for goaltender Harry Lumley—and no one else. Less than a year later Gardner was traded to Boston for cash. He never missed a single game with the Bruins until his retirement once the 1956–57 season was in the books. Gardner was also offensively consistent, scoring 14, 16, 15 and 12 goals in his four campaigns with the Bruins. During the 1970s, Gardner found work as a hockey broadcaster on a Toronto radio station. Two of Gardner's sons, Paul and Dave, both became professional hockey players and had substantial careers. Cal Gardner died at age 76 on October 10, 2001, about five months after the surviving members of the 1951 Stanley Cup champions were honored on the fiftieth anniversary of their triumph by the Maple Leafs' organization.

Goalie **Jack Gelineau** never played another game for the Boston Bruins following the 1950–51 NHL season—a season in which he played all 70 of Boston's games and four of their six semifinal playoff games versus Toronto. The 26-year-old was unable to reach a contract deal with Art Ross despite posting very decent starts for a mediocre club that struggled mightily all season long to stay within the top four teams in the league. Unlike many of his hockey contemporaries, Gelineau had post-secondary education on which to fall back. The NHL's Rookie of the Year in 1949–50, Gelineau walked away from the spotlight of the NHL, opting instead for a position at Sun Life Insurance in Montreal. During the 1947–48 season, Gelineau had attended McGill University while playing occasionally for Boston. He thus became the first player in three decades to simultaneously combine university attendance and NHL hockey. He obtained a Bachelor of Commerce degree. Ken Dryden of the Montreal Canadiens would famously duplicate the feat by obtaining a law degree in 1970–71. (He was also a McGill alum.) Gelineau, the insurance man, was content to play senior amateur hockey with the formidable Quebec Aces for a few winters, but he did return to the NHL once. During the 1954–55 season, Gelineau played a pair of games for the Chicago Black Hawks—and allowed 18 goals in two one-sided losses. He died one day after his 74th birthday in 1998.

Bernie Geoffrion, who shone offensively but struggled defensively during the 1951 playoffs, became a huge star with the Montreal Canadiens. Sill retaining rookie status in 1951–52 because of how few games he played in the NHL in 1950–51, the ruggedly handsome Geoffrion won the Calder Trophy as Rookie of the Year. He played 14 seasons for Montreal—often battling serious injuries along the way—and scored 371 regular-season goals. A good team player, he also picked up 388 assists. He finished out his playing career with two seasons as a New York Ranger. A fiercely proud man, Geoffrion was openly devastated when Jean Béliveau was named the Habs' captain in 1961 instead of him. Beginning in 1972, Geoffrion coached the expansion Atlanta Flames for the club's first two and a half seasons in the NHL. His longtime ambition to coach the Canadiens came true in 1979, but it lasted a mere 30 games. Severe stomach ulcers, his old-school attitude regarding pampered modern players, and Montreal's uncharacteristic mediocre play to begin the 1979–80 season combined to cause the embittered Geoffrion to resign around Christmastime. Geoffrion's #5 was retired by the Canadiens on March 11, 2006. Too ill from stomach cancer to attend the ceremony, Geoffrion died that very day in an Atlanta hospital at age 75. Fun fact: Geoffrion was the son-in-law of Howie Morenz, a Hab superstar from the 1920s and 1930s. The two hockey greats never met, however, as Morenz died at age 34 in 1937 when Geoffrion was just six years old.

Ebbie Goodfellow lasted one more dismal season as the coach of the Chicago Black Hawks. After his club went 12–47–10 in 1950–51, there was only a marginal improvement in 1951–52. That season Chicago again finished last in the league standings, this time with a 17–44–9 record. Goodfellow did leave on something of a high note, however. On March 23, 1952, in the third period of his final game, one of Goodfellow's players, Bill Mosienko, scored three goals in just 21 seconds against the New York Rangers to set an NHL record for the fastest hattrick. As of 2023, it still stands. Goodfellow never coached again. He died from cancer in Florida on September 10, 1985, at age 76.

Doug Harvey was largely regarded as the greatest defenseman in NHL history until Bobby Orr came along. He posted Orr-like numbers regarding the Norris Trophy, winning the award for the league's top defensemen seven times, the first one coming in 1955. (Theoretically Harvey could have won more, as the trophy was first presented after the 1953–54 season. The first recipient was Red Kelly.) Unlike Orr, Harvey was not nearly as much of an offensive threat; he never achieved double digits in goals scored in any NHL season. However, Harvey was known to make daring rushes up the ice on occasion. His true value was in strong, reliable, positional play. His usual defensive partner in Montreal, Tom Johnson, once said that Harvey was unrivaled as a defenseman in his era and could control the tempo of a game at will. Harvey was an excellent all-round athlete who often played football and semipro baseball in hockey's offseason. (He was offered a minor league contract by the Boston Braves in 1952, which he declined.) Harvey is also famous for an infamous (albeit unintentional) blunder. During the overtime period of Game #7 of the 1954 Cup finals versus Detroit, Harvey raised his glove to try to knock down a seemingly harmless dump-in from Detroit's Tony Leswick who lobbed the puck from near the red line and skated toward his team's bench. Harvey only got a piece of it—but it was enough to redirect the puck past his startled goaltender Gerry McNeil, giving Detroit the flukiest of Stanley Cup–winning goals. Despite his obvious hockey talents, Harvey was a problematic player for Montreal. He was frequently critical of the hockey establishment and its reserve clause that kept players' salaries artificially low. Prior to the 1960–61 season, Harvey was voted captain of the Canadiens by his teammates. The club's management was less than thrilled by this development, as they had been displeased with Harvey's actions both on and off the ice. The Canadiens were unhappy with Harvey's play during their semifinal loss to Chicago that spring and dealt him to the New York Rangers—where he won the Norris Trophy again as the team's playing-coach. His NHL career ended, it was thought, when the Rangers cut him loose after the 1963–64 season when his three-year contract expired. However, Harvey continued to play in the minor leagues and made occasional comebacks to the big league. He played 70 games for the 1968–69 St. Louis Blues when he was 44 years old and then retired for good. Harvey was elected to the Hall of Fame in 1973. Unfortunately, Harvey's later years were marred by struggles with alcoholism and failed business ventures. He died shortly after his 65th birthday, in Montreal, on December 26, 1989.

Gordon (Red) Henry had to wait another two years before he played goal again for the Boston Bruins. He played three games in the 1953 Stanley Cup playoffs, compiled a 1–2 record, and was never seen in the NHL again. He died at the young age of 46 in October 1972. Neither Jack Gelineau nor Red Henry was Boston's frontline goaltender in 1951–52. Coincidentally, it was another fellow named Henry—Sugar Jim Henry—who got the job. The Winnipeg native played in all 70 games for the Bruins during the regular season, along with their seven postseason games. His contract was purchased by the Bruins from the Detroit Red Wings just prior to the season's start, in September 1951.

Suffice to say **Gordie Howe** made a complete recovery from his near fatal head injury during the 1950 Stanley Cup semifinals. One of the most remarkable athletes in sports history, Howe played in Detroit for 25 seasons, through the 1970–71 campaign. Four of those clubs were Cup winners. Along the way he established daunting NHL records for scoring and longevity. (In his final campaign with the Red Wings, he scored 23 goals while approaching his 43rd birthday.) Cheerful and engaging off the ice, Howe was famous for his excellent memory, terrifying mean streak while playing, and his ability to hold on to grudges for years. During the 1957–58 season, rugged Toronto defenseman Bobby Baun nailed Howe with a heavy bodycheck. A decade later, Baun was playing for the expansion Oakland Seals when Howe cut to the middle of the ice. Howe released his shot and held his follow-through long enough for his stick blade to carve a gash in Baun's throat. As Baun gasped for breath, Howe coolly called him an SOB and informed him they were now even. After a short hiatus from hockey, Howe was persuaded to return to the sport to play alongside his sons on the World Hockey Association's Houston Aeros. He played

16. Postscripts

six WHA seasons and scored 174 goals! When that league folded in 1979, Howe, age 52, returned to the NHL and played one season with the Hartford Whalers, appearing in all 80 of the team's regular-season games and its three playoff games. He scored 15 goals to give him 801 in NHL competition. Howe's professional career remarkably spanned five decades. (It is six decades if one counts the two shifts Howe played at age 69 in a 1997 game for the International Hockey League's Detroit Vipers—an obvious publicity stunt which drew a rare capacity crowd for the club.) Aptly known as Mr. Hockey, Howe died as a much-beloved icon of the sport at age 88 on June 10, 2016.

Prior to becoming an esteemed NHL coach, **Dick Irvin** played professional hockey from 1915 to 1926 in the Pacific Coast Hockey League and the Western Canada Hockey League. He then spent three years with the Chicago Black Hawks before retiring as a player. From 1931 to 1940, Irvin coached the Toronto Maple Leafs. Beginning in 1940, he coached the Montreal Canadiens through the 1954–55 season, winning the Stanley Cup in 1953. Irvin's 15 years behind the Habs' bench remains the longest tenure for any coach in that storied club's impressive history. However, Irvin was dismissed by the club for the high crime of losing to the Detroit Red Wings in the seventh game of the Stanley Cup finals two seasons in a row. Irvin was replaced by Hector (Toe) Blake who immediately led the Habs to five consecutive Cups. The Canadiens' surprise trip to the 1951 Stanley Cup finals marked the first of 10 straight appearances the club made in the championship round of the playoffs—a record unlikely to be matched anytime soon in the modern, 32-team NHL. Irvin, who staunchly avoided tobacco and alcohol throughout his life, died from what was often described in the press as a "lingering illness" (it was later learned to be bone cancer) in May 1957. He was 64 years old. His son, Dick Irvin, Jr., was a likable and longtime fixture on the English-language telecasts of *Hockey Night in Canada* from Montreal who has published numerous books about his career and the history of the Habs.

Today, Detroit's **Tommy Ivan** is perhaps the least appreciated coach and general manager in NHL history. (Some experts knew his worth, however. Hockey historian Stan Fischler ranked Ivan among his Top 10 NHL coaches of all-time.) A facial injury that befell him as an amateur player prevented him from attaining a professional career on the ice, so he shifted his passion for hockey to creating and molding championship teams. Possessing a keen judgement of talent, Ivan's record of building excellent teams has few rivals. He coached three Stanley Cup winners in Detroit in his stint there from 1947 to 1954. In all seven of his seasons with the Red Wings, Ivan's club qualified for the playoffs. Moreover, Detroit finished in first place six consecutive times—an impressive achievement.

With Jack Adams solidly ensconced as the Wings' general manager, Ivan felt there was no room for further advancement in Detroit—but there certainly was in Chicago where the lackluster club was thrilled to offer him the position. Taking over the woebegone Black Hawks in 1954, Ivan rebuilt the entire franchise, adding new farm teams and securing new prospects. He hired Rudy Pilous as the team's coach. Eventually Ivan's system produced a Stanley Cup winner for Chicago in 1961. The Hawks would also be Cup finalists in 1962, 1965, 1971 and 1973. Altogether, he was a member of the Black Hawks' front office for 23 seasons before retiring. Later, Ivan helped to organize a huge prospect camp that provided more than 90 hopeful amateur players for coach Herb Brooks to examine for his famous gold-medal-winning 1980 U.S. Olympic team. Ivan died in June 1999 of a kidney ailment at age 88.

Defenseman **Tom Johnson** had an impressive rookie season with the Montreal Canadiens in 1950–51, playing in all 70 of the Habs' regular-season games and all 11 playoff matches, winning much praise along the way. He would remain in the NHL through the 1964–65 season, playing in nearly 1,100 total games if postseason appearances are included. All but Johnson's final two seasons were as a member of the Canadiens, where he was on six Stanley Cup champions. (Johnson is one of a dozen Habs to play on the teams that won five consecutive Cups from 1955–56 to 1959–60. He was probably the most underappreciated of the bunch.) Johnson was a stay-at-home blueliner who was especially good at killing penalties. When he won the Norris Trophy in 1958–59 as the NHL's best defenseman, Johnson interrupted a long winning streak by his teammate, Doug Harvey. According to the Canadiens' website, Johnson was "an adept stickhandler and effective passer. He was instrumental in launching the powerful Montreal transition game, coolly relieving opponents of the puck and directing play back up the ice. Never the fastest skater, Johnson relied instead on his anticipation and hockey sense and was rarely outplayed or caught out of position." Johnson finished his playing career in Boston, playing on Bruin teams that never qualified for the playoffs. He had a long post-playing career in Boston in several capacities. Johnson became the team's coach in 1970 following the unexpected resignation of Harry Sinden after the latter led the team to the Stanley Cup in May. He took over a dominant club that featured Bobby Orr, Phil Esposito and Johnny Bucyk. Johnson coached Boston to the 1972 Stanley Cup. Over his two and a half years behind the bench, Johnson compiled the best winning percentage (.738) of any coach in NHL history who has a minimum of 200 games on his résumé. Before stepping down as coach partway through the 1972–73 season to resume his former job as Boston's assistant general manager, Johnson had won 142 games while losing just 43 and tying 23. At age 79, Johnson died of heart failure on November 21, 2007, while chopping wood at his home in Falmouth, Massachusetts. He had been elected to the Hockey Hall of Fame as a player in 1970.

After the 1951 Stanley Cup triumph, defenseman **Bill Juzda** spent one more season in Toronto, playing 46 games for the Maple Leafs in 1951–52. That was the final chapter in his NHL career. The following season Juzda was on the roster of the Pittsburgh Hornets of the AHL. Renowned in his prime as one of the NHL's hardest hitters—one of his bodychecks ended Toe Blake's playing career—Juzda kept active in the game by playing senior amateur hockey for his hometown Winnipeg Maroons for the next decade. He appeared in two Allan Cup finals before hanging up his skates at age 43. Juzda lived to be 87 years old. He died in Winnipeg on February 17, 2008.

Ted (Teeder) Kennedy—the hockey player—was famous long before the American politician of the same name ever was. He got off to a disadvantaged start in life. Eleven days before Ted's birth in Humberstone (now part of Port Colborne), Ontario, in 1925, his father was killed in a tragic hunting accident, leaving a widow to raise four children. To help make ends meet, as a youth Ted worked with his mother at the concession booth at the local hockey arena. When the building officially closed each night, Kennedy and his siblings were permitted to use the ice surface. It was virtually his second home during his formative years. He developed excellent all-around hockey skills there. Not noted for being a particularly great skater, Kennedy mastered other important skills and the art of positional play. He was good enough to play in the NHL as an 18-year-old during the Second World War. By 1948 he had succeeded Syl Apps as captain of the Toronto Maple Leafs. Many hockey historians rank Kennedy as the most skillful faceoff man in NHL history. He won the Hart Trophy as the NHL's MVP in 1954–55. The next Maple Leaf to be so honored was Auston Matthews in 2021–22. After his retirement from hockey, Kennedy was an official with the Ontario Racing Commission. In 1979 he made headlines as one of three stewards at the $100,000 Canadian Oaks race to scratch a horse named Come Lucky Chance for throwing its rider before the race. The infuriated horse's owner was Kennedy's former boss, 84-year-old Conn Smythe, who grumbled, "I'll raise hell with only two of the stewards."[6] A lifelong teetotaler, Kennedy appeared in a public-service film made by the Ontario government alerting youngsters to the dangers of alcohol and drug abuse. He died at age 83 in August 2009 of congestive heart failure in a Port Colborne nursing home. How did Kennedy get the odd nickname Teeder? As a child, many of his young friends could not pronounce Kennedy's legal first name (Theodore). "Teeder" was as close as they got—and the moniker stuck.

Forward **Joe Klukay** spent one more season in Toronto before being acquired by Boston in a cash transaction prior to the 1952–53 season. *Boston Globe* sports writer Tom Fitzgerald would later categorize Klukay's acquisition as being extremely important as the dependable veteran was a surprise hero in the club's surprise playoff victory over Detroit in Klukay's first season with the Bruins. Klukay scored 20 goals with the Bruins in 1953–54, his highest offensive output for a single NHL campaign. He was shipped back to Toronto the following season in a trade for Leo Boivin—who, at age 22, was 10 years younger than Klukay. That was the beginning of the end for Klukay; he was out of the NHL at the end of 1955–56. Klukay continued to play high-level senior amateur hockey in Canada for several more years. He was part of an Allan Cup–winning team in 1963 with the Windsor Bulldogs. Klukay was 83 years old when he died in February 2006.

Elmer Lach played his entire 14-year NHL career with the Montreal Canadiens. Born in Nokomis, Saskatchewan in 1918, Lach was rejected by the Toronto Maple Leafs for being too small—even though he was listed as 5'10". Montreal paid just $100 for Lach's rights. It was money very well spent. In his rookie season of 1942–43, Lach had six assists on February 6 versus the Boston Bruins to set a team record for a single game that still stands. He was eventually teamed with Toe Blake and Maurice Richard as the center on the formidable Punch Line—an offensive unit that dominated the NHL for four seasons. Lach was named the Hart Trophy winner in 1944–45 as the NHL's MVP. He was the league's scoring champion in 1947–48—a rare season in which Montreal did not qualify for the Stanley Cup playoffs. He thus became the first scoring champion to be awarded the Art Ross Trophy. He announced his retirement after suffering a fractured jaw near the end of the 1948–49 season, but he was later persuaded to return to the Habs. He remained on the Canadiens' roster until the end of the 1953–54 season. By that time, Lach had been reduced to a parttime player but he was the NHL's all-time scoring leader. All that season, the Habs assigned Lach to tutor budding star Jean Béliveau on the game's subtleties. Lach scored 215 goals for Montreal in regular-season competition and another 19 in Stanley Cup play. His most famous tally occurred in Game Five of the 1953 Stanley Cup final versus Boston. His goal at 1:22 of overtime won the Stanley Cup for the Habs. It was the game's only goal. Moments afterward, in the rowdy, postgame celebration, Maurice Richard accidentally broke Lach's nose with his stick. Frequently injured due to his willingness to fight for the puck in the corners, that was one of seven times Lach's nose was broken during his hockey career. Many of his injuries were undoubtedly of the payback variety. A *Saturday Evening Post* article from 1950 noted, "To some, [Lach] is hockey's greatest competitor. To others, he is the nastiest so-and-so in the league."⁷ Twice widowed, Lach lived to be 97 years old. He attended Jean Béliveau's funeral in December 2014. It was his last public appearance. Lach himself passed away four months later on April 4, 2015. He had been the Habs' oldest living player prior to his death.

Calum (Baldy) MacKay's peak year in the NHL was easily the 1950–51 campaign. The 24-year-old forward, who was born in Toronto, played in all 70 games of the Habs' regular-season schedule along with all 11 of their postseason contests. MacKay had started his professional hockey career by playing five games for the Detroit Red Wings in 1947. In 1950, his rights were acquired by the Montreal Canadiens. He was a tough customer who routinely got far more penalty minutes than points in any given season. MacKay spent three years with the Habs before being demoted to the minor league Buffalo Bisons. He rejoined the Canadiens in a timely manner in the 1952–53 season for the playoffs; he had participated in no regular-season games for Montreal that year. They won the Stanley Cup—and MacKay got his name engraved on it—as the Habs defeated Boston in five games in the finals. MacKay played two more seasons for the Canadiens before he suffered a career-ending knee injury on September 30, 1955, during the team's training camp. MacKay died at age 74 in August 2001.

Fleming Mackell was a talented Montreal resident who somehow was not recruited by his hometown Canadiens. "Fleming was the best amateur hockey player in Quebec,"⁸ Hall of Famer Dickie Moore claimed in a 1986 *Montreal Gazette* feature article. Instead, he ended up as a Maple Leaf, winning two Cups with Toronto, in 1949 and 1951. He was traded from the Leafs to the Boston Bruins midway through the 1951–52 season. He excelled in his nine years as a Bruin. Following the 1952–53 campaign, Mackell was selected to the NHL's First All-Star team and was the recipient of the Elizabeth C. Dufresne Trophy as Boston's top performer in home games. He was the center on a Boston line featuring his former Maple Leaf teammate Cal Gardner and future Leaf Larry Regan. During the 1958 Stanley Cup playoffs, Mackell set a new NHL record with 14 assists in 12 games, leading all players in that year's postseason scoring with 19 points. When his NHL career ended, Mackell became a playing coach for the Quebec Aces of the American Hockey League. He was the son of Jack Mackell, who played two seasons for the original Ottawa Senators in 1919–20 and 1920–21. He won the Stanley Cup in both those years. Fleming Mackell died at age 86 on October 19, 2015.

(James) Bud MacPherson was one of those few athletes who made it to the big time in his sport and then seemed to vanish completely. Born in Edmonton in 1927, he played in 259 NHL games from 1948 to 1957—all for the Montreal Canadiens. When his NHL days ended, MacPherson continued to play professionally in the minor leagues through the 1960–61 season. After that point, the trail goes cold. Some hockey websites list his date of death as 1988 with a question mark. Others list the date as August 31 of that year. Assuming that at least the year is correct, he passed away—very quietly, it seems—at age 61. In 2005, MacPherson was inducted into the Alberta Sports Hall of Fame, presumably posthumously, as a member of the 1947–48 Edmonton Flyers who were Allan Cup finalists that season.

Paul Masnick, the youthful player from Regina, seemed to be a bright, upcoming star for the Canadiens. However, he ended up having a very spotty professional hockey career. Masnick played in 220 games in the NHL, but he was often shuttled back and forth between the Canadiens and their minor league clubs. (Masnick ended up playing for the Chicago Blacks Hawks and Toronto before hanging up his skates.) As of August 2023, the 92-year-old Masnick was the last surviving member of the Canadiens' 1952–53 Stanley Cup team and the last living player from either the Maple Leafs or the Canadiens who played in the 1951 Cup finals. When Masnick was interviewed by a local reporter at his Barrie, Ontario, condo just prior to the 2021 Stanley Cup finals at age 90, he told the scribe he would not be watching any of it because he did not own a television and had not seen a hockey game in many years. He died in March 2024.

Gerry McNeil, the rookie Montreal goaltender who played every minute of every game in 1950–51 (and famously allowed Bill Barilko's Stanley Cup–winning goal), seemed to be poised for a long career with the Habs. McNeil again played in every one of his team's 70 games in 1951–52 and appeared 66 times the following season. He promptly retired after the 1953–54 season in which he played 53 games—and the emergence of another goaltender was clearly on the horizon. (Author Kevin Shea accurately referred to McNeil's tenure as the Canadiens' netminder as the club's "brief interregnum between the Hall-of-Fame careers of Bill Durnan and Jacques Plante."[9]) He did return to the club, but he was slowly replaced by Plante as the Habs' go-to netminder by 1954. McNeil played minor league hockey with the Montreal Royals and Rochester Americans for a time. McNeil's last NHL games were in the 1956–57 season when he was just 31 years old. He died of cancer in June 2004 at age 78. Throughout his life, McNeil never stopped receiving autograph requests in the mail—quite frequently from Toronto fans wanting him to sign the famous photograph of Barilko's Cup-winning goal entering the net beside him.

Howie Meeker did not retire from hockey to become the manager of the Kitchener Memorial Auditorium as was rumored during the 1951 Stanley Cup playoffs. A month after the Leafs' triumph, Meeker had a personal victory of a different type. Making an unexpected foray into politics,

Meeker ran as a Progressive Conservative candidate in a federal byelection in the Ontario riding of Waterloo South (now Cambridge). He was elected, getting more than 42 percent of the vote in a three-person race. (Because of his election victory, on the same weekend that Bill Barilko vanished, Meeker was made an honorary member of the Ohsweken tribe and was given the native name Flying Cloud.) Remarkably, Meeker worked as both a Member of Parliament and as an NHL hockey player for two years. He did not run for reelection when his term as MP ended in 1953. Meeker returned to hockey and was briefly the Toronto Maple Leafs coach and then the team's general manager in the mid–1950s. Beginning in the 1970s, Meeker became known to a new generation of fans as an easily excitable but thoroughly lovable between-periods analyst on *Hockey Night in Canada*'s English-language telecasts. He was a pioneer in the use of a telestrator to analyze points of interest from the previous period. (Meeker constantly gave impromptu instructions to the videotape crew to "Stop it right here!" and "Roll it back!" in order to clearly emphasize his points.) "One thing Howie brought to every telecast was his undying enthusiasm for the game," recalled one colleague. That he did. His childlike interjections, such as "Golly gee!" and "Gee willikers!" endeared him to many fans, as did his catch phrase "Keep your stick on the ice!" Meeker often publicly decried the lack of fundamentals in many aspiring players. "Howie's two passions were hockey and teaching the game," broadcast partner Jim Hughson noted. "He kept hammering away at how we were falling behind the Russians in teaching the skills to our youngsters. It was a message a lot of people didn't want to hear, but he was right. When we [Canadians] lost our superiority, it was a rude awakening. But Howie saw it was coming."[10] In response to his concerns about the game's grassroots, Meeker ran his own summer hockey schools for many years. CBC Television produced more than a hundred 15-minute episodes of *Howie Meeker's Hockey School* between 1973 and 1977; they were instructional programs generally geared toward coaches. Meeker died in a Nanaimo, BC hospital in November 2020, not long after his 97th birthday.

Paul Meger, the 21-year-old Hab who got his team's second goal in Game Five of the finals—the last marker for Montreal in the series—returned to the Canadiens' roster the following season and impressively scored 24 goals for them in 1951–52. That was the high point of his professional hockey career. In the three seasons that followed, Meger only scored 13 more times. He was part of the Habs' Cup-winning squad of 1952–53. By the end of the 1954–55 season, Meger was out of the NHL and organized hockey altogether. He died on August 27, 2019, at the age of 90.

The **Montreal Canadiens** did not let the disappointment of losing in the 1951 Stanley Cup final hurt their enthusiasm for the 1951–52 season. They again advanced to the Cup finals as they would every season until 1961. They lost in 1952, 1954 and 1955, but the won six Stanley Cups—including five straight from 1956 to 1960. It could be argued that the dynasty lasted until the year of their most recent Cup triumph: 1993. Given how dominant the Habs were for more than four decades, their current Stanley Cup drought seems downright unfathomable.

Defenseman (**Angus**) **Gus Mortson** of New Liskeard, Ontario, spent one more season with the Toronto Maple Leafs—in which he scored one goal and picked up 106 minutes in penalties—before being shipped to the Chicago Black Hawks prior to the 1952–53 campaign in the deal for Harry Lumley. Nicknamed "Old Hardrock," Mortson spent six years with the Hawks—the same length of time he had been on the Maple Leafs' roster. He finished his NHL career by playing a single season with Detroit. After retiring from hockey, Mortson became involved in the food services industry and, for a time, was employed as a stockbroker, then as a mining company representative in Timmins. Mortson died at age 90 in August 2015. His obituary in the *Detroit Free Press* mentioned that he engaged in a scrap with Gordie Howe during the 1948 All-Star Game. To date, it is the only fight in the history of the exhibition game.

After starting his NHL days with the almost-forgotten Brooklyn Americans in 1941–42, **Ken Mosdell** remained a center on the Canadiens' roster for most of his career. A trade sent him to Chicago in 1956 for one season. Mosdell later returned to the Habs and played just two games in the 1957–58 season before being sent to the minors. He was surprisingly summoned to the Canadiens for the 1959 playoffs. Mosdell played three postseason games, but that qualified him to have his name inscribed on the Stanley Cup for the fourth time. He accrued 141 regular-season goals, all but nine of them with Montreal. Highlighting how poorly NHL players were paid, his 1954 Parkhurst hockey card noted that Mosdell worked summers "building boxcars and swinging a sledgehammer all day to keep in top physical shape." Mosdell died in January 2006 at age 83. He had been in declining health for about three years after suffering a stroke.

Bert Olmstead began the 1950–51 season as a member of the Chicago Black Hawks. On December 2, a trade sent him to Detroit, but he never played a game with the Red Wings. Seventeen days later another deal sent Olmstead to Montreal where he stayed with the Canadiens until 1958. As a long-serving Hab, he won four Stanley Cups. The last four seasons of Olmstead's NHL playing career were spent in Toronto where Olmstead won the Cup as a member of the Maple Leafs in 1962. In total, Olmstead appeared in a remarkable 11 Stanley Cup finals. A left winger, he scored 181 goals in regular-season play. Olmstead would be classified as a "power forward" in today's NHL, battling for pucks and merrily dishing out hard checks along the way. Olmstead's occasional rough play earned him the amusing and unflattering nickname "Dirty Bertie." His lone NHL coaching foray was a disaster. He lasted 64 games as the man behind the bench for the expansion Oakland Seals in 1967–68. Olmstead earned a hugely unpleasant reputation as a brutally hard taskmaster who was despised by his players, but it was his dismal record of 11-36-17 more than anything else that cost him his job. Olmstead died from a stroke on November 16, 2015. He was 89 years old.

Lynn Patrick remained the coach of the Boston Bruins until about halfway through the 1954–55 campaign. Oddly, 30 games into that season, he was fired as Boston's man behind the bench—but promoted to the team's general manager! He served in that capacity until 1964. In 1958, with the assistance of *Boston Herald* sports writer Leo Monahan, Patrick co-authored an instructional book titled *Let's Play Hockey!* that was aimed at the sport's youth coaches. In 1967, Patrick was hired by the expansion St. Louis Blues for double duty as both coach and general manager, but he quickly—and wisely—handed over the coaching duties to Scotty Bowman after just 16 games. Bowman led the Blues to three consecutive Stanley Cup finals in those seasons when one of the six NHL expansion teams was guaranteed a berth in the championship series. Patrick was employed by the Blues until 1977, rising as high as senior vice-president in the organization. On January 26, 1980, Patrick left a Blues home game versus Colorado not feeling very well. He died in a car crash on the way home. It was discovered that Patrick had suffered a fatal heart attack while driving. He was 67 years old. Nine years later, Patrick was posthumously awarded the trophy named after his famous father, Lester, for his lifetime contributions to hockey in the United States.

Johnny Peirson, the Boston Bruin forward who was seriously injured in the semifinal series versus Toronto, remained a mainstay on the B's until retiring after the 1957–58 season—his 11th NHL campaign. Four times Peirson was a 20-goal scorer for Boston; he managed 153 total goals in his solid career. He told an interviewer in 2012 that he retired at age 33 because his legs "sort of disappeared."[11] Peirson likely could have extended his career on the roster of a minor league team, but he did not want to uproot his family to continue as a hockey player with diminishing skills. For a time, he worked at the furniture factory owned by his father-in-law. Later, Peirson was a familiar television color commentator on Bruins games during the glory years of the Bobby Orr era and beyond. At one point he was the oldest living ex–Bruin. Peirson was 95 years old when died on April 16, 2021.

Joe Primeau did not immediately step down as the coach of the Toronto Maple Leafs, as Milt Dunnell had boldly predicted in his *Toronto*

Star column at the end of the Stanley Cup finals. In fact, Primeau lasted two more seasons behind the bench with the club, both of which were largely unsuccessful. In those two campaigns, his Maple Leafs posted a mediocre combined regular-season record of 56–55–29. Primeau never won another playoff game as Toronto's coach after the night of Bill Barilko's heroics, going 0–4 in 1952 and not qualifying for the postseason at all in 1953. "I had the conviction that Joe couldn't [win the Stanley Cup] again with the same team," Toronto owner Conn Smythe wrote in his autobiography. "But I was determined that he should keep on coaching."[12] The easy-going Primeau voluntarily retired as Toronto's coach after the 1952–53 season and entered the business world. He was replaced by another former Toronto star player from bygone days: Francis (King) Clancy. Primeau's unique achievement of having coached the winners of the Allan Cup, Memorial Cup and Stanley Cup will likely remain unequaled because the once-vibrant senior amateur hockey ranks in Canada are now verging on extinction. The Allan Cup, with its rich lore, may soon sadly pass into history. Primeau died on May 14, 1989, in Toronto at the age of 83.

Billy Reay, who had an excellent postseason for Montreal in 1951, ended up playing 10 seasons in the NHL, mostly with the Canadiens. Afterward, he became much better known as an NHL coach. His second career did not start out especially well. Reay's 1957–58 Toronto Maple Leafs finished dead last in the league. The next season he was fired by Toronto after just 20 games. Five years would pass before Reay returned to the NHL as coach of the Chicago Black Hawks in 1963. He led the Hawks to three Stanley Cup finals, but failed each time in his quest to capture the elusive Cup. All three of the losses were at the hands of the Montreal Canadiens. Nevertheless, by the time Reay was callously dismissed by the Black Hawks in December 1976 (via a pink slip left under his apartment door three days before Christmas), he had won 542 regular-season games. That sizable total put him in second place among all NHL coaches in history at the that time, with only Dick Irvin ahead of him. (As of August 2023, Reay's ranking had dropped considerably in 47 years to 26th place.) Reay died of liver cancer on September 23, 2004, at the age of 86.

Leo Reise, the Detroit defenseman who was perhaps the Red Wings' best performer in their semifinal loss to Montreal, was actually Leo Reise, Jr.—the son of another NHL player. (His father had played eight NHL seasons in the 1920s with the old Hamilton Tigers, New York Americans and New York Rangers.) The younger Reise was a dominant athlete. As a teen, he once won five different events at a high school track meet. Reise was a very capable blueliner who notched 28 goals in 494 NHL games, the vast majority with the Red Wings. His most famous accomplishment was scoring the game-winning goal in Game Seven of Detroit's semifinal triumph

16. Postscripts

over Toronto in 1950 to knock the three-time defending champions out of the Stanley Cup playoffs. Upon retiring from hockey, Reise managed a plumbing business. He died of cancer at age 93 on July 26, 2015.

Maurice Richard remained the favorite son of Quebec through his retirement at the end of the 1959–60 season and well beyond. Between 1951 and 1960, Richard was on six Cup-winning teams in Montreal. When Richard hung up his skates, he was the NHL's all-time leader in goals scored with 544 and points with 966; he had easily overtaken Nels Stewart's previous record of 324 career goals during the 1952–53 season. Interestingly, Richard never captured an individual season's scoring title—a stat which gives equal weight to both goals and assists. (His goal mark was eventually surpassed by Gordie Howe in 1963.) He became an important cultural icon for French-Canadians who felt marginalized by perceived English-Canadian elitism. Possessing fire in his eyes and a famously quick temper, Richard's most notorious incident occurred late in the 1954–55 season when he punched linesman Cliff Thompson in Boston during a late-season scuffle with the Bruins' Hal Laycoe when the official tried to intervene. (Laycoe was a former Montreal teammate of Richard for several seasons.) Clarence Campbell promptly suspended Richard for the rest of the regular season and the playoffs, outraging Hab supporters. During the Habs' next game at the Forum against Detroit on March 17, Campbell was assaulted by a fan. Someone set off a tear gas bomb as what became known to history as the "Richard Riot" broke out. The game was forfeited to the Red Wings, but violence spilled onto the streets of Montreal and resulted in $500,000 in property damage. Richard, at the request of the police, made a public plea by radio for the rioting to stop. It did. However, Richard's absence from the Montreal lineup cost him the season's scoring title as he was overtaken by teammate Bernie Geoffrion. (He and Richard each notched 38 goals, but Geoffrion had 37 assists to Richard's 36.) When the Montreal Forum hosted its final game on March 11, 1996, Richard was the last dignitary introduced. He received a 16-minute standing ovation. In 2012, Bleacher Report rated it the #1 moment in the 72-year history of the Montreal Forum, noting, "There's not much else to say on the matter except for the fact that if the moment brought a player known for having fire in his eyes to tears, you may not be able to watch [the video clip] and keep your eyes dry."[13] When Richard died in May 2000 at age 79 of abdominal cancer, he was given a state funeral—something unprecedented for a Canadian athlete in any sport. Beginning in 1998–99, the Maurice (Rocket) Richard Trophy has been annually awarded to the NHL's seasonal leader in goals scored.

Al Rollins, the 1950–51 Vezina Trophy winner, played just one more season with the Toronto Maple Leafs. On September 11, 1952, Rollins was traded with three teammates to Chicago for just one player: highly regarded goaltender Harry Lumley. Rollins spent almost the rest of his NHL career with a woeful Black Hawks team that seldom made the playoffs, much less threatened to win the Stanley Cup. Nevertheless, in 1953-54, Rollins remarkably won the Hart Trophy as the NHL's Most Valuable Player despite only winning 12 games for last-place Chicago that season. As of 2023, he is just one of three players to be named a seasonal MVP in the NHL and *not* later be enshrined in the Hockey Hall of Fame once eligible. (Tommy Anderson and José Théodore are the other two.) Rollins died at age 69 in July 1996.

During the Stanley Cup finals, it was reported by the Red Wings that Detroit's young superstar netminder **Terry Sawchuk** had successfully undergone surgery. The operation was to remove a large bone chip from an area of his right arm near the elbow. It was not a new injury. Sawchuk had damaged it as a youth and had already had some chips removed in a previous surgical procedure. (The injury had mildly retarded that arm's growth. When observing their goaltender preparing for games, keen-eyed teammates noticed that Sawchuk's left arm was markedly longer than his right one.) Physicians estimated that Sawchuk would not be able to use his right arm for about a month. He recovered nicely. Sawchuk would eventually play 21 seasons for five different NHL teams and record 103 career shutouts—a record that stood until Martin Brodeur eclipsed it in 2009. His undisputed greatness as a goaltender obscured an often-turbulent private life. Sawchuk died under odd circumstances from a pulmonary embolism about seven weeks after his New York Rangers were eliminated from the 1970 Stanley Cup playoffs. He was just 40 years old.

Milt Schmidt, with his two ailing knees, was voted the winner of the NHL's Hart Trophy for the 1950-51 season. The award is often mischaracterized as the league's MVP award; that is only half true. The trophy is presented to the player judged to be the most valuable *to his team*. Often the last three words are ignored—and the distinction is important. Thus, while hockey fans engaged in lively discussions about the merits of Maurice Richard and Gordie Howe as to which one was the NHL's best player, Schmidt was declared to be the most valuable cog to his club, the Boston Bruins. (Nineteen years later in 1970, Schmidt, would present the Hart Trophy to 22-year-old Bobby Orr.) Schmidt would play for a few more seasons and accumulate 229 career goals. Partway through the 1954-55 season, however, Schmidt retired as a player and took over the Boston coaching reins from Lynn Patrick. He held that job until 1966 when he was promoted to the club's general manager, a job he held until 1973. Schmidt left Boston for a brief stint with the expansion Washington Capitals as that club's first general manager. He even coached them, a thoroughly hapless squad, for part of two seasons before being fired. Schmidt officially retired from hockey management, but he retained a strong connection to the Bruins, especially their alumni. In his later years, Schmidt was lovingly referred to as "Uncle Miltie" (as comedian Milton Berle once was). His jersey #15 was retired by the team. Schmidt died of a stroke in January 2017 at the age of 98. Before his death, Schmidt was the oldest living ex–NHL player, the last remaining man to have played in the league in the 1930s, and the last player to have participated in the American Hockey League's inaugural season of 1936–37. "There were two guys over there in Boston that I played against and respected," Gordie Howe once said. "Two guys that I really admired as well: Bobby Orr and Uncle Miltie. He [Schmidt] was a hard-nosed player, a great skater, a great playmaker, and a great competitor."[14]

Tod Sloan, one of Toronto's important scoring heroes of the 1951 Stanley Cup playoffs, typically put up only average offensive totals for the rest of his career. After scoring 31 goals in 1950–51, Sloan's tally total dropped to 25, 15, 11 and 13 over the next four seasons with the Maple Leafs, before rebounding dramatically to 37 goals in 1955–56. However, Sloan ran afoul of Toronto management in 1958 when he was one of several NHL players who tried to form the union which eventually became the National Hockey League Players' Association. As punishment, Sloan was traded to Chicago—which was often considered the Siberia of the NHL at the time. He spent his final three NHL seasons there as the team improved. His last NHL game was Chicago's Stanley Cup-winning triumph in 1961 versus Detroit—the club's first championship since 1938. His name was incorrectly engraved on the Cup as "Martin A. Sloan." (Sloan's legal name was Aloysius Martin Sloan. He acquired the nickname Tod as a youth because of the famous American jockey of the 1890s with that name.) The following season, Sloan was reinstated as an amateur and played a handful of games for the Galt Terriers, Canada's representative at the 1962 IIHF world championship tournament in Colorado where he was a silver medalist. Sloan retired shortly afterward. A cousin of later Toronto great Dave Keon, he died on July 12, 2017, at the age of 89.

Sid Smith made a memorable splash with the Toronto Maple Leafs when it counted most. He had played just one regular-season game for them during the 1948–49 season, having spent most of that campaign playing for the Leafs' top minor league club in Pittsburgh where he scored 55 goals. Smith was recalled for the playoffs—and promptly scored a hat-trick in Game Two of the Stanley Cup finals against the heavily favored Detroit Red Wings, accounting for all the Toronto goals in the Maple Leafs' 3–1 road victory. Described by Jack Sullivan of the Canadian Press as "a chunky 24 year old," Smith was decreed to be "the whole show. He was going both ways all the time, proving to the Leafs it was their best move to call on him."¹⁵ Smith was a mainstay with the Maple Leafs from that point forward until he retired from the NHL in 1958. Smith became the Toronto captain in 1955, replacing Ted Kennedy, and twice won the Lady Byng Trophy for gentlemanly play combined with high skill. The thoroughly reliable Smith scored at least 20 goals per season for six consecutive years—a feat only Gordie Howe had accomplished in the NHL at that time. His highest seasonal total was 33 in 1955-56. After he quit the NHL, Smith became the playing coach of the very successful Whitby Dunlops senior amateur team that had won the Allan Cup and IIHF world championship. Smith died at age 78 in 2004.

Conn Smythe had built the foundation for the expansion New York Rangers in 1926, but he was fired before his team had played a single game. Not long afterward he moved back to his hometown in Toronto and became part of the ownership group that acquired the Toronto St. Patricks—which were quickly renamed the Maple Leafs. They became a winning outfit with Smythe assuming near dictatorial powers over the team. Milt Dunnell of the *Toronto Star* once joked in a piece about Smythe's smothering leadership style, "The rules are simple. Aside from what you wear, what you say, what you eat, what you drink, who you're with, where you're going, how much you weigh and what you think, the club has little, if any, interest in the hired help, outside working hours."¹⁶ It worked, however. Smythe's Leafs won their first Stanley Cup in 1932—beating the New York Rangers in three straight games (to Smythe's great delight)—and then won six more Cups between 1942 and 1951. After an uncharacteristic down period for the rest of the 1950s, the Maple Leafs experienced a renaissance and won four more Cups between 1962 and 1967. By 1966, Smythe, now in his seventies, had sold his interest in the team but stayed on as a member of the board of directors for Maple Leaf Gardens. He resigned that post later that same year when the famous arena was the site for the heavyweight championship fight between Muhammad Ali and Canada's George Chuvalo. Ali had basically been forced to compete outside the United States because of his very public stance against the Vietnam War—and having him defend the world title at the arena Smythe had built was completely outrageous to the hockey mogul. Smythe, who served in the Canadian military in both world wars, angrily told the press, "The Gardens was founded by men—sportsmen—who fought for their country. It is no place for those want to evade conscription in their own country. The Gardens was built for many things, but not for picking up things that no one else wants."¹⁷ Smythe died on November 18, 1980, at age 85.

No one knew it at the time, of course, but the **Toronto Maple Leafs'** 1951 Cup triumph marked the end of an era for that storied NHL club. The

16. Postscripts

team generally dropped to mediocrity for more than half a decade, even missing the playoffs on a couple of occasions. They did not win another playoff series until 1959. The early 1960s, however, saw a renaissance of hockey excellence in Toronto with three straight Stanley Cups from 1962 through 1964 under the leadership of coach Punch Imlach. Another Cup triumph, an upset win over Montreal in the finals, came in 1967—the last season of the six-team NHL. (Fittingly, it was Canada's centennial year, too.) As of 2023, that was the Maple Leafs' most recent appearance in the Stanley Cup finals. Twenty different teams have won the Stanley Cup since Toronto last achieved the feat. Fifteen of those clubs were not in existence in 1967. Remarkably, the two Original Six teams that have presently gone the longest without winning the Stanley Cup are Toronto and Montreal.

Harry Watson, as an 18-year-old rookie in 1941–42, was one of very few NHL players who could claim the first club he played for was the Brooklyn Americans. (They were the New York Americans from 1925 to 1926 to 1940–41. Although they retained Madison Square Garden as their home building, the club played just one season as a "Brooklyn" team before folding.) Watson, a native of Saskatoon, had the good fortune of being picked up in a special dispersal draft by the Detroit Red Wings and won a Stanley Cup in 1942–43. Watson served in the Royal Canadian Air Force in the Second World War and played some hockey on the RCAF service team that was situated in Winnipeg. After the war, Watson returned to the roster of the Red Wings. "At 6-foot-1 and 207 pounds," said one obituary when he passed away in 2002, "Watson was among the biggest skaters in the NHL. Fast and powerful, the left winger was a solid scorer, a tough forechecker, and a sound defensive worker."[18] Just prior to the start of the 1946–47 season, Watson was traded by the Red Wings to the Toronto Maple Leafs—just in time to be part of a dynastic team. By 1948–49, he was the club's leading scorer, with 26 goals and 19 assists for 45 total points. Furthermore, Watson had zero penalty minutes for the entire 60-game regular season. Watson reached the milestone of 200 career goals in his final season with Toronto, the 200th coming against Montreal on October 21, 1954. Not long afterward he was traded to Chicago and spent most of three years with the Black Hawks. Watson finished his career with 236 goals and 207 assists in 809 games. A five-time Stanley Cup winner, Watson was in the NHL's top 15 all-time goal scorers at the time of his retirement. He was elected to the Hall of Fame in 1994. Watson died on November 19, 2002, at age 79, after a short illness.

17

1951 Stanley Cup Finals
Series Statistics

Montreal Canadiens

Players	G	A	PTS	PIM
Maurice Richard	5	2	7	4
Bill Reay	1	2	3	10
Doug Harvey	0	3	3	2
Paul Masnick	2	0	2	4
Paul Meger	1	1	2	2
Bert Olmstead	0	2	2	7
Elmer Lach	1	0	1	2
Butch Bouchard	0	1	1	0
Bud MacPherson	0	1	1	4
Ken Mosdell	0	0	0	2
Tom Johnson	0	0	0	2
Bernie Geoffrion	0	0	0	4
Bob Dawes	0	0	0	2
Floyd Curry	0	0	0	2
Totals	10	12	22	47

(Other Canadiens who appeared in the series but had no points or penalty minutes were Calum MacKay, Eddie Mazur and Ross Lowe.)

Goaltender	GP	W	L	GA
Gerry McNeil	5	1	4	13

17. 1951 Stanley Cup Finals

Toronto Maple Leafs

Players	G	A	PTS	PIM
Tod Sloan	3	4	7	7
Sid Smith	5	1	6	0
Ted Kennedy	2	4	6	2
Max Bentley	0	4	4	2
Harry Watson	1	2	3	4
Howie Meeker	1	1	2	10
Bill Barilko	1	0	1	6
Gus Mortson	0	1	1	0
Fern Flaman	0	0	0	6
Bill Juzda	0	0	0	2
Fleming Mackell	0	0	0	2
Jimmy Thomson	0	0	0	4
Totals	13	17	30	45

(Other Maple Leafs who appeared in the series but had no points or penalty minutes were Cal Gardner, Joe Klukay, Danny Lewicki and Ray Timgren.)

Goaltenders	GP	W	L	GA
Turk Broda	2	1	1	5
Al Rollins	3	3	0	5
Totals	5	4	1	10

Chapter Notes

Introduction

1. "Barilko's Sudden Death Goal Beats Montreal Six," *Boston Globe*, April 22, 1951, 49.
2. Dink Carroll, "Playing the Field," *Montreal Gazette*, April 2, 1951, 22.
3. Kevin Shea, *Barilko: Without a Trace* (Bolton, ON: Fenn Publishing Company Ltd., 2004), 139.

Chapter 1

1. Dink Carroll, "Playing the Field," *Montreal Gazette*, March 29, 1950, 18.
2. "National Hockey League Opens with Rangers Visiting Detroit," *Montreal Gazette*, October 11, 1950, 16.
3. Dink Carroll, "Canadiens, Hawks Launch Season Here with 3-3 Draw," *Montreal Gazette*, October 13, 1950, 18.
4. "Toronto's Al Rollins in Line for Vezina and Rookie Cups," *Ottawa Citizen*, February 28, 1951, 21.
5. Stan Fischler, "From the Archives: Rangers Hypnotist Ruled Offside," TheHockeyNews.com, August 17, 2022.
6. Ibid.
7. Ibid.
8. Ibid.
9. Ibid.
10. Dink Carroll, "Playing the Field," *Montreal Gazette*, January 1, 1951, 14.
11. "Howe, Wings Star, Seriously Hurt; Has Brain Operation," *Boston Globe*, March 29, 1950, 15.
12. Red Burnett, "Butt-End Injured Howe, Detroit Coach Claims, but Teeder Denies," *Toronto Daily Star*, March 29, 1950, 19.
13. "Writer's View on the Howe Case," *Ottawa Citizen*, March 30, 1950, 24.
14. Ibid.
15. Ibid.
16. Dink Carroll, "Playing the Field," *Montreal Gazette*, March 30, 1951, 16.
17. Stan Fischler, "From the Archives: The Magic Elixir That Amazed the Rangers," TheHockeyNews.com, May 18, 2022.
18. Dink Carroll, "The Rocket Banished as Habs Go Down 3-1," *Montreal Gazette*, March 5, 1951, 18.
19. "Richard Admits Scuffle—'A Man Can Take So Much,'" *Boston Globe*, March 5, 1951," 10.
20. Ibid.
21. Dink Carroll, "The Rocket Banished as Habs Go Down 3-1," *Montreal Gazette*, March 5, 1951, 18.
22. Mel Suffrin, "Leafs Shut Out Canadiens Which Tightens Vezina Trophy Race," *Galt Evening Reporter*, March 22, 1951, 17.
23. Baz O'Meara, "The Passing Sport Show," *Montreal Star*, April 12, 1951, 54.
24. Baz O'Meara, "The Passing Sport Show," *Montreal Star*, March 26, 1951, 26.

Chapter 2

1. "Are Wings Best in History?" *Ottawa Citizen*, March 27, 1951, 15.
2. Marshall Dann, "'Everything to Win, Nothing to Lose'—Irvin," *Montreal Gazette*, March 27, 1951, 18.
3. Ibid.
4. Ibid.
5. Dink Carroll, "Rocket Provides Thriller Finish for Canadiens Win," *Montreal Gazette*, March 28, 1951, 20.
6. Brian Kendall, *Shutout: The Legend of Terry Sawchuk* (Toronto: Penguin, 1996), 42.

Chapter Notes

7. Dink Carroll, "Rocket Provides Thriller Finish for Canadiens Win," *Montreal Gazette*, March 28, 1951, 20.
8. "Richard Goal Beats Wings, 3–2, in 4th Overtime Period," *Boston Globe*, March 28, 1951, 18.
9. Ibid.
10. Dink Carroll, "Rocket Provides Thriller Finish for Canadiens Win," *Montreal Gazette*, March 28, 1951, 20.
11. "Richard Goal Beats Wings, 3–2, in 4th Overtime Period," *Boston Globe*, March 28,1951, 18.
12. Ibid.
13. Dink Carroll, "Playing the Field," *Montreal Gazette*, April 2, 1951, 22.
14. Dink Carroll, "Wings Back in Playoff Hunt After Beating Canadiens 2–0 on Forum Ice," *Montreal Gazette*, April 2, 1951, 22.
15. Ibid.
16. Ibid.
17. Ibid.
18. "Wings Spill Montreal on Howe, Abel Goals," *Boston Globe*, April 1, 1951, 47.
19. Dink Carroll, "Playing the Field," *Montreal Gazette*, April 2, 1951, 22.
20. Baz O'Meara, "The Passing Sport Show," *Montreal Star*, April 2, 1951, 33.
21. Doug Vaughan, "On the Rebound," *Windsor Daily Star*, April 3, 1951 (Section II) 3.
22. "Wings Beat Montreal, 4–1, Square Series 2-All," *Boston Globe*, April 5, 1951, 10.
23. Ibid.
24. Harold Atkins, "Detroit Boys Out to Bury Habs in Hurry," *Montreal Star*, April 4, 1952, 32.
25. Dink Carroll, "Canadiens Overcome Early 2-Goal Deficit to Conquer Red Wings 5–2," *Montreal Gazette*, April 6, 1951, 20.
26. Ibid.
27. Baz O'Meara, "The Passing Sport Show," *Montreal Star*, April 5, 1951, 31.
28. Dink Carroll, "Canadiens Overcome Early 2-Goal Deficit to Conquer Red Wings 5–2," *Montreal Gazette*, April 6, 1951, 20.
29. Ibid.
30. "Canadiens Spot Wings 2 Goals, Rally for 5–2 Victory," *Boston Globe*, April 6, 1951, 20.
31. Baz O'Meara, "The Passing Sport Show," *Montreal Star*, April 5, 1951, 31.
32. "Canadiens Down Wings, 3–2, Gain Finals of Cup Playoffs," *Boston Globe*, April 8, 1951, 46.
33. Dink Carroll, "Canadiens in Stanley Cup Final with Leafs by Defeating Wings 3–2," *Montreal Gazette*, April 9, 1951, 22.
34. "Canadiens Down Wings, 3–2, Gain Finals of Cup Playoffs," *Boston Globe*, April 8, 1951, 46.
35. Brian McFarlane, *The Lively World of Hockey* (New York: Signet, 1968), 109.
36. Dink Carroll, "Canadiens in Stanley Cup Final with Leafs by Defeating Wings 3–2," *Montreal Gazette*, April 9, 1951, 22.
37. "Canadiens Down Wings, 3–2, Gain Finals of Cup Playoffs," *Boston Globe*, April 8, 1951, 46.
38. Dink Carroll, "Playing the Field," *Montreal Gazette*, April 9, 1951, 22.
39. "Show Over Wings Boosts Hab Stock," *Calgary Herald*, April 9, 1951, 18.
40. "1951: The Most Closely Matched Stanley Cup Final," TheHockeyWriters.com, April 1, 2019.
41. Jack Koffman, "Along Sport Row," *Ottawa Citizen*, April 9, 1951, 17.

Chapter 3

1. Tom Fitzgerald, "Bruins See Rough Series with Leafs," *Boston Globe*, March 27, 1951, 10.
2. Tom Fitzgerald, "Leafs' Watson Unable to Face Bruins Tonight in Series Opener," *Boston Globe*, March 28, 1951, 18.
3. Ibid.
4. "Watson Missing for First Game," *Montreal Gazette*, March 28, 1951, 20.
5. Tom Fitzgerald, "Bruins See Rough Series with Leafs," *Boston Globe*, March 27, 1951, 10.
6. Tom Fitzgerald, "Gelineau Great as Bruins Upset Leafs, 2–0, in Opener," *Boston Globe*, March 29, 1951, 10.
7. Ibid.
8. Fraser MacDougall, "Boston Takes First Game Against Favored Leafs," *Ottawa Citizen*, March 29, 1951, 23.
9. Gerald Lougheed, "Bruins Blank Leafs in Upset," *Galt Evening Reporter*, March 29, 1951, 22.
10. Fraser MacDougall, "Boston Takes First Game Against Favored Leafs," *Ottawa Citizen*, March 29, 1951, 23.

11. *Ibid.*
12. Tom Fitzgerald, "Bruins, Leafs Tie, 1–1, in Overtime Bruiser," *Boston Globe*, April 1, 1951, 1.
13. *Ibid.*
14. *Ibid.*
15. Gerald Lougheed, "Leafs Even Series After Riotous Week-end," *Ottawa Journal*, April 2, 1951, 17.
16. Tom Fitzgerald, "Bruins, Leafs Tie, 1–1, in Overtime Bruiser," *Boston Globe*, April 1, 1951, 1.
17. Tom Fitzgerald, "Leafs Beat Bruins, 3–0, to Square Cup Series," *Boston Globe*, April 2, 1951, 1.
18. *Ibid.*
19. *Ibid.*
20. Red Burnett, "Leafs Hold Whip Over Bruins Again," *Toronto Star*, April 2, 1951, 16.
21. Tom Fitzgerald, "Leafs Beat Bruins, 3–0, to Square Cup Series," *Boston Globe*, April 2, 1951, 1.
22. *Ibid.*
23. "Leafs Score in Boston to Square Series," *Ottawa Citizen*, April 2, 1951, 21.
24. Kevin Shea, *Barilko: Without a Trace* (Bolton, ON: Fenn Publishing Company Ltd., 2004), 121.
25. Tom Fitzgerald, "Toronto Takes Playoff Lead, Scores 3–1 Win," *Boston Globe*, April 7, 1951, 10.
26. Herb Ralby, "Patrick Weighs Lineup in Bid to Even Series," *Boston Globe*, April 7, 1951, 4.
27. *Ibid.*
28. Tom Fitzgerald, "Bruins Lose, 4–1; Canadiens Win, Eliminate Wings," *Boston Globe*, April 8, 1951, 1.
29. Tom Fitzgerald, "Bruins Eliminated from Cup Play," *Boston Globe*, April 9, 1951, 1.
30. *Ibid.*
31. "Broda Gets Shutout as Leafs Reach Finals," *Ottawa Citizen*, April 9, 1951, 17.
32. Tom Fitzgerald, "Bruins Eliminated from Cup Play," *Boston Globe*, April 9, 1951, 1.
33. *Ibid.*
34. *Ibid.*
35. *Ibid.*
36. Dink Carroll, "Playing the Field," *Montreal Gazette*, April 12, 1951, 18.
37. *Ibid.*
38. Jack Koffman, "Along Sport Row," *Ottawa Citizen*, April 9, 1951, 17.

Chapter 4

1. Doug Vaughan, "On the Rebound," *Windsor Daily Star*, April 18, 1949 (Section II), 3.
2. Doug Vaughan, "On the Rebound," *Windsor Daily Star*, April 9, 1950 (Section II), 3.
3. Brian McFarlane, *The Lively World of Hockey* (New York: Signet, 1968), 103.
4. Doug Vaughan, "Leafs Deliver a 2–1 Kayo to Win Stanley Cup," *Windsor Daily Star*, April 21, 1947 (Section II), 3.
5. Brian McFarlane, *The Lively World of Hockey* (New York: Signet, 1968), 87.
6. Dink Carroll, "Last Ditch Rally Falls Goal Short," *Montreal Gazette*, April 1, 1945, 16.
7. Jack Koffman, "Along Sports Row," *Ottawa Citizen*, April 9, 1951, 17.

Chapter 5

1. Jack Koffman, "Along Sports Row," *Ottawa Citizen*, April 9, 1951, 17.
2. Dink Carroll, "Hockey Elite Meet," *Montreal Gazette*, April 12, 1951, 18.
3. *Ibid.*
4. *Ibid.*
5. *Ibid.*
6. *Ibid.*
7. *Ibid.*
8. Jack Koffman, "Along Sports Row," *Ottawa Citizen*, April 9, 1951, 17.
9. Baz O'Meara, "The Passing Sport Show," *Montreal Star*, April 11, 1951, 33.
10. Maurice Smith, "Time Out," *Winnipeg Free Press*, April 11, 1951, 22.
11. Kevin Shea, *Barilko: Without a Trace* (Bolton, ON: Fenn Publishing Company Ltd., 2004), 122.
12. "Harvey and Geoffrion May Miss First Playoff," *Ottawa Citizen*, April 10, 1951, 18.
13. Jack Koffman, "Along Sports Row," *Ottawa Citizen*, April 11, 1951, 24.

Chapter 6

1. Baz O'Meara, "Leafs Grab Series Lead as Smith Fires Clincher," *Montreal Star*, April 12, 1951, 54.
2. Kevin Shea, *Barilko: Without a Trace* (Bolton, ON: Fenn Publishing Company Ltd., 2004), 123.
3. Dink Carroll, "Second Goal by Sid

Smith Ends Extra Period Battle," *Montreal Gazette*, April 12, 1951, 18.
4. *Ibid.*
5. Kevin Shea, *Barilko: Without a Trace* (Bolton, ON: Fenn Publishing Company Ltd., 2004), 123.
6. *Ibid.*
7. *Ibid.*
8. Dink Carroll, "Second Goal by Sid Smith Ends Extra Period Battle," *Montreal Gazette*, April 12, 1951, 18.
9. *Ibid.*
10. *Ibid.*
11. "Leafs Win by 3-2 in Overtime," *Ottawa Citizen*, April 12, 1951, 25.
12. Dink Carroll, "Second Goal by Sid Smith Ends Extra Period Battle," *Montreal Gazette*, April 12, 1951, 18.
13. Fraser MacDougall, "Habs' Bad Break on Curry's Shot," *Ottawa Citizen*, April 12, 1951, 25.
14. *Ibid.*
15. Jack Koffman, "Along Sport Row," *Ottawa Citizen*, April 12, 1951, 24.
16. Doug Vaughan, "On the Rebound," *Windsor Daily Star*, April 12, 1951 (Section II), 3.

Chapter 7

1. Dink Carroll, "Playing the Field," *Montreal Gazette*, April 16, 1951, 22.
2. Dink Carroll, "Playing the Field," *Montreal Gazette*, April 13, 1951, 20.
3. *Ibid.*
4. *Ibid.*
5. *Ibid.*
6. *Ibid.*
7. *Ibid.*
8. *Ibid.*
9. *Ibid.*
10. Dink Carroll, "Richard's Early Overtime Goal Enables Canadiens to Down Toronto 3-2," *Montreal Gazette*, April 16, 1951, 22.
11. *Ibid.*
12. *Ibid.*
13. *Ibid.*
14. Fraser MacDougall, "Rocket Breaks Up Game with Overtime Tally," *Ottawa Citizen*, April 16, 1951, 21.
15. Dink Carroll, "Playing the Field," *Montreal Gazette*, April 16, 1951, 22.
16. Jack Koffman, "Along Sport Row," *Ottawa Citizen*, April 16, 1951, 21.
17. Dink Carroll, "Playing the Field," *Montreal Gazette*, April 16, 1951, 22.
18. *Ibid.*
19. Gerry Lougheed, "Richard Greatest in the Game Today," *Ottawa Citizen*, April 16, 1951, 21.
20. Doug Vaughan, "On the Rebound," *Windsor Daily Star*, April 16, 1951 (Section II), 3.
21. Dink Carroll, "Richard's Early Overtime Goal Enables Canadiens to Down Toronto 3-2," *Montreal Gazette*, April 16, 1951, 22.
22. Doug Vaughan, "On the Rebound," *Windsor Daily Star*, April 16, 1951 (Section II), 3.
23. Fraser MacDougall, "Rocket Breaks Up Game with Overtime Tally," *Ottawa Citizen*, April 16, 1951, 21.
24. Dink Carroll, "Playing the Field," *Montreal Gazette*, April 16, 1951, 22.
25. "Sudden Death Goal Ties Stanley Cup Series at 1–1," *Boston Globe*, April 15, 1951, 46.
26. Gerry Lougheed, "Richard Greatest in the Game Today," *Ottawa Citizen*, April 16, 1951, 21.
27. Red Burnett, "Rocket, McNeil, Irvin's Not-So-Secret Weapons," *Toronto Star*, April 16, 1951, 18.
28. Dink Carroll, "Playing the Field," *Montreal Gazette*, April 16, 1951, 22.
29. Doug Vaughan, "On the Rebound," *Windsor Daily Star*, April 16, 1951 (Section II), 3.
30. Jack Koffman, "Along Sport Row," *Ottawa Citizen*, April 9, 1951, 17.
31. "Béliveau May Be Successor to the Rocket," *Galt Evening Reporter*, April 16, 1951, 12.
32. Dink Carroll, "Playing the Field," *Montreal Gazette*, April 16, 1951, 22.
33. Doug Vaughan, "'Richard in Overtime'—A Great Script Played Again," *Windsor Daily Star*, April 16, 1951 (Section II), 3.
34. Jack Koffman, "Along Sport Row," *Ottawa Citizen*, April 16, 1951, 21.

Chapter 8

1. Kevin Shea, *Barilko: Without a Trace* (Bolton, ON: Fenn Publishing Company Ltd., 2004), 124.
2. Red Burnett, "Leafs Need Breaks to Overpower Stubborn Habs," *Toronto Star*, April 18, 1951, 16.

Chapter Notes

3. Dink Carroll, "Playing the Field," *Montreal Gazette*, April 17, 1951, 20.
4. *Ibid.*
5. *Ibid.*
6. *Ibid.*
7. *Ibid.*
8. *Ibid.*
9. *Ibid.*
10. "'Edge Is on Our Side,' Says Dick Irvin," *Montreal Gazette*, April 17, 1951, 20.
11. *Ibid.*
12. *Ibid.*
13. *Ibid.*
14. Milt Dunnell, "Speaking on Sport," *Toronto Star*, April 16, 1951, 18.
15. *Ibid.*
16. *Ibid.*
17. Jack Koffman, "Along Sport Row," *Ottawa Citizen*, April 16, 1951, 21.
18. *Ibid.*
19. Dink Carroll, "Ted Kennedy Nets Extra Period Goal," *Montreal Gazette*, April 18, 1951, 22.
20. *Ibid.*
21. *Ibid.*
22. W.R. Wheatley, "Leafs Beat Canucks in Overtime," *Ottawa Citizen*, April 18, 1951, 25.
23. "Leafs Top Canadiens, 2-1, on Kennedy's Overtime Goal," *Boston Globe*, April 18, 1951, 22.
24. "Leafs Win 2-1 in Overtime; Canadiens Again Underdogs," *Calgary Herald*, April 18, 1951, 26.
25. Jack Koffman, "Along Sport Row," *Ottawa Citizen*, April 18, 1951, 24.
26. Dink Carroll, "Ted Kennedy Nets Extra Period Goal," *Montreal Gazette*, April 18, 1951, 22.
27. *Ibid.*
28. "Leafs Captain Modest; Gives Rollins Credit," *Montreal Gazette*, April 18, 1951, 22.
29. "Leafs Win 2-1 in Overtime, Canadiens Again Underdogs," *Calgary Herald*, April 18, 1951, 26.
30. "Leafs Captain Modest; Gives Rollins Credit," *Montreal Gazette*, April 18, 1951, 22.
31. Jack Koffman, "Along Sport Row," *Ottawa Citizen*, April 18, 1951, 24.
32. "Leafs Captain Modest; Gives Rollins Credit," *Montreal Gazette*, April 18, 1951, 22.
33. *Ibid.*
34. *Ibid.*
35. "Leafs Gain with 2-1 Victory," *Windsor Star*, April 18, 1951, Section III, 1.
36. "Leafs Captain Modest; Gives Rollins Credit," *Montreal Gazette*, April 18, 1951, 22.
37. Jack Koffman, "Along Sport Row," *Ottawa Citizen*, April 18, 1951, 24.

Chapter 9

1. Baz O'Meara, "Toronto Thieves Filch Pucks to Beat Canucks," *Montreal Star*, April 20, 1951, 36
2. Baz O'Meara, "The Passing Sport Show," *Montreal Star*, April 19, 1951, 37.
3. Dink Carroll, "Playing the Field," *Montreal Gazette*, April 19, 1951, 20.
4. Baz O'Meara, "The Passing Sport Show," *Montreal Star*, April 19, 1951, 37.
5. Dink Carroll, "Playing the Field," *Montreal Gazette*, April 19, 1951, 20.
6. Jack Koffman, "Along Sport Row," *Ottawa Citizen*, April 18, 1951, 24.
7. *Ibid.*
8. Bob Mamini, "Calgary Herald Sports," *Calgary Herald*, April 19, 1951, 23.
9. "Amusing Wire from Students Tickles Leafs," *Toronto Telegram* digital archives, April 20, 1951.
10. Baz O'Meara, "Toronto Thieves Filch Pucks to Beat Canucks," *Montreal Star*, April 20, 1951, 36.
11. *Ibid.*
12. *Ibid.*
13. Harold Atkins, "Smythe Adds Fiery Touch to Playoffs," *Montreal Star*, April 20, 1951, 36.
14. *Ibid.*
15. Baz O'Meara, "The Passing Sport Show," *Montreal Star*, April 20, 1951, 36.
16. Baz O'Meara, "Toronto Thieves Filch Pucks to Beat Canucks," *Montreal Star*, April 20, 1951, 36.
17. Kevin Shea, *Barilko: Without a Trace* (Bolton, ON: Fenn Publishing Company Ltd., 2004), 125.
18. Baz O'Meara, "Toronto Thieves Filch Pucks to Beat Canucks," *Montreal Star*, April 20, 1951, 36.
19. *Ibid.*
20. *Ibid.*
21. Red Burnett, "Rookie Rollins Is Leafs' Iron Man," *Toronto Star*, April 20, 1951, 16.

22. *Ibid.*
23. *Ibid.*
24. Baz O'Meara, "Toronto Thieves Filch Pucks to Beat Canucks," *Montreal Star*, April 20, 1951, 36.
25. Baz O'Meara, "The Passing Sport Show," *Montreal Star*, April 20, 1951, 36.
26. Baz O'Meara, "Toronto Thieves Filch Pucks to Beat Canucks," *Montreal Star*, April 20, 1951, 36.
27. Milt Dunnell, "Speaking on Sport," *Toronto Star*, April 20, 1951, 16.
28. *Ibid.*
29. Baz O'Meara, "The Passing Sport Show," *Montreal Star*, April 20, 1951, 36.
30. *Ibid.*
31. Harold Atkins, "Smythe Adds Fiery Touch to Playoffs," *Montreal Star*, April 20, 1951, 36.
32. "Canadiens State Dick Irvin to Be Retained," *Calgary Herald*, April 21, 1951, 24.
33. Baz O'Meara, "The Passing Sport Show," *Montreal Star*, April 20, 1951, 36.
34. *Ibid.*

Chapter 10

1. "Leafs Take Cup in Five Thrillers," *The Hockey News* online archives, May 8, 1951.
2. "Wotta Series," *Toronto Star*, April 21, 1951, 18.
3. Joe Perlove, "Leafs Get Stanley Cup—Now They Have to Make It Stick," *Toronto Star*, April 21, 1951, 18.
4. *Ibid.*
5. "Toronto Fans Will Settle for Ted Kennedy," *Ottawa Citizen*, April 21, 1951, 20.
6. Mel Sufrin, "Reckoning May Be with Curfew Time," *Windsor Star*, April 21, 1951, Section II, 3.
7. *Ibid.*
8. *Ibid.*
9. *Ibid.*
10. "Leafs Dread 'The Rocket' in Seeking Clincher," *Boston Globe*, April 21, 1951, 4.
11. *Ibid.*
12. Brian McFarlane, *The Lively World of Hockey* (New York: Signet, 1968), 109.
13. Kevin Shea, *Barilko: Without a Trace* (Bolton, ON: Fenn Publishing Company Ltd., 2004), 127.
14. *Ibid.*, 129.
15. *Ibid.*
16. *Ibid.*
17. Carola Vynhak, "The 11-Year Mystery of Leafs' 'Bashin' Bill Barilko,'" *Toronto Star* (online archives), June 1, 2017.
18. "Barilko's Sudden Death Goal Beats Montreal Six," *Boston Globe*, April 22, 1951, 49.
19. *Ibid.*
20. James Marsh, "My Hero: Bill Barilko, Frozen in Time," nationalpost.com, April 21, 2010.
21. Foster Hewitt, 1951 Stanley Cup Finals; Game Five, CBC Radio Archives, April 21, 1951
22. Kevin Shea, *Barilko: Without a Trace* (Bolton, ON: Fenn Publishing Company Ltd., 2004), 135.
23. "Barilko's Sudden Death Goal Beats Montreal Six," *Boston Globe*, April 22, 1951, 49.
24. Kevin Shea, *Barilko: Without a Trace* (Bolton, ON: Fenn Publishing Company Ltd., 2004), 132.
25. *Ibid.*, 135.
26. *Ibid.*, 134.
27. "Toronto Wins Stanley Cup Fourth Time in Five Years," *Calgary Herald*, April 23, 1951, 20.
28. John Devaney and Burt Goldblatt, *The Stanley Cup: A Complete Pictorial History* (Chicago: Rand McNally & Company, 1975), 132.
29. "Toronto Wins Stanley Cup Fourth Time in Five Years," *Calgary Herald*, April 23, 1951, 20.
30. Stan Fischler, "From the Archives: Defeat Not Easy for Habs During 1951 Stanley Cup Final," TheHockeyNews.com, June 15, 2022.
31. Milt Dunnell, "Gentleman Joe to Become One-Punch Primeau," *Toronto Star*, April 23, 1951, 14.
32. Kevin Shea, *Barilko: Without a Trace* (Bolton, ON: Fenn Publishing Company Ltd., 2004), 139.
33. Gerry Lougheed, "Boys Become Men for Leafs; Prize Is the Stanley Cup," *Galt Evening Reporter*, April 23, 1951, 12.
34. Tommy Shields, "Hats Off to the Leafs," *Ottawa Citizen*, April 23, 1951, 17.
35. "1951: The Most Closely Matched Stanley Cup Final," TheHockeyWriters.com, April 1, 2019.

Chapter 11

1. Dink Carroll, "Playing the Field," *Montreal Gazette*, April 24, 1951, 20.
2. *Ibid.*
3. *Ibid.*

Chapter 12

1. "Kareem Abdul-Jabbar Quotes," Brainyquote.com.

Chapter 13

1. Mark Fera, Interview. Conducted by John G. Robertson and Carl T. Madden, June 29, 2023.
2. Jamie Hayes, "They Didn't Win Another Til 1962: The Maple Leafs and the Disappearance of Bill Barilko," factinate.com.
3. Kevin Shea, *Barilko: Without a Trace* (Bolton, ON: Fenn Publishing Company Ltd., 2004), 58.
4. *Ibid.*, 57.
5. Was El-Halabi, "The Legend of Bill Barilko," BelacherReport.com, November 29, 1008.
6. "Search Shifts," *Ottawa Citizen*, August 29, 1951, 16.
7. Kevin Shea, *Barilko: Without a Trace* (Bolton, ON: Fenn Publishing Company Ltd., 2004), 220.
8. *Ibid.*, 226.
9. Kevin Shea, "Barilko—A 70th Anniversary Documentary," YouTube video, 2021.
10. Kevin Shea, *Barilko: Without a Trace* (Bolton, ON: Fenn Publishing Company Ltd., 2004), 212.
11. Peter Worthington, "Hope of a Miracle Dies After 11 Years," *Toronto Telegram* digital archives, June 7, 1962.
12. *Ibid.*
13. *Ibid.*
14. *Ibid.*
15. "One Body Barilko's," *Montreal Gazette*, June 7, 1962, 1.
16. Kevin Shea, *Barilko: Without a Trace* (Bolton, ON: Fenn Publishing Company Ltd., 2004), 219.
17. Bill Steer, "Barilko Legend to Get New Monument," Baytoday.ca, August 6, 2020.
18. Kevin Shea, *Barilko: Without a Trace* (Bolton, ON: Fenn Publishing Company Ltd., 2004), 225.
19. *Ibid.*, 226.
20. Mark Fera, "Barilko—A 70th Anniversary Documentary," YouTube video, 2021.
21. Kevin Shea, *Barilko: Without a Trace* (Bolton, ON: Fenn Publishing Company Ltd., 2004), 199.
22. Mark Fera, "Barilko—A 70th Anniversary Documentary," YouTube video, 2021.
23. Bill Steer, "Breaking a Trail in Search of the Place a Great Leaf Fell," SooToday.com, December 15, 2021.
24. Mark Fera, "Barilko—A 70th Anniversary Documentary," YouTube video, 2021.

Chapter 14

1. Brian Costello, "Has the Mystery Behind Barilko's Cup-Winning Puck Been Solved in Zapruder-Like Fashion? You Be the Judge," TheHockeyNews.com, April 19, 2016.
2. *Ibid.*
3. Brian Costello, "Barilko Mystery Grows as Leafs Fan Claims to Have Puck from Historic OT Goal," TheHockeyNews.com, December 20, 2015.
4. Mark Fera, Interview. Conducted by John G. Robertson and Carl T. Madden, June 29, 2023.
5. *Ibid.*
6. *Ibid.*
7. *Ibid.*
8. *Ibid.*

Chapter 16

1. John Devaney and Burt Goldblatt, *The Stanley Cup: A Complete Pictorial History* (Chicago: Rand McNally & Company, 1975), 36.
2. Ken Campbell, *Hab Heroes: The Greatest Canadiens Ever from 1 to 100* (Toronto: Transcontinental Books, 2008), 115.
3. John Halligan, "'The Big Whistle' Passes Away at Age 94," NHL.com, October 24, 2009.
4. *Ibid.*
5. Marvin Pave, "Fern Flaman, 85, Bruins Star and Legendary Coach at

Northeastern," *Boston Globe* (online archives), June 26, 2012.

6. Milt Dunnell, "How Taylor Rates His Win at the Plate," *Toronto Star*, June 29, 1979, B1.

7. Trent Frayne, "You Can't Kill a Hockey Player," Saturdayeveningpost.com, 1950.

8. Dave Stubbs, "In Appreciation of Fleming Mackell, From NCG to Two Stanley Cups with Toronto Maple Leafs," Montrealgazette.com, October 21, 2015.

9. Kevin Shea, *Barilko: Without a Trace* (Bolton, ON: Fenn Publishing Company Ltd., 2004), 142.

10. Lyndon Little, "Famed NHL Player and Broadcaster Howie Meeker Passes Away at Age 97," TheProvince.com, November 8, 2020.

11. Earl Zukerman and Joe Pelletier, "This Date in History: Former McGill Star and NHL Player Johnny Peirson was Born," *McGill University News and Events* (online newsletter), July 21, 2012.

12. Stan Fischler, "From the Archives: Goodbye Gentleman Joe, Hello King!" thehockeynews.com, May 4, 2022.

13. Ryan Szporer, "Montreal Canadiens: Top 10 Moments from the Montreal Forum," Bleacherreport.com, December 30, 2012.

14. Mark Feeney, "Bruin Great Milt Schmidt Dies at 98," *Boston Globe* (online archives), January 4, 2017.

15. Jack Sullivan, "Smith Scores All Three Goals as Leafs Trim Wings," *Ottawa Citizen*, April 11, 1949, 20.

16. Kelly McPartland, *The Lives of Conn Smythe: From the Battlefield to Maple Leaf Gardens* (Toronto: McClelland and Stewart, 2011), 264.

17. Conn Smythe and Scott Young, *Conn Smythe: If You Can't Beat Them in the Alley* (Toronto: McClelland and Stewart, 1981), 232.

18. "Hockey Hall of Famer Watson Dies," Theintelligencer.com, November 20, 2002.

Bibliography

Books

Campbell, Ken. *Hab Heroes: The Greatest Canadiens Ever From 1 to 100*. Toronto: Transcontinental Books, 2008.
Devaney, John, and Burt Goldblatt. *The Stanley Cup: A Complete Pictorial History*. Chicago: Rand McNally & Company, 1975.
Gaston, Tom. *A Fan for All Seasons*. Bolton, ON: Fenn Publishing Company Ltd., 2001.
Kendall, Brian. *Shutout: The Legend of Terry Sawchuk*. Toronto: Penguin, 1996.
McFarlane, Brian. *The Leafs*. Toronto: Prospero, 2008.
_____. *The Lively World of Hockey*. New York: Signet, 1968.
McPartland, Kelly. *The Lives of Conn Smythe: From the Battlefield to Maple Leaf Gardens*. Toronto: McClelland and Stewart, 2011.
Shea, Kevin. *Barilko: Without a Trace*. Bolton, ON: Fenn Publishing Company Ltd., 2004.
Smythe, Conn, and Scott Young. *Conn Smythe: If You Can't Beat Them in the Alley*. Toronto: McClelland and Stewart, 1981.

Newspaper/Periodical Archives

Boston Globe
Boston Herald
Calgary Herald
Detroit Free Press
Fitchburg Sentinel
Galt Evening Reporter
Montreal Gazette
Montreal Star
National Post
New York Daily News
New York Telegram-Sun
New York Times
Ottawa Citizen
Ottawa Journal
Pittsburgh Press
Timmins Daily Press
Toronto Globe & Mail
Toronto Star
Toronto Sun
Toronto Telegram
Windsor Daily Star
Winnipeg Free Press

Online Resources

BayToday.ca
BleacherReport.com
Calgary.ca
CBC.ca
EliteProspects.com
Factinate.com
HHOF.com
HockeyReference.com
NationalPost.com
NHL.com
OriginalHockeyHallofFame.com
PolishSportsHallofFame.com
SaturdayEveningPost.com
SooToday.com
TheHockeyNews.com
TheHockeyWriters.com

TheIntelligencer.com
TheProvince.com

Yardbarker.com
YouTube.com

Personal Interview

Fera, Mark. Interview. Conducted by John G. Robertson and Carl T. Madden. June 29, 2023.

Index

Abdul-Jabbar, Kareem 137
Alexander, Viscount Harold 49
Ali, Muhammad 196
"Alouette" (song) 89
Anderson, Tommy 194
Apps, Syl 90, 185
Atkins, Harold 39, 108, 112

Babando, Pete 8, 37, 68
Babcock, Sam 85
Baun, Bobby 182
Bentley, Doug 23, 174
Black, Steve 10
Blake, Hector (Toe) 85, 98, 107, 129, 185, 186
Bodnar, Gus 90-91
Boivin, Leo 186
Boucher, George 5-6
Bower, Johnny 127
Boyd, Ron 154
Brodeur, Martin 194
Brown, Adam 21
Bruneteau, Modere (Mud) 2
Bucyk, Johnny 184

Cain, Herbie 16
Calder, Frank 64
Cattarello, Sandra 156
Chenier, Archie 147, 156
Chuvalo, George 196
Clancy, King 192
Clapper, Dit 177
Collins, John 132
Colville, Mac 177
Conacher, Charlie 10
Conacher, Roy 21
Connor, Cam 2
Costello, Brian 166
Couture, Gerry 39
Crawford, Jack 87, 105
Crawford, James 148-149
Creighton, Dave 55
Crosby, Sidney 2

Dann, Marshall 31
Dawes, Bob 118

Day, Hap 8, 67, 69, 74, 126, 127
Dever, Paul A 52
Dewsbury, Al 8
Donohue, Dan 164
Donohue, Harry 162-164, 166
Donohue, Jeremiah 163-164, 167
Doraty, Ken 2, 111
Downie, Gord 160-162
Dryden, Ken 180
Dumart, Woody 23, 47, 48, 57
Duncan, Art 73
Dye, Babe 65

El-Halabi, Was 146
Elizabeth, Princess 178
Esposito, Phil 174
Ezinicki, Bill 21, 53, 55, 57, 74

Ferguson, Elmer 20
Ferguson, Lorne 47
Ferrier, Joe 80
Fields, Gary 153-156
"Fifty Mission Cap" (song) 160-162
Fischler, Stan 183
Fisher, Dunc 51, 53, 55
Fletcher, George 164
Fogolin, Lee 10

Garant, Gaston 157
Gaston, Tom 124
Gilbert, Rod 64
Goldham, Bob 9, 36
Goodfellow, Ebbie 10, 21, 181
Gorman, Tommy 106, 131
Gravelle, Leo 10
Gretzky, Wayne 3, 174

Hainsworth, Alma 12
Hainsworth, George 12
Hall, Ted 154
Harmon, Glen 95
Hassard, Bob 159
Hastings, Louise 158
Hayes, Jamie 145
Heard, Ted 113

Index

Henderson, Murray 46
Henry, Gordon (Red) 57
Henry, Jim 9, 59–60, 182
Hewitt, Foster 97, 122, 123, 127
Hildebrand, George 113
Hill, Mel 2–3, 86–87
Hirshberg, Al 25–26
Holly, Buddy 146
Horeck, Pete 47–48, 50
Horton, Tim 151, 157
Huber, Fred 37
Hudson, Lou 158
Hudson, Phyllis 151
Hughes, Carl 115

Imlach, Punch 197

Juzda, Bill 46, 185

Kaleta, Alex 16
Kane, Evander 2
Kelley, Dr. Tom 51
Kelly, Red 181
Keon, Dave 195
Klisanich, Frank 147, 152
Kraftcheck, Steve

Lalonde, Newsy 62
Landis, Kenesaw Mountain 113
Laviolette, Jack 62
Laycoe, Hal 193
Layne, Rex 80
Leone, Gene 19
Leprade, Edgar 19
Leswick, Tony 15–16
Lincoln, Abraham 110
Livingstone, Eddie 62
Lougheed, Gerry 47, 51, 125, 128
Lund, Pentti 16

MacArthur, Douglas 4
MacBrien, William A.H. 171
MacCabe, Edward 38
Mackell, Jack 187
Mahovlich, Frank 2
Main, Jimmy 166
Mamini, Bob 106
March, James 121
Martin, Pit 64
Matthews, Auston 185
Matthews, Harry 80
Mazur, Eddie 111
Mazydlo, Jeff 3
McCool, Frank 67
McFarlane, Brian 40, 117, 121
McGirr, Dave 156
McIntyre, Jack 57, 58
McLean, Hugh 20–21
Mephan, Eddie 20
Mickoski, Nick 16, 19

Mikan, George 80
Monahan, Leo 191
Morenz, Howie 63, 181
Morrison, Bill 104–105
Morrison, Don 8
Mosienko, Bill 181

Neale, Harry 17, 123, 126
Nickleson, Al 93, 95, 121, 124, 126
Norris, James (Jim) 33

O'Connor, Buddy 16
Orr, Bobby 2, 174, 181, 184, 191, 194, 195

Paterick, Ray 153
Patrick, Lester 7, 191
Pavelich, Marty 35
Perlove, Joe 114–115
Perry, Corey 2
Pitre, Didier 62
Plante, Jacques 188
Powers, Eddie 21
Pratt, Babe 21, 111
Primeau, Jim 20
Pronovost, Marcel 64
Prystai, Metro 9, 39

Quackenbush, Bill 46
Quackenbush, Max 53

Ralby, Herb 23, 50
Ratelle, Jean 64
Rayner, Charlie 10, 16, 19
Reeve, Ted 18
Regan, Larry 187
Reise, Leo, Sr. 192
Rindone, Joe 11
Robinson, Sugar Ray 10–11
Ronty, Paul 47
Roosevelt, Theodore 24
Ross, Art 6, 8, 80, 180

Sakic, Joe 2
Scott, Barbara Ann 107
Sellars, John 131
Shibicky, Alex 177
Shields, Tommy 129
Sinden, Harry 184
Skrudland, Brian 2
Smith, Maurice 74
Smythe, Stafford 156
Spooner, J.W. 154
Stanley, Allan 144, 149, 151, 157
Stasiuk, Vic 10
Steer, Bill 160
Stewart, Gaye 9
Stewart, Jack 8, 17
Stewart, Nels 193
Storey, Red 34, 51
Sufrin, Mel 24, 116

Index

Sullivan, Jack 195
Sullivan, Red 57, 58

Taylor, Zack 15
Terrion, Greg 168
Théodore, José 194
Thompson, Cliff 193
Tobin, Bill 9, 85, 132
Tracy, Dr. David F. 14–16, 18
Truman, Harry 4
Tunney, Gene 126
Turofsky, Lou 121
Turofsky, Nat 121–122

Vaughan, Doug 90
Vézina, Georges 62
Vincent, Kevin 157–158
Voss, Carl 51

Weston, Phil 154
Wheatley, W.R. 99
Wheeler, Dan 148
Worthington, Peter 155, 159

www.ingramcontent.com/pod-product-compliance
Lightning Source LLC
Chambersburg PA
CBHW032042300426
44117CB00009B/1162